Zbigniew Borysiuk

Modern Saber Fencing

Technique – Tactics – Training – Research

by
Zbigniew Borysiuk, Ph.D.

Also from SwordPlay Books

Laszlo Szabo, *Fencing and the Master*
Istvan Lukovich, *Fencing: the modern international style*
Istvan Lukovich, *Electric Foil Fencing*
   Advanced competitive training
Imre Vass, *Epee Fencing: a complete system*
Zbigniew Czajkowski, *Understanding Fencing*
Aladar Kogler, *One Touch at a Time*
Sergei Golubitsky, *Fencing Is My Life*
Harry James, *Strength Training for Fencers*
Johan Harmenberg, *Epee 2.0: the Birth of the
   New Fencing Paradigm*

Published by SKA SwordPlay Books
3939 Victory Boulevard
Staten Island, NY 10314
1.718.761.3305
www.swordplaybooks.com

Cover photograph: Tan Xue of China, left, vs. Elena Netchaeva of Russia, at the 2005 Las Vegas Grand Prix in women's saber. Photograph © Serge Timacheff/FencingPhotos.com.

Copyright © 2009 Zbigniew Borysiuk
ISBN 978-0-9789022-3-0
All rights reserved
Photographs by Zbigniew Werema
DVD Video production by Zbigniew Werema
Translated from the Polish by Tomasz Skirecki, Ph.D
Edited by Stephan Khinoy

*This book is dedicated
to my wife Iwona and my daughter Kate
for their unfailing love and patience
throughout my career as a fencing coach
and my life as a researcher.*

Acknowledgements

The original idea behind Modern Saber Fencing was to link my years of experience as a fencing coach with the extensive research I have conducted. I am convinced that this approach to the dynamic changes in fencing, including saber – changes that have transformed fencing and are still taking place – can be a source for further fencing development.

However, achieving the final shape of this book would not have been possible without many contributions.

The person who inspired me to write my first work destined for fencing instructors and trainers was Jadwiga Kwiatkowska from "Coach's Library" in Warsaw. I also want to direct special appreciation to Professor Zbigniew Czajkowski, who gave me encouragement and support to write this book and who has encouraged me in many publications and managed major scientific deomnstrations and lectures for coaches on my behalf. I would like to thank the master of saber and Professor of Architecture Wojciech Zablocki for his contribution to Chapter Two of this book, which are devoted to the story of how saber transformed itself through the ages. Additionally, the European Women's Saber Champion, Aleksandra Socha and her colleague from the AZS Warsaw Club, Monika Kościucha, played an outstanding role in presenting saber technique for the photographs included in this book. I would like to offer great thanks to National Women's Saber coach Arkadiusz Roszak and the members of Polish saber team, such as Irena Więckowska, Marta Wątor , Katarzyna Karpińska, and Izabela Sajewicz, who took part in training sessions, and especially in the fencing lessons which make up so much of the material on the DVD.. In the same context, I thank the Polish Saber Coach, Ryszard Czaja, and his pupils Wojciech Marczak and Jan

Karkosz who also appear on the DVD and took part in the preparation of its material. The DVD itself was made by the very talented and creative Zbigniew Werema, to whom I offer considerable gratitude. I would like to acknowledge to Jason Sheridan, founder of his Sheridan Fencing Academy in New York City, for his very valuable cooperation in translating of DVD material, including all of the specialized fencing terminology, from Polish into American English.

I must thank my friends from the United States, Janusz Smolenski, Wieslaw Głon, and my pupil Dariusz Gilman, who supported the idea of publishing the present book for English-speaking readers.

I express my great thanks to Tomasz Skirecki, Ph.D., of Poznań University for his invaluable contribution to the process of translating the whole text from the Polish language to American English.

It is a particular honor for me to direct my thanks to the prominent American Coach, Edward Korfanty who wrote the very deep, professional and analytical preface to this book. He has successfully planted Polish fencing roots on the American soil, the fruit of which is now visible in the form of gold medals for the United States Olympic Fencing Team.

Last but not least, I thank Steve Khinoy, the editor and publisher at SwordPlay Books, for his professional approach and very creative role in the process of preparing and publishing *Modern Saber Fencing*. I especially thank him for helping in the comprehensive conception of the book which provides the opportunity of reaching different categories of readers, from novices to advanced fencers – including their parents, coaches, and fans – as well as the sports scientists searching for an inspiration for further work. The shape of this book and its profile: *Technique – Tactics – Training – Research* is Steve Khinoy's concept and merit.

Zbigniew Borysiuk
Opole, Poland 2009

Contents

Acknowledgements   6

Preface
by Edward Korfanty, U.S. Olympic Coach   13

Chapter 1.
Saber reflections: Beijing 2008   19

Chapter 2.
The History of Saber Fencing and the Rise of Polish Saber   25
2.1   Sport fencing and the national fencing schools   25
2.2   Fencing in the modern Olympics   26
2.3   The transformations of competitive fencing   27
2.3.1   History of swordplay   28
2.4   The Polish saber school in the 18th and 19th centuries   29
2.5   The rise of the Italian saber school in the late 19th century   31
2.6   The Hungarian School   32
2.7   Saber fencing in Poland, 1909-1968   34

Chapter 3.
The Impact of Electronic Scoring on Saber   37
3.1   The crisis of non-electric saber   37
3.2   Reforming tendencies   39
3.3   Tactical analysis of some top saber bouts of the 1990s   41
3.4   Tactical trends as of the mid 1990's   43
3.5   Technical developments of the mid 1990's   44
3.6   Combat styles of top world saber fencers studied   46
3.7   Current trends   47

Chapter 4.
Modern Saber: Technique — 48

Part I: Footwork training — 48
4.1.1 General considerations — 48
4.1.2 Some of the special features of modern saber: — 49
4.1.3 Elements of footwork — 49

Part II. The Saber — 58
4.2.1 The parts of the saber — 58
4.2.2 Holding the saber — 58
4.2.3 The saber target — 60

Part III. Basic Fencing Positions — 62
4.3.1 Initial position: Point in line. Varying senses of "line." — 62
4.3.2 Basic position – On guard — 63
4.3.3 Invitations — 64
4.4.4 Positions of the hand and blade — 65
4.3.5 Actions on the blade: Engagements, beats, binds — 69

Part IV. Basic Fencing Actions — 71
4.4.1 Hits — 71
4.4.2 Offensive actions — 71
4.4.3 Ripostes and counter-ripostes — 77
4.4.4 Counter-time — 78
4.4.5 Renewed offensive actions — 78
4.4.6 Offensive-defensive actions — 81
4.4.7 Counter-attacks — 82
4.4.8 Defensive actions — 85
4.4.9 Defense by retreat — 87

Part V. Overview of Tendencies in Modern Saber — 88
4.5 The transformation of saber — 88

Chapter 5.
Modern Saber Training — 90
5.1 Forms of fencing training — 90
5.2 The individual fencing lesson — 93

5.3	Outlines of individual lessons	94
5.4	The introductory training level	94
5.5	The intermediate training level	96
5.6	Advanced, or specialized training level	98
5.7	Championship training level	101
5.8	Pair exercises	102
5.9	Queue exercises and fencing dummy training	107
5.10	Exercises with a fencing dummy; mirror fencing	108
5.11	Training cycles and the fencing year	109
5.12	Training sessions	111
5.13	Training loads	112

Chapter 6.
Nutrition of fencers — 116

6.1	The role of nutrition in fencing	117
	Carbohydrate	117
	Fat	118
	Protein	120
6.2	Energy reference values and nutritional requirements	120
6.3	Intensity of performance and types of energy sources	121
6.4	Water and electrolyte balance	122
6.5	Nutrition during competition and recovery	124
6.6	Doping and stimulants	125

Chapter 7.
Recent Fencing Research: Concepts and Highlights — 127

7.1	Identifying fencing potential and assessing progress	127
7.2	Body type	128
7.3	Aerobic and anaerobic potential	129
7.4	Personality type	129
7.5	Psychomotor ability	130
7.6	Types of reactions and their application in fencing lessons	130

Chapter 8.
Fencing talent identification and selection — 134

8.1	Review of previous models of talent Identification	134
8.2	Criticism of earlier models and new directions	134

8.3	Goals of the present study: identification and assessment of fencing-specific talent	136
8.4	Conclusions and indications of the present study	137
8.5	Selection in fencing	139
8.5.1	Somatic determinants	141
8.5.2	Physical capacity parameters	142
8.5.3	Tools for assessment of fencing predispositions	145

Chapter 9.
Diagnostic tools in fencing research — **148**

9.1	Assessment of somatic and physiological predispositions; Significance of subjects' age.	149
9.1.1	Measurement tools for assessment of somatic and coordination parameters	150
9.1.2	Somatic examination results	151
9.1.3	Physiological examination results	154
9.2	Practical tools and for assessing fencing preparation	158
9.2.1	Fencing preparation assessment results	160
9.3	Assessment of psychomotor predispositions	162
9.3.1	Methods and tools of assessment of psychomotor predispositions	164
9.3.2	Psychomotor examination results	166
9.4	Assessment of psychological predispositions	169
9.4.1	Methods and tools of assessment of psychological predispositions	172
9.4.2	Psychological assessment results	173

Chapter 10.
Reaction time and movement time. Types of sensori-motor responses. Fencing tempo (the "sense of timing"). — **176**

10.1	Reaction time and movement time	177
10.2	Classification of sensori-motor responses	180
10.3	Novice – expert paradigm	189
10.4	Fencing tempo (sense of timing)	191

Chapter 11.
Information processes, stimulation and perceptual training — **195**

11.1	Information processes	195

11.2	Stage of response choice	199
11.3	Stage of response programming	201
11.4	Stimulation types (tactile, acoustic, visual, kinesthetic) and time of sensori-motor responses	203
11.5	Integration of data from different senses.	209
11.6	Perceptual training	210

Chapter 12
The DVD: Description and Commentary — **214**

12.1	Technical lesson [Roszak – Więckowska].	215
12.2	Technical-tactical lesson [Borysiuk – Wator].	216
12.3	Technical-tactical lesson [Borysiuk – Karpińska].	217
12.4	Technical-tactical lesson – championship level [Roszak – Więckowska]	219
12.5	Group footwork training of the Polish national team	221
12.6	Individual footwork training.	222
12.7	Queue training.	223
12.8	Pair exercises.	224
12.9	Individual lessons with members of the Polish national men's saber team	226
12.9.1	Technical lesson (Jan Karkosz)	226
12.9.2	Tactical lesson before competition (Wojciech Marczak)	227

References   **229**

Preface

by Edward Korfanty, U.S. Olympic Coach

Zbigniew Borysiuk's *Modern Saber Fencing* is the product of the author's many years experience, both as a fencing coach and as a researcher of psycho-motorics and coaching. Zbigniew Borysiuk's particular research interests include information processes, perception, different reaction types, spatio-temporal anticipation, selection in sport, and fencing training at all stages of an athlete's development. One of its greatest assets is the wealth of illustrations and photographs, not to mention as the presentations of technical and tactical actions by elite saber fencers on a DVD. This book will be extremely useful in fencing training and should attract the interest of the fencing community throughout the English-speaking world – and beyond.

After a successful career as a fencer – his AZS Warsaw Club team won a bronze medal in the Polish national championships – Borysiuk went on to an equally successful career in coaching and research. He holds a doctor's degree in physical culture sciences and is a first- class fencing coach at the same time. His trainees have been members of the Polish National Team at the cadet, junior and senior fencing world championship levels. One of his best students, Dariusz Gilman, became Cadet World Champion and Junior European Champion in saber. (Dariusz now coaches at the DC Fencers Club in Silver Springs, Maryland.)

As a researcher, Borysiuk holds a doctorate and is currently an assistant professor in the Faculty of Physical Education and Physiotherapy at the Opole Technical University, where his research and teaching interests include sport theory, anthropo-motorics, psycho-motorics, exercise diagnosis and motor training. He has published numerous papers and is the author of three previous books.

In the past two decades, saber has been transformed as the result of the introduction of electronic scoring equipment, a new prominence of fencing in the media – and above all, the application of new rules and techniques of judging. In other words, Saber has undergone a revolution. How can saber fencers and their coaches adapt to these changes and succeed? This is the main theme of the book.

The book derives from Borysiuk's copious notes, observations, and video footage from training sessions and fencing competitions. They are the product both of his long-term coaching in Opole and his work with the junior and senior Polish saber teams durin the 1980's and 1990's, i.e. at the time of the greatest transformations in saber fencing, when, along with many coaches in Poland, he initiated the training of very young fencers. His experiences forced Borysiuk and others to adopt a new approach to previously unquestioned training methods. Against the traditionalists, who were skeptical about the new saber revolution, Borysiuk and his colleagues embraced the "new saber."

The book incorporates the most recent advances in training theory, methodology and motor control, which have effectively and positively influenced fencing research.

The book's structure is logical. Particularly important are Chapter 4 on saber method and Chapter 5, devoted to the methodology of saber training. A welcomed innovation is a chapter on nutrition and dietary supplements in fencing.

Modern Saber Fencing consists of eleven chapters set in logical order, plus a twelfth chapter explaining the contents of the DVD. The subjects range from the historical transformations of the saber, leading to the emergence of its modern Olympic version, problems of talent identification in fencing, to fencing methodology and training. The key parts of the book are descriptions of the scientific foundations of the training process involving the knowledge of information processes and perceptual training. They are enriched by discussion of problems of diagnosis and control of the training process as well as different types of sensori-motor skill of reactions and sense of timing in fencing. These issues are thoroughly discussed from the point of view of the application of modern diagnostic tools such as surface electromyography and devices for measuring athletes' aerobic and anaerobic capacity.

In Chapter One, the author discusses the historical evolution of the saber. The author provides particularly detailed descriptions of 19th-century fencing weapons. At that time the evolution of fencing towards a competitive sport began, following the introduction of first competitive fencing rules. Borysiuk stresses the Polish aspects of saber fencing historical development, especially the historically important Polish fencing school. Contemporary saber fencing has been, however, predominantly influenced by the Italian school and, from the 1920's, by the Hungarian school, which triggered the proliferation of competitive saber fencing all over Europe. These traditions underlay the international successes of the Polish saber fencing school in the late 1950's and in the 1960's, in particular, Jerzy Pawłowski's gold medal in saber at the 1968 Olympic Games in Mexico City. Many medals, including gold in team and individual competition, were won by Polish and Hungarian saber fencers, and later on by the Soviet fencers.

Chapter Two contains a detailed analysis of changes in saber technique and tactics in the late 1980's and in the 1990's following the introduction of electronic scoring an also new competition rules. The chapter contains interesting figures and tables illustrating technical and tactical actions of world elite saber fencers, complete with the descriptions of combat styles of selected fencers. The author concludes that these changes contributed greatly to the reduction of the duration of bouts, limited the range of technical actions and made saber fencing less attractive to the spectators. However, the new developments in saber constitute a reasonable compromise between tradition and requirements of referees' objectivity. The lack of progress in this field would have posed the danger of total marginalization of saber events.

Chapters Four and Five are devoted to fencers' technical and tactical preparation and coaching methodology. This is one of the key parts of the book. It contains a detailed analysis of the most essential saber actions as well as outlines of tutorials designed for novice and advanced fencers. Many different fencing methods are presented such as: individual lessons, collective lessons, pair exercise, queue exercises, practice before mirror, before dummy, footwork exercise etc. The author analyzes different offensive, defensive and counter offensive actions. He puts emphasis on proper fencing terminology (basic classification of fencing actions, tactical classification) as well as justifies the significance of the practical classification of fencing skills into technical, tactical and tactical-technical on the basis of the concept of sensori-motor skills (motor habit patterns) using extrinsic and intrinsic motor feedback.

He discusses fencing training cycles, placing a great emphasis on the optimization of energy fitness coordination abilities, fencer's technical and tactical skills, especially before the most important competitions. This leads to issues such as successive stages of fencing development starting from the beginner stage and progressing through the intermediate up to the master level of fencing advancement. Additionally, the chapter presents methods of achieving the optimal predisposition before taking part in crucial tournaments.

Chapter Six, devoted to nutrition in fencing, is a kind of novelty in publications on fencing. It discusses the most important dietary and nutritional principles in fencing training and competitions. One of the chapter's assets is a valuable discussion about the link between different aspects of nutrition, including hydration, and the energy needs of fencers during training or competition. The author reveals the most common errors and bad habits in fencing diet and condemns the use of stimulants and alcohol as well as banned performance-enhancing substances.

Chapter Seven is an introduction to the research and theoretical section of the book. It is a valuable "executive summary" of some of the main concepts and conclusions in the chapters that follow.

Chapter Eight, the first of these chapter, is concerned with the problem of talent identification in fencing. It is based on the paradigm of talent identification used in the theory of sport training. The author calls into question the so-called "master model" and emphasizes specific predispositions the best fencers should possess. According to Borysiuk, talent identification in fencing should rely to a greater degree on one's psychomotor abilities rather than fitness predispositions. Borysiuk claims that each fencer features his or her individual temperament and personality profile as well as other abilities dependent on his or her somatic build. All these elements should be considered by the coaches in the process of development and training of talented fencers.

Chapter Nine presents diagnostic methods, tests and tools which can be extremely useful in the selection and assessment of fencers at every stage of training. He considers five aspects, including somatic build, energetic predispositions, psychomotor abilities, personality and temperament traits and technical and tactical skills. The chapter includes the author's own project of a test assessing fencers' predispositions consisting of seven diagnostic tasks.

In Chapter Ten and Eleven, the theoretical foundations of information processes and perception are discussed including the results of studies. Additionally the author presents different types of reactions and timing in fencing using a scientific approach with a practical implementation of surface electromyography (SEMG). The chapter describes the results a long-term study of novice and advanced fencers: testing their simple and other varieties of senso-motor reactions using: visual, tactile and acoustic stimuli. He also discusses the fencers' responses to two types of anticipatory signals: spatial and temporal, as well as their senso-motor responses. The author's original and innovative research ideas can be effectively implemented in perceptual training and training of motor habits.

One of the strongest features of this book is the plethora of photographs illustrating the most important technical actions used in modern saber fencing. The high-quality illustrations as well as the professionally made footage on the accompnying DVD were prepared with valuable contributions from the European women's saber champion Aleksandra Socha and Monika Kosciucha from the AZS Warszawa Athletic Club. The DVD contains tutorials with fencers from the Polish women Olympic fencing team prepared by the national coach and the author. The footage also contains footwork training techniques, tutorials and technical-tactical exercises carried out by the author with two saber fencers from the Polish National Team–Wojciech Marczak and Jan Karkosz.

It gives me great satisfaction to state that Zbigniew Borysiuk's publication will definitely meet the expectations of the fencing community. Olympic fencing, especially women saber fencing, is currently in its heyday. Saber fencing is becoming popular among female fencers from Poland, Korea, China, Russia and the United States, who have achieve numerous international successes at tournaments.

Modern Saber Fencing book also emphasizes problems of coaching practice and research into sport theory and practice. It can be treated both as a valuable training manual and an updated report on the implementation of the newest diagnostic techniques. I sincerely hope it will attract great interest from the entire fencing community as well as of young researchers seeking inspiration for their own studies – not only of fencing and combat sports generally, but of all sports based on open sensori-motor skills, of cognitive motor type, in which perception, attention, reaction and tactics play an important part.

Edward Korfanty
United States Fencing Association
National Women's Saber Coach

Chapter 1.

Saber reflections: Beijing 2008

We begin with the saber trends of the most recent Olympics, since these will be of the widest interest. These trends, however, are only the latest developments of a long history, which will be discussed in subsequent chapters.

The Olympic fencing tournament in Beijing, especially women's saber fencing, was unique. The tournament marked the tenth anniversary of the international debut of women's saber: the first women's saber world championships had taken place in Seoul in 1998. In 2004, the first Olympic women's saber competition took place, and in 2008, women's team saber competition entered the Olympic program. It is very appropriate that this book and its DVD are primarily illustrated with women saber fencers!

Recently there have been many transformations in men's and women's saber fencing, especially the way new fencing powers are superseding the old, traditional ones. The Beijing Summer Olympics clearly confirmed this tendency. Since the Athens Olympics, U.S. saber fencers have entered the saber elite. In Beijing U.S. women won all three medals in the individual competition and the bronze medal in the team event, while the U.S. men's saber team won the silver medal. This caused a genuine sensation, especially considering the Olympic medal tables from the last half-century. Undoubtedly, the American saber fencer Mariel Zagunis has become a world fencing star. A pupil of Polish fencing Master Ed Korfanty, Zagunis is now a two-time Olympic gold medalist (first time in Athens in 2004) and she presses on the heels of foil champion Valentina Vezzali, who has won three individual foil gold medals at three consecutive Olympics. Zagunis will be only 27 in London in 2012 and she stands a good chance to equal the Italian's Olympic record.

Another emerging world saber fencing power is China. Chinese fencer Man Zhong won the gold medal in individual saber, and the Chinese women's team lost the gold medal to Ukraine (!!) by only one point. Just before the Beijing Olympics, Man Zhong had won the "Wolodyjowski's Saber" World Cup Tournament in Warsaw. The Chinese fencer, a pupil of French fencing master Christian Bauer, was surely one of the favorites of the Olympic tournament. Historically, his gold medal was only the second Chinese Olympic medal in fencing. The first was won at the 1984 Olympics in Los Angeles by a foil fencer Juije Luan, who also, at the age of 50, took part in the Beijing Olympics as a member of the Canadian team. She won the 32nd place, and her feat can be regarded as an irrefutable proof of the longevity of a fencing career.

For the first time, for decades, Russian and Hungarian men saber fencers did not collect any medals. One of the favorites in the Beijing fencing tournament, Stanisław Pozdniakov, a five-time world champion and three-time Olympic champion, was defeated and announced the end of his spectacular sports career at the age of 35. One fencer who definitely influenced Pozdniakov's decision was the American Keeth Smart, who defeated the Russian champion in the semi-finals of the team competition 10 – 4, securing a U.S. victory over Russia 45 –44. The American saber team had also defeated the Hungarian team in a similar manner earlier and advanced to the semi-finals with this victory. The Olympic preparation of the U.S. team, both physical and psychological, was truly impressive. It seems that the decades-long era of Hungarian and Russian supremacy in saber has ended. At present, about eight European countries plus the USA and China seem to form the saber fencing elite. The French and Italian saber fencers won Olympic medals in Beijing (gold and bronze, respectively). Thus, the only saber fencer who won two Olympic medals was Frenchman Nicolas Lopez: gold in the team event and silver in individual event. It should be noted that the bronze medal in the individual men's event was won by the former Olympic champion from Sydney (2000) Michail Covaliu of Romania, who defeated Frenchman Julien Pillet.

The apparent decline of the traditional saber fencing world powers is surely an indication of the growing popularity of fencing all over the world. One of the highlights of the Beijing saber tournament was the semifinal bout between the American Becca Ward and the Tunisian Azza Bezbes, with the latter losing by only one point (14 – 15). It now seems that African saber fencers may also become well-known international stars. Seven countries had fencers in the quarterfinals of the men's individual saber competition (China, France, Romania Italy, USA, Spain, Belarus), and there were five countries in the quarterfinals of the women's competition (USA, Ukraine, Russia, China, Tunisia). Truly, this was a world-wide contest!

In terms of saber technique and tactics, many positive developments could be noticed, which are significant for spectators' perception and better understanding of saber fencing, as well as the appreciation of the event. Saber bouts tend to last longer. The fencers, both men and women, no longer attack every time, as soon as the referee says "Allez!," in order to gain the right of way. They are more confident about their skills at counter-attacks, parries and counter-ripostes; they engage in combat all along the piste and score valid touches in defense as well as through counter-time and their own simple and compound attacks. Characteristically, these tendencies were more visible among female saber fencers. These are definitely optimistic developments in terms of the attractiveness of saber fencing: the number of double hits has gone down, and saber bouts have become more understandable to an average spectator. There is no doubt that the limitation of the lockout time to 120 milliseconds in saber fits the modern, more versatile physical preparation of fencers. A saber fencer today must hit 120 ms sooner than his or her opponent for a one-light valid touch to be registered by the electronic scoring apparatus. This has greatly contributed to more frequent uses of parries and ripostes, which now register as a single light and do not require the referee's interpretation. (Such actions had often been ambiguous before the introduction of the scoring apparatus and the new change in timing. The new style of saber combat requires coaches and fencers to closely observe and anticipate the opponent's tactical intentions. In modern saber, fencers absolutely need a high level of perception and high reaction speed, as well as perfect footwork and timing training.

A detailed analysis of valid hits scored during selected fencing bouts at the Beijing Olympics: two individual saber finals Mariel Zagunis – Sada Jacobson 15 – 8 and Man Zhong – Nicolas Lopez 15 – 9; and the women's team saber final Ukraine – China 45 – 44, yields the following observations.

- In fencing tactics, the problem of double touches (which had to be disallowed by by the referees) has been practically eliminated. Statistically, there were only two simultaneous actions per bout. The fencers, however, often pretended to try to take the opponent's blade in simultaneous actions, provoking the opponent to commit finish his attack prematurely and allowing the fencer to initiate simple attacks, mostly cuts to the torso with a lunge, or quite often, epee-like stop-hits with opposition. Fencers did not rush to get bouts over with in a hurry: stopping the bout every 2-3 seconds, as had often happened earlier, was very rare. Usually, a hit was scored after 3 to 10 seconds. The longest time for a single hit was noted in the team saber match between Bao (China) and Khomorowa (Ukraine): 20 seconds at the score of 40 – 36. Interestingly, fencers from different countries displayed their own styles of preparatory actions. The American female saber fencers started their preparatory actions with a feinted step in place, whereas the Chinese began with a rhythmic two-step and stopping.

- In offense, feint attacks were intertwined with renewals of offensive actions, mostly simple attacks and actions on the blade. Incorrect feint attacks aimed at the opponent's valid target area often resulted in the opponent's counter-time.

- Defensive actions were dominated by counter-attacks, with the French saber fencers leading the way with their cut-over actions to forearm. Very few parries were used, mostly tierce and quarte, and only three parries of quinte in all of the observed bouts (these were employed by the Chinese fencers.) The effectiveness of these parries relied on the perfect adjustment of their distance from the fencer's body. The footage of the bouts in slow motion showed that the most efficient were tierce and quarte, taken fairly close to the body. Inaccurate parries often resulted in the appearance of a single light on the electronic apparatus against the defending fencer with no possibility of scoring double hits in case of a riposte.

- As far as the valid target area was concerned very few hits on the head were registered. The most common hits were on the chest and the torso. About 30% of valid touches were hits to forearm by cut over. Present-day saber fencing prefers the so-called "advanced, or near" target area, which benefits tall fencers with a long arms span. For example, the mean height of the Chinese national men's saber team was about 190 cm – nearly 6'3". The coupé-like actions that are becoming more and more common are best performed by tall, strong fencers, who can fully utilize their physical advantage.

- Readers may be interested in contrasting these developments with the trends in the early days of electric saber discussed in Chapter 3 and summarized in Table 3.1.

The novel tennis-like developments in refereeing are most welcome. When in doubt, referees and fencers can now check (challenge) a decision by reviewing the video recording of the bout. The use of video footage in slow motion in saber fencing – which is a conventional weapon – has greatly increased the objectivity of the referees' judgments. At present the referees do not have problems deciding the priority rule in saber, and a technical error, e.g. commencing an attack with a foot movement, is easy to spot in slow motion. In contrast, while watching other Olympic combat sports events such as taekwondo, boxing, judo, and wrestling, one may conclude that these sports suffer from a deep crisis in terms of the intelligibility of referees' decisions. The refereeing of combat sports has become incredibly difficult, and many times referees have taken controversial decisions. A case in point was the scandal involving the Swedish wrestler Ara Abrahamian who protested against what he thought was an unfair referee's ruling by dropping his bronze medal on the mat. The Cuban taekwondo athlete Angel Matos was banned for life for kicking a referee in the face. His action, and the referee's decision that led to it, may be highly detrimental to the sport of taekwondo in general, since it risks being dropped from the Olympic program. Fencing, which uses electronic registration of hits and video review, is becoming one of the most objective combat sports.

Another novelty that positively affected the spectators' and journalists' perception of saber fencing was the widely approved use of clear visor masks, allowing observation of emotions on fencers' faces. The new mask was first introduced four years ago during the Athens Summer Olympics, but at that time it raised many doubts. Recent studies have shown that the visor does not reduce a fencer's field of vision, nor had any negative influence on the gas exchange in fencers's lungs or oxygen uptake by dueling fencers. It remains to be seen whether these masks will ever be welcomed in epee, where the face is valid target for a heavier thrusting weapon.

These positive developments point to some bright prospects for saber fencing and are definitely contributing to the popularization of fencing among the young people from different countries. There is, however, still much to be done to increase the attractiveness of this one and only Olympic cutting and thrusting weapon. There are still many connoisseurs of the "old" saber who remain nostalgic about the spectacular exchanges of parries, ripostes, and counter-ripostes. Some even fondly remember the spectacular fleches performed by the old-time fencing champions. For them, the modern saber appears too fast and too purely physical. It is worth recalling here the idea of Polish four-time saber world champion from the 1960's, Wojciech Zabłocki. According to him a good way to "slow down" a saber bout and bring out the beauty of the sport, i.e.the vast array of saber parries and ripostes, could be the use of a saber twice as heavy as existing fencing weapons (up to 1 kg) with a stiffer blade. In my opinion, it is a very interesting concept; however, using a 750 gram saber would be more optimal.

The World Congress of Science and Technology in Fencing held in Barcelona in February and March 2008 foresaw further technical innovations in fencing. Most likely, the fencers' body cords will be soon replaced in all three weapons with wireless technology, employing telemetric registration of hits. This will definitely increase the attractiveness of saber fencing, characterized by the highest dynamics and the greatest variability of actions.

Chapter 2.

The History of Saber Fencing and the Rise of Polish Saber

2.1 Sport fencing and the national fencing schools

Fencing as a sport developed from swordplay as a combat art for the battlefield and for personal self-defense. The predecessors of our contemporary fencing masters were the Masters of Fence from the late 16th century, who authored some of the earliest treatises on fencing. These were the earliest manuals of fencing methodology in the modern sense. They included descriptions of the characteristics of particular weapon types: saber, rapier, epee and – later – foil, as well as instructions on how to teach cuts, thrusts, attacks, and parries. They also discussed the differences between national schools of swordsmanship: Italian, French and Spanish. A turning point in the development of competitive fencing was the 18th century, which witnessed the invention of the fencing mask and the introduction of the foil, which made fencing practice much safer. The 18th century also saw the culmination of a trend toward lighter and lighter combat weapons: the transition to court swords (smallswords) from rapiers, which had in their turn replaced the heavy battlefield swords of the Middle Ages.

These innovations, as well as the social transformations of the nineteenth century, made swordsmanship more of a sport than a method of armed combat, although swords still played a formal role in the "duels of honor," of western and central Europe.

By the late 19th century, the most famous fencing schools were located in Italy, France and Austria-Hungary (Barbasetti 1900). This period also saw the heyday of the Polish saber school, which incorporated many progressive elements into fencing instruction. The Polish

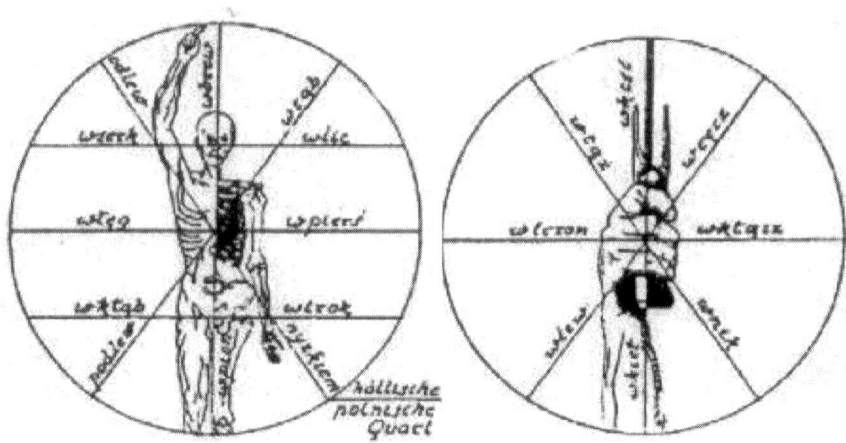

Fig. 2.1: Saber cuts of the 18th and 19th-century Polish School (Starzewski)

fencing school became popular in Hungary and Germany, and many Polish fencing masters were invited to the royal courts of Western Europe to share the secrets of Polish saber fencing (Fig. 2.1).

By the end of the 19th century, fencing tournaments, attended by top fencing masters, had become very popular within the Austro-Hungarian Empire, which included parts of Poland and Italy (and five other nationalities as well.) Although foil was generally the dominant fencing weapon until the outbreak of World War II, saber was more popular in Hungary and parts of Italy. In the early 20th century, the Italian saber school enjoyed its greatest international successes, only to fall behind the Hungarian school in the late 1920's. The latter had a profound impact on the development of Polish saber, and Polish saber fencers became well-known worldwide in the interwar period and after World War Two. In 1959, the Polish saber fencers challenged the supremacy of Hungarians in Budapest and won the world team championship. They continued their sport successes until the late 1960's. The crowning achievement of Polish saber fencing was Jerzy Pawlowski's gold medal at the 1968 Olympic Games in Mexico City.

2.2 Fencing in the modern Olympics

The revival of the Olympic Games in 1896 represented the triumph of sport fencing over its military variant. Individual men's saber and foil events date back to the first Modern Olympic Games in Athens. Since then, saber has always been included in the Olympic program as a separate fencing event. (Significantly, it was only during the 2004

Olympic Games in Athens, 108 years after the start of the Games, that women's saber became part of the Olympic program.)

The Modern Olympics were founded by Baron Pierre de Coubertin, a keen saber fencer and equestrian. Interestingly, 1896, the year of the first Modern Olympics in Athens, was also the year of the first modern competitive fencing tournament with a new refereeing system. As part of the observance of the thousandth anniversary of Hungarian statehood, a saber and foil tournament for fencing masters and amateur fencers took place in Budapest. The historic winner of the competition was Italo Santelli, a student of Master Radaelli's Italian saber school. The rapid development and immense popularity of fencing in the 19th century vastly contributed to the sport's permanent inclusion in the Olympic program. Today, fencing is one of only five sports to have been included in every official Olympic program. (The others are athletics (track and field), cycling, gymnastics, and swimming.)

The first Olympic fencing champions were the Greek I. Georgiadis in saber and Frenchman Gravelotte in foil. The first Olympic epee event took place at the 1900 Olympic Games in Paris. The individual epee champion was the Cuban R. Fonst, who also won two Olympic gold medals in foil in 1904 in St. Louis (in individual and team events). Fonst was undoubtedly the best competitive fencer in the world at that time. The first Olympic team fencing events took place at the 1904 Olympics in St. Louis, but only in foil. The first Olympic team fencing champion was Fonst's Cuban team, whose victory demonstrated that because of the colonial policies of France and Spain, fencing had become a global sport. Team saber and epee events were held for the first time during the 1908 London Olympics; the winners were the Hungarians in saber and the French in epee.

These were all men's events. Although women had been taking part in sport fencing for decades, women's individual foil had to wait until the 1924 Games and women's team foil until 1960. Women's individual and team epee were not added until 1996, while women's individual saber was added in 2004 and finally women's team saber in 2008.

2.3 The transformations of competitive fencing

The end of the 19th century brought profound changes in competitive fencing, thanks mostly to improvements in the refereeing of fencing bouts. Apart from dueling, most competitive fencing had taken the form of exhibitions for prizes or prestige, or to demonstrate superiority of one fencing school over another. But this was part of an evolutionary process that had stretched over millennia.

2.3.1 History of swordplay

Military training in ancient Egypt already included fencing bouts with wooden swords. The ancient Greeks and Romans, like other ancient civilizations throughout Europe and Asia, used cutting and thrusting swords in warfare. A turning point in the evolution of fencing was the introduction of gunpowder (a Chinese invention) to the European battlefield, which made armor obsolescent. The heavy armor of the European Middle Ages had lost its raison d'être, and the rapier, which was lighter and more suitable for daily wear, replaced the medieval broadsword. The rapier had a long double-edged blade used for both cutting and thrusting and had a complex hilt consisting of a large crosspiece, knuckle bow and various protective rings. Meanwhile, the saber, a weapon with a curved blade originally from the East (particularly Turkey,) became the dominant weapon in Poland, Muscovy and Hungary, from which it spread into Western Europe. Both the broadsword and the saber were one-handed weapons of offense, whereas the shield was used for defense. Once the shield was no longer carried, the saber and rapier (which evolved into the epee) became both defensive and offensive weapons.

The turn of the 15th century witnessed the foundation of fencing societies, which provided the ground for systematic fencing instruction. A great number of fencing treatises appeared in Spain, Italy and France. Numerous chroniclers described the views and opinions of the famous masters of their time. The most frequently mentioned name was perhaps that of Achille Marozzo of Bologna, the founder of the Italian school of swordsmanship.

In the 17th century the development of fencing was heavily influenced by French fencing masters, such as Besnard la Touche. Their major contribution was to hasten, theoretize, and systematize the replacement of the rapier. The rapier represented compromise between two demands: a gentleman had to manifest his connection with the feudal aristocracy by carrying a sword that was deadly, but the weapon he carried could not be so clumsy as to disgrace a ballroom. At that time, the art of fencing had reached a heyday, mostly thanks to a number of Italian masters who greatly contributed in theory, practice and methodology to the development of rapier fencing, e.g. Marozzo, Viggiani, Fabris, Cavalcabo, Agrippa, Ferro, Giganti, Saviolo and many others.

The 17th century brought new developments in fencing, e.g. the invention of what was to become the modern foil for use in practice. Another transformative invention, the fencing mask, first appeared in the 18th century. The foil and the mask transformed fencing even more into a competitive sport. The concept of priority, or right of way, originated at that time. The speed of fencing movements increased; new elements of combat such as exchanges of parries, ripostes and counter-ripostes, and various types of counter-attacks appeared; and finally the target area in saber was enlarged to include the head, chest, arms, wrists, and the lower parts of the trunk.

In the 19th century, after the Napoleonic Wars, many new fencing schools were founded. Of special importance are the following: In 1824, the first Hungarian fencing school was founded in Kolozsvar. One year later, the Pest Fencing Institute was established in Pest (the eastern part of modern Budapest). In 1852, the Fencing Masters' School of the Austro-Hungarian Empire was founded in Wiener-Neustadt, south of Vienna. This was a principal training ground for Austrian and Hungarian officers and non-commissioned officers. It was followed in 1872 by the French Joinville-le-Pont School for fencing masters, founded in a suburb of Paris,, and in that same year by the Italian Fencing Masters' School in Rome – the Scuola Magistrale.

2.4   The Polish saber school in the 18th and 19th centuries

The Polish saber school was most comprehensively described in 19th century treatise by Michal Ostoja Starzewski who, as a non-commissioned officer of the Volhynia Mounted Rifles, had fought in the tragic November Uprising against Russian rule in 1831. His fencing treatise was published by his grandson in 1932 and is an invaluable source for Polish fencing history. The Polish school introduced a number of progressive elements into saber fencing including the wielding of the saber with an immovable elbow. The system was widely used and became implemented in many countries, e.g. in Hungary, where it was known as the Kerestessy school. Bouts took place within a space limited by the constraints of the duel. The outcome depended on the dexterity of the fencer's hand. Footwork was

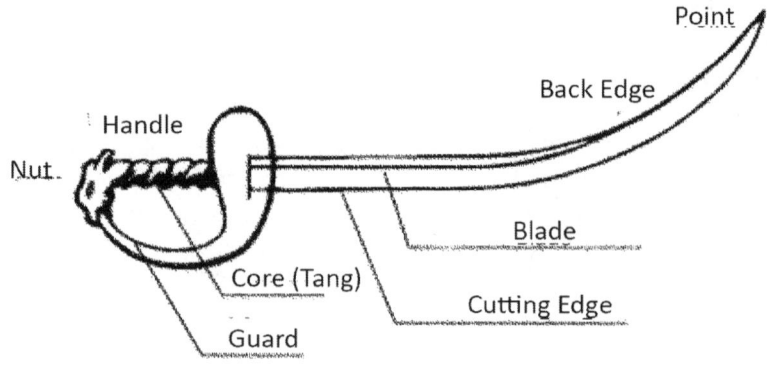

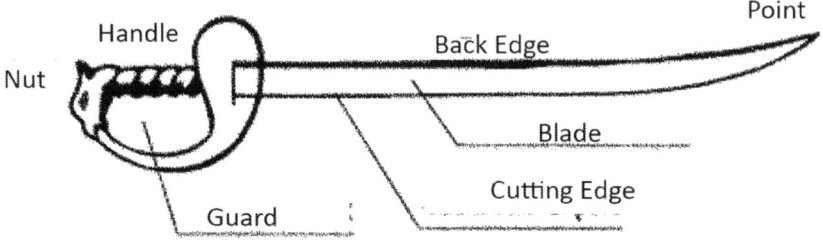

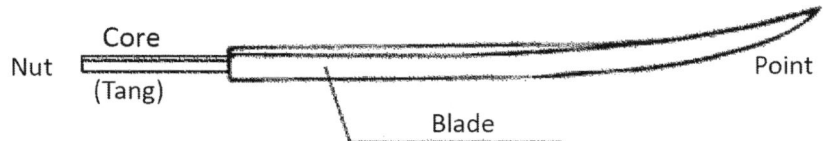

Fig. 2.2: Nineteenth-century Polish Sabers (Starzewski)
Overall length 1.05m – 1.25m (41.3 – 49.2 inches)

limited by both the weight of the weapon and that of the protective gear: a heavily padded fencing jacket and a heavy face-mask.

Starzewski described a number of fencing positions associated with this school. The most basic was the "forward" position. The position of the feet was similar to the present-day on-guard position. The rear hand was stuck behind the back inside the belt, and the sword arm was extended, with the point aimed at the opponent's right eye. From this position, fencers carried out attacks and parries, and recovered to it after the completion of their actions. Different cuts had traditional Polish names, e.g. *ciecia wreczne* (cuts on the arm) and *ciecia rdzenne* (cuts on the torso, head and shoulders). Also "triple cuts" were used, which resembled contemporary compound attacks. The parries included high prime and seconde. The attacks were executed over shorter distances, mostly with the lunge; defense relied on retreats and evasions as well as parries. Counter-attacks and counter-time were not used, and Starzewski makes no mention of thrusts. (The shape of the Polish saber made it a typical cutting weapon (Fig. 2.2).

The first half of the 19th century was the heyday of Polish fencing. Many Polish fencing masters were invited to Western Europe, mostly to Germany, where they taught the arcana of traditional Polish saber fencing. Although many of the aforementioned elements had been known for a long time in dueling fencing, by the end of the 19th century a new era in competitive fencing had surely begun.

2.5   The rise of the Italian saber school in the late 19th century

The founder of the modern Italian saber school was Fencing Master Giuseppe Radaelli. In Italy, saber schools were divided into Southern (Neapolitan and Sicilian), Roman, and Northern (Tuscan). The last school included such famous 20th century fencers and fencing masters as Nedo and Aldo Nadi, as well as Eugenio Pini who was never defeated in any fencing tournament. Italo Santelli, who later became a noted fencing master and coach of many Hungarian teams, also came from the Northern Italian school. Radaelli's method called for executing cuts from the elbow with a stiff wrist. The new Italian saber ("Sciabola") weighed only 800 grams (about 27 oz.) and allowed natural movements and much faster fencing. The grip rested between the thumb and the index finger. The main parries of the Italian school were prime, seconde and quinte; tierce and quarte were auxiliary parries, while sixte and septime were used only occasionally. The initial positions were high tierce and seconde; thus, the aim of most attacks was the opponent's cheek. Photographs and drawings from the Italian school show that tierce and quarte were executed low and forward because of the fear of circular parries.

The Italian system showed a marked progress in saber fencing. It gave rise to hitherto unknown counter-attacks, counter-time, second intention actions, and thrusts. The footwork became immensely flexible, including steps, advance lunges, and retreats (but as yet no fleches), and perfect maintenance of distance became an art in itself. The Italian masters developed the principles of fencing instruction, methodology and fencing terminology with the aid of modern manuals. One such fencing master was a student of Radaelli, Luigi Barbasetti, the author of two books on saber and foil fencing, who in 1894 became the Headmaster of the Wiener-Neustadt Fencing Academy. Many Italian fencers moved to Hungary, where they spread their swordsmanship skills. The Italo Santelli, winner of the historic 1896 Hungarian fencing tournament, became the coach of the Hungarian national team and often competed against Polish fencers at the Olympic Games (Paris, Amsterdam, Los Angeles) and European Championships.

Within a short time, the Italian fencing school was world famous.

2.6 The Hungarian School

Even as Italian saber was spreading worldwide, the Hungarians were making a thorough revision of the Italian schools and introducing a number of key improvements. Paradoxically, it was Italian fencing masters in Hungary, who, together with their Hungarian fencers, brought an end to the dominance of the Italian school as early as the 1908 Olympics in London. (Later, a similar transfer of pre-eminence took place when some of the leading Polish fencing masters (Aleksander Wójcicki, Zbigniew Czajkowski) along with the Hungarian Janos Kevey broke the long-lasting supremacy of Hungarian saber fencers, when the Polish team won the gold medal at the World Championships in Budapest in 1959.) The objective of the new Hungarian system was to improve the quality of bladework in order to avoid excessive movements from the elbow, which together with the forearm had become a common target for counter-attacks. The idea was to keep the forearm and the bell guard in the line of attack. Furthermore, in the Hungarian school the center of rotation was the wrist, not the elbow as in the Italian school (Schenker 1967). Thanks to the interaction between the elbow and wrist joints, fencing movements became softer and more flexible. The Hungarian school featured a great improvement in footwork quality and an increase in the speed of actions, which had made it easier to execute hits on the unguarded hand when held on guard in seconde. The better-defended tierce and quarte therefore became the basic positions in the new system. Their added advantage was the lack of interaction among the shoulder girdle muscles, so that stiffening of the shoulder was avoided and the intention to assume a given parry was concealed. There were no revolutionary changes in footwork mechanics or exercises; however, in the Hungarian system, footwork was smoother and the moves less perceptible than in the Italian system. Typical Hungarian footwork, as exemplified by the Olympic champion Jeno Fuchs (1908 and 1912) was called "stealthy." In addition, the theory of fencing tactics gained a number of hitherto unknown elements (Lukovich 1975):

- *Foot tempo.* The notion of foot tempo, understood as the ability to seize the moment of attack by taking advantage of opponent's foot movement (exploiting his inertia at the start of offensive action) became immensely significant. From that time onward, the feeling of fencing tempo – the sense of the right moment – has been a key test of whether a fencer possesses the potential to practice saber fencing on a high level.
- *Rhythm.* A great emphasis was placed on the rhythm of movements, which some Hungarian fencing masters demonstrated in the form of musical notes.
- *Parrying system and bladework.* Hungarian fencing technique used the "triangle" of parries tierce, quarte and quinte, as well as characteristic speed and precision of bladework, combining wrist movements with delicate finger play.

These improvements did not appear suddenly or simultaneously, but were the results of the long-term development of the Hungarian fencing system.

- *The fleche.* In the 1920's, the Hungarian fencer Attila Petschauer introduced the fleche into fencing footwork. Soon it became very popular among a number of fencers. The fleche was employed by Olympic champions Aladar Gerevich (London, 1948) and Pal Kovacs (Helsinki, 1952). (However, Rudolf Karpati (Melbourne, 1956 and Rome, 1960) preferred classical footwork and fleched only sporadically.) Polish saber fencers like Wojciech Zablocki, Jerzy Pawlowski used a particularly dynamic form of fleche. They finished their fleche in the air, cutting opponents with maximal speed in the final action and landing on the forward leg.

(This spectacular bit of footwork is now a closed chapter in the history of saber fencing. In 1993, the FIE banned the fleche due to its abuse in the form of the so-called "running attacks" in the 1980's and the 1990's. Because referees found themselves unable (or unwilling) to discern the end of continuous running attacks, they brought about a crisis in saber fencing which finally led to the outlawing of the fleche, but was not resolved until the introduction of the electronic scoring apparatus.)

The Hungarian fencing system, however, was not perfect, as the British master Roger Crosnier pointed out at the time (1956). Overconfident fencing masters and fencers often fell into routine bladework and frequently overused the fleche, evasions and retreats. The stagnation and crisis of Hungarian saber school followed, caused by a lack of impulse to develop new ideas. A new tendency, particularly in saber technique and physical preparation, emerged from Poland and Russia, which dominated on the fencing circuits during the 1960's (Poles) and 1970's (Russians).

2.7 Saber fencing in Poland, 1909-1968

Saber fencing began to develop rapidly in Poland after the country regained its independence in 1918. The first mentions of Polish competitive fencing clubs date from the end of the 19th century, when Poland was still partitioned among Russia, Germany, and Austria-Hungary. In 1909, the first official fencing club opened in Kraków. The outbreak of World War I interrupted its activities, but the club revived in 1922 as AZS Kraków. The major figure among the Kraków fencing masters was Eugeniusz Linneman, a graduate of the Wiener-Neustadt Fencing Academy. Others included Antoni Bakowski, Jerzy Zabielski, Wladyslaw Segda and Adam Papee. Papee's first coach was the renowned painter and art critic Konrad Winkler. In Lvov, then part of Poland (now part of Ukraine,) the main figures were Mankowski, Sobolewski, Sedlaczek and Vambera – the first President of the Polish Fencing Association, founded in Lvov in 1922. Another famous fencing master in Poland at that time was Horace

Santelli, a relative of Italo Santelli, the famous progenitor of the Italo-Hungarian fencing family.

The Italian system (with some modifications from the Wiener-Neustadt school) dominated Polish saber fencing in the interwar period. Polish fencing literature emphasized following the Italian system in Polish saber fencing. Mankowski, in his work *Saber Fencing* (1929), as well as Sobolewski and Zytny in their fencing manuals, used only Italian fencing terminology without any Polish equivalents.

By that time the Italian school (which the Poles still favored) was already somewhat outdated; the Hungarian system had superseded it. An important lesson for the Polish saber fencers came with their bitter defeat at the Paris Olympic Games in 1924. Expectations and ambitions under the domination of the Italian coaches had been much higher than real achievements. Subsequent changes in fencing training methodology and the hiring of the Hungarian fencing master Bella Szombathely to work with the Polish national team brought some success. In 1928 at the Olympic Games in Amsterdam the Polish national saber team (Segda, Malecki, Laskowski, Fnedrich, Zabielski, Papee) made their historic achievement: the team Olympic bronze medal. Adam Papee recalled the preparation for the Olympic contest and the influence of the Hungarian fencing master: "We practiced the fleche, tempo and unpremeditated actions." This was a crucial moment in the development of saber tactics. Before then, fencers had trained using set sequences of actions; from then on, actions with an unknown ending have been added to the arsenal. After Kraków and Lvov, new fencing centers, e.g. in the Central School of Gymnastics and Sport in Poznan, were established with top fencing masters: Berski, Laskowski, Kozarski and many others. Kozarski also worked in Katowice, founded new fencing clubs and trained such prominent fencers as Sobik, Zaczyk, Paszek and Radecki.

The fencing center in Warsaw became very significant after the Central School of Gymnastics and Sport moved there and became the Central Institute of Physical Education. New fencing clubs founded in Warsaw included Legia, Warszawianka, AZS and Policyjny Klub Sportowy (Police Sport Club). In 1929, the first course for fencing masters was organized under Szombathely's guidance. In 1934, the World Fencing Championships were held in Warsaw. They turned out to be a great organizational and sport success: the Polish saber team won the bronze medal. The preparation for the event took the form of a professionally organized one-week training camp at the Central Institute of Physical Education in Bielany.

Although epee and foil competitions had taken place in Poland since the National Championships in 1924, Polish epeeists and foilists did not achieve any international successes in the interwar period. The Polish saber team won another Olympic bronze medal in Los Angeles in 1932 and a bronze medal at the European Fencing Championships in Liege, Belgium in 1930. The Berlin Olympic Games of 1936 and their propaganda setting portended the impending war. A number of Polish fencers, e.g. Nycz, Malecki, and Radecki were killed during World War Two; others became prisoners of war, e.g. Segda and Zabielski. After the war the old masters: Papee, Friedrich, Laskowski, Sobik, Zaczyk and many others enthusiastically revived saber fencing in Poland and provided the ground for the future, outstanding international achievements of Polish fencers. The first significant success after the second World War was caused by the Polish saber team in Brussels in 1953. The main creators of the new stage in history of Polish saber school were Aleksander Wojcicki and Zbigniew Czajkowski. The first spectacular and individual success was the silver medal in 1956 Olympic Game in Melbourne won by Jerzy Pawlowski. After this event, Polish saber fencers have won four World Championships. The absolute champion of saber and a contender for the title "The best saber fencer ever" was above mentioned Jerzy Pawłowski, three times the individual World Champion and gold medalist at the 1968 Mexico City Olympic Games.

Chapter 3.

The Impact of Electronic Scoring on Saber

3.1   The crisis of non-electric saber

The next major development in the history of saber was the advent of electric scoring, which transformed saber, as it had foil and epee. Saber was the last fencing weapon to start using electronic scoring equipment. After many attempts, an electronic scoring apparatus was approved, and by the end of the 1980s, its use became mandatory in all international events. (Electronic scoring had been first introduced to epee in the 1930s and to foil in the 1950s.)

For those too young to remember visually-judged saber, these were some of its features:

- As in epee, the piste was a theoretical 18 meters in length. Since bouts were actually fenced on a 14 meter piste, this meant that a fencer retreating off the back of the piste for the first time was placed on guard at the two-meter line. This interrupted the flow of the bout and introduced extraneous tactical considerations.

- A referee (director, president) presided over four side judges (two side judges in the case of less formal competitions).

- The priority (right-of-way) conventions were essentially the same as those in foil. In particular, a hit with priority stopped the action, even if it was off-target (compare the white light in foil).

- The only valid hits were those made by a thrust with the point or by a solid cut from anywhere on the front edge of the blade or the first third of the sides or back of the blade. The hit needed to be clearly visible and often audible.

- Hits "through steel" – those that whipped over a defender's guard or blade after being parried – did not count as valid.

- Mere grazes, that is, cuts or thrusts with no substantial force behind them, did not count. Given the speed of saber actions, this often meant that judges had to hear hits, rather than see them.

- The technical difficulty in registering these distinctions reliably on an electronic apparatus (the scoring machine) made saber the last weapon to adopt electronic scoring. Saber devotees insisted on retaining all of these features until a deep crisis beginning in the 1970's.

The cause of the crisis was the referees' misinterpretations of attacks. Referees were not able to cope with the increasing dynamics and speed of saber bouts, so that increasingly they saw all forward movement as an attack. The result was a progressive limitation of the repertoire of fencing actions, excessive use of simultaneous actions, and the reduction of classical footwork to simply running along the piste.

At that time, the main offensive technique in saber was the fleche, or rather the continuous running attack. This put the attacking fencer in a privileged position because referees were unwilling to call successive running steps a preparation rather than a continuous attack. As a result, defenders were not able to utilize the rich array of counter-attacks because the referees awarded continuous priority (right of way) to the fencer running down the strip. Therefore, fencers felt forced to charge down the strip at each other, resorting sometimes to as many as several dozen (!) simultaneous actions during a single bout. They used these tactics frequently, hoping to overcome the opponent psychologically. Finally, saber fencers ceased executing real feints and simply pretended to attack, confusing the referees, frustrating each other, and boring the spectators.

All of the above inevitably led to a declining interest in saber and made saber into an increasingly marginal fencing event. The International Fencing Federation (FIE) became seriously worried about the future of saber after the International Olympic Committee threatened to exclude saber from the Olympic program.

3.2   Reforming tendencies

Following long-term tests, the first electronic saber devices were developed in the late 1980's. Saber fencers started to wear conductive masks and jackets (lamés). It proved impractical to retain certain features of visually judged saber. At first, special capteurs (motion sensors) inside the guard were intended to eliminate accidental hits caused by grazes and whip-overs. The capteurs proved unreliable, however, and present-day electric saber (perhaps unfortunately) does not use any sensors. In addition, the off-target light was eliminated, so that a hit on a non-valid surface simply did not register: It counted as a miss. The result was a faster bout and one that was more comprehensible to the spectators.

At the 1989 World Championships in Denver, saber fencers used only electric weapons for the first time. It was a moment long anticipated by the entire fencing community. The electronic equipment made refereeing a lot simpler: there was only one referee instead of five during a bout, the same as in the thrusting weapons. Referees' decisions were more objective. Finally, electronic scoring made saber bouts more comprehensible and attractive to the spectators.

Earlier, a rule that randomized right-of-way had been introduced to prevent the excessive use of simultaneous attacks. After a few simultaneous attacks, the referee would warn both fencers and then order a coin toss for the subsequent right-of-way. This forced the defending fencer to use defensive actions and counter-attacks. Saber fencers themselves welcomed the new rule, because it opened up a range of new tactical possibilities. However, in the opinion of many spectators, it was incomprehensible and ridiculous, and it aroused suspicion of favoritism by the officials. A case in point was the popular French fencer Jean Francois Lamour and his fight for a medal at the 1992 Olympic Games in Barcelona. During the event, spectators called French TV, asking for the entire bout to be decided by a coin toss.

The situation was not improved by a proposal in the spring of 1993 to count double touches, as in epee. This was a total failure and the authorities quickly discarded the idea.

There were positive changes as well. These included limiting the piste length by abandoning the "two-meter rule." Today, a fencer backing off the end of the strip gets an immediate touch against him. Eliminating this feature intensified saber bouts and forced saber fencers to stay constantly alert on any part of the strip and make decisions without the possibility of stopping the attack simply by running away.

Despite a number of obvious positive changes, electronic scoring still caused problems for referees. Chief among them was the difficulty of judging whether a parry was sufficient. A parry – riposte is probably the most spectacular fencing action. The technical limitation of the cutout time to 0.2 seconds eliminated the registration of hits received by the defender during a parry – riposte. However, there was no revolutionary change, since inept referees still regarded such situations as "malparé." In November 1991, at the Junior Fencing World Cup in Dourdan, Prieur Sports demonstrated a scoring apparatus that seemed to offer a solution to the problem. It used a pulsed light to signal a "false" hit during a correct riposte. However, other manufacturers did not follow suit, and other proposals for solving the problem gained little support. To date the problem of the two lights remains open: was the attack successful? Was the parry – riposte in time? It is a difficult and controversial decision, even with video replay.

Other regulation changes in saber fencing aimed to make fencing bouts easier for spectators to understand. New reforms were introduced. The most significant was the FIE decision to prohibit the fleche and cross-over steps in saber fencing in the fall of 1993. The first tournament without them was the Category B World Cup in Munich in November 1993. The ban, although received skeptically by traditionalists, very soon turned beneficial for saber fencing. Before the ban, the real combat time during a bout was only 30 – 40 seconds on average. Now it was significantly longer. Saber fencers started to make frequent use of ripostes, counter-ripostes, simple attacks, compound attacks, actions on the blade and counter-attacks. The problem of excessive simultaneous attacks was largely resolved and the number of tactical possibilities increased. The hated coin toss for right-of way also disappeared from the regulations. Saber fencing also benefited from changes in bout duration in fencing in general. The new fencing bout regulations replaced the earlier best-of-three

5-touch rounds in a bout with a 15-touch bout consisting of 3-minute rounds with 1-minute breaks between them for rest, consultations with the coach, and of course, television commercials. These changes were very positive and resulted in an increase in the popularity of saber fencing. At the World Championships in The Hague in 1995, the number of participating saber fencers equaled the number of epeeists and foilists for the first time in years.

All the above changes increased the popularity of saber fencing among women. Women's saber was an exhibition event at the 2000 Olympic Games in Sydney, and it was officially included in the program of the Athens Olympic Games in 2004. The development of women's saber fencing shows a number of positive tendencies. Unlike men, female saber fencers had not experienced the slow and painful evolution of the technique and tactics of electric saber, so they were open to the new possibilities of the evolved electronic weapon. Women's saber bouts display well-considered tactics and are often longer than men's bouts. Female saber fencers make use of a wide range of technical actions, including a great variety of parries, counter-attacks, counter-ripostes, and counter-time.

3.3 Tactical analysis of some top saber bouts of the 1990s

The following sections report on saber technique and tactics as they had evolved a half-decade after the introduction of electronically-scored saber. The reader will find it instructive to compare this analysis with the chapter on the 2008 Beijing Olympics and decide which trends are permanent parts of the saber scene, which changes represent positive developments, and which may simply be passing fads.

The analysis below is based on video footage of actions performed by some top world saber fencers. Five bouts from the footage considered the most representative of different styles of fencing combat were selected for the analysis (Borysiuk 1996).

Bouts selected for Table 3.1
1. Felix Becker (Germany) v. Stanislav Pozdniakov (Russia), score: 15-14, Final, World Championships, Athens, 1994.

2. Felix Becker (Germany) v. Grigorij Kirienko (Russia), score: 15-10, Semi-final, World Championships, Athens, 1994.

Table 3.1: Fencing actions of top world saber fencers (in percentages)

BOUT	Attacks					Counter-attacks					Ripostes, Ctr-ripostes			Penalties	Target Hit			Simultaneous hits
	Simple	On blade	Feinted	Counter-time	Renewed	Simple	Feinted	With opposition	On blade	Point in line	Simple	Feinted	Counter-riposte		Arm	Head	Trunk (chest, flank)	
Becker - Pozdniakov 15-14	2	0	12	4	0	4	1	0	0	4	1	0	0	1	4	1	23	13
Becker - Kirienko 15 - 10	3	0	5	3	0	7	0	1	0	0	5	0	1	0	6	4	15	18
Szabo - Sznajder 15 - 7	2	0	5	5	1	4	0	0	2	0	2	0	1	0	4	7	11	7
Gilman - Olech 5, 4-4	4	0	3	1	0	2	0	1	1	0	4	1	1	0	6	3	9	0
Kirienko - Wiesinger 15 - 11	3	1	4	1	1	2	2	1	3	0	2	3	1	0	4	8	14	7
%	12	0.8	24	12	1.7	16	2.5	2.5	5	3.3	13	3.3	3.3	-	20	19	60	38
%	50.1					29.1					19.9			0.8				

3. Bence Szabo (Hungary) v. Rafal Sznajder (Poland), score: 15-7, Semi-final, Category B World Cup, Munich, 1993.

4. Dariusz Gilman (Poland) v. Janusz Olech (Poland), score: 5-4, 5-4, training bouts of the Polish National Team before the World Championships in The Hague, 1995.

5. Grigorij Kirienko (Russia) v. Steffen Wiesinger (Germany), score: 15-11, Semi-final, Category A World Cup, Madrid, 1995.

Table 3.1 presents a percentage analysis of 120 fencing actions resulting in valid touches (including one penalty hit for Pozdniakov for execution of a fleche) as well as 45 simultaneous hits. All the bouts took place in the mid-1990's, i.e. 5 – 6 years after the introduction of electronic scoring. The analysis of the bouts was based on numerous observations and video recordings. Some interesting conclusions emerged.

3.4 Tactical trends as of the mid 1990's

The prohibition of the fleche and crossover steps led to limited speed of footwork and longer bouts that kept the spectators uncertain of the result until the very last actions on the piste. Stanislav Pozdniakov experienced this aspect when he fenced Becker in the finals of the 1994 World Championships in Athens. Pozdniakov led Becker at 12 – 3, but ultimately lost 14 –15.

The percentage analysis of hits reveals an "ideal" equilibrium between attacks (50.1%), counter-attacks (29.1%), and ripostes and counter-ripostes (19.9%). This equilibrium is highly significant from the tactical point of view. The studied fencers often made first-intention feint attacks, shortened the distance, and used simple attacks, counter-attacks, or parries. The percentage of counter-attacks in the total number of hits (almost 30%) was a sign of their increased effectiveness. In the Becker – Pozdniakov bout, Becker, while in a "critical situation," executed eight counter-attacks, including four stop-hits to arm and four points-in-line. Many saber experts regarded this as proof of the highest tactical artistry.

The most common offensive action was feint attack (24.2%). This is hardly surprising. What was significant was the manner of its execution: an attack consisted of a series of short feints with an emphasis on the final feint provoking the opponent's response. Simple attacks and counter-time actions comprised equal 11.7% proportions of offensive actions. The latter often included the co-called "concealed counter-time," that is, the attacker changed his preparation into a final action on seeing the opponent's counter-attack. The concealed counter-time was a special skill of Olympic champion Bence Szabo, who scored five touches in this way in his bout against Rafal Sznajder— in three actions, he initially feinted a quinte parry, provoking a delayed response from his opponent.

The observed percentage of ripostes and counter-ripostes (19.9%) was decidedly below expectations for any saber connoisseur. Recent observations confirm more frequent and bolder use of parries in saber. Characteristically a significant number of ripostes and counter-ripostes were executed by Gregorij Kirienko, the world's best saber fencer at the turn of the 1980's.

The above tactical analysis would not be complete without mentioning the ratio between the number of simultaneous hits (45) and valid touches (120), which amounted to "merely" 37.5% simultaneous actions. In the most prestigious bouts, the number of simultaneous hits was proportionally larger. Out of 27 valid touches in the bout between Becker and Kirienko there were 18 simultaneous hits. These were not consecutive, but were rather interludes that preceded some interesting actions. When the pressure was lower, the number of simultaneous actions per bout was significantly less, e.g. none were registered during the Gilman-Olech bout. The number of simultaneous hits in saber also illustrates the poor level of tactical and technical advancement, especially in top-level bouts. Too many simultaneous hits can be an indication of the fencers' lack of confidence in technical actions and reliance on the opponent's errors rather than applying one's own technical and tactical solutions. A bout involving excessive use of simultaneous actions is passive and unattractive to spectators.

3.5 Technical developments of the mid 1990's

The analysis revealed a surprisingly low number of hits to the head. This may be an indication of some epee-like tendencies in saber; in epee, most hits are to the forearm, arm, and trunk. The saber fencers in this study displayed particular creativity in executing cuts on arm both in defensive and offensive actions, using all sides of the blade. The parrying movements were mostly beat parries, taken in front of the body. Parries seconde and prime were popular as well as circular: counter-quinte, counter-quarte and counter-tierce. Counter-ripostes were rare, but they occurred.

The blade-work techniques were also significant. The cuts were dynamic, clean and executed with sufficient force. The distance between fencers was shorter, and the feinting technique emphasized the foible (the part of the blade near the tip), rather than the forearm, which had to be "concealed" to prevent an attack. The world's top fencers, mostly Russians (Kirienko, Sharikov), performed their final cuts with just as the leading foot landed on the piste; occasionally, the tap of the front foot even followed the cut during feint ripostes. The change of distance had no effect, however, on the relatively small number of actions on the blade. What was characteristic was a very low percent of point-in-line actions (one of the most basic offensive-defensive actions.) Formerly, the point-in-line was used too often and referees' interpretations caused controversies among coaches and fencers. At present, the short distance makes it easy to neutralize this threatening movement with beat attacks to the forearm.

The changes in fencing technique and tactics discussed above were the consequences of footwork limitations. It is a paradox, therefore, that the role of footwork has significantly increased over recent years. One can often hear opinions concerning elite saber fencers such as Grigorij Kirienko from Russia or Philippe Daurelle from France that they won their bouts "on foot." Modern footwork techniques in saber consist of various combinations of steps, double-steps, glides and lunges, all with varying rhythm. During the execution of a simple action, experienced fencers start advancing slowly and imperceptibly to make a quick lunge in the end. During the execution of compound feint attacks, they use a series of rhythmic steps in each phase of the movement. The classic lunge was also significantly altered. Depending on the situation on the piste, it can play the role of the fleche: a fencer who realizes he would fail to reach the opponent can re-lunge and land on the leading foot. This is the so-called saber fleche, which United States fencers colloquially call a "flunge." A novel element in saber footwork is the riposte – counter-time, which is actually a counter-attack. While performing this action the defending fencer feints a stop-hit, which forces the opponent to finish the attack. After that, he increases the distance with a step or jump backwards, avoids a hit and seizes the initiative ("takes over" the attack.)

3.6 Combat styles of top world saber fencers studied

Grigorij Kirienko – four-time world champion, was a "total" fencer, using a vast array of perfectly executed offensive and defensive actions. Kirienko often used parries, especially in risky situations during simultaneous actions. He featured perfect footwork technique, which allowed him to execute accurate simple attacks and counter-attacks, and took merciless advantage of his opponent's errors. Kirienko's psychological ability to overcome difficulties during top-level bouts made him one of the most stress-resistant fencers in history.

Bence Szabo – Olympic and world champion, preferred attacks with effective counter-time. With his excellent somatic parameters – long arm span in particular – Szabo often used compound attacks with a feint preceding the final cut. He often cut to the flank or under the arm with the outer flat of the blade. Szabo's cunning solution of the problem of simultaneous actions consisted of a delayed feint attack and a quick lunge to stop-hit the opponent. His favorite parries included the classic system of tierce, quarte and quinte as well as seconde.

The technique of Felix Becker – world gold, silver, and bronze medalist – was not spectacular, but it was highly efficient. One of his specialties was a stop cut to arm. Becker was one of the very few top saber fencers to succeed in using point in line combined with derobement-thrusts. Fiery by temperament, Becker displayed an impulsive combat style. He was a great individualist who did rather poorly in team events.

Stanislav Pozdniakov – many-time world and Olympic champion, displayed a profile similar to Kirienko's, representative of the Russian saber fencing school. He performed compound attacks excellently, often ended with cuts on chest with the edge, which were very difficult to parry. His attacks commenced with a short jump forwards, increasing the series of steps, depending on the distance to the opponent. Thanks to his excellent sense of distance, he often took the initiative and forced his opponents to shorten their offensive actions. Due to his technique of holding the guard close to his hip, Pozdniakov was rarely taken by surprise with a stop-hit to arm.

He was extremely stress-resistant and could change the score to his advantage in the last moments of the top-level Olympic and world championships bouts.

All the world's top saber fencers of the last decade discussed above started their sport careers in the era of dry saber. They all adapted to the new conditions very well and achieved great successes in electric saber. In my opinion, the studied fencers were the most representative for new tendencies in saber following the introduction of electronic scoring equipment into saber fencing.

3.7　Current trends

Nowadays we can observe positive tendencies connected with the introduction of new lockout time, defined as 120 ms. A saber fencer today must hit 120 ms earlier than his or her opponent for a single touch to be registered by the electronic scoring apparatus. This results in the use of more defensive actions, including parries and counter-parries. Currently we can observe that approximately 30% of touches are executed to the forearm, most of them as a counter-attack in cut-over manner. Generally, the courses of actions are longer. The time needed to score one touch is extended. Practically, simultaneous touches have ceased. The judges' decisions, particularly in top-level competitions, have become more objective, thanks to the introduction of video and replay systems.

Chapter 4.

Modern Saber: Technique

PART I: FOOTWORK TRAINING

The quality of footwork determines success in modern fencing!

The significance of footwork in fencing has grown because of the changes in the rules designed to make fencing more attractive and comprehensible to the spectators. These changes particularly affected the development of saber fencing, which used to be the most conservative of all the three weapons. At present, saber footwork is extremely dynamic. The elimination of the old form of the fleche and the cross-over step have profoundly improved the quality of footwork in saber. In order to meet the speed demands of modern saber, fencers have invented the so-called "saber fleche," called the "flunge" in the United States, and replaced the cross-over step with combinations of glides, jumps forward and the rhythmic steps characteristic of the patinando.

Footwork techniques in saber include:
- Step forward, step backward
- Jump forward, jump backward
- Slide
- Lunge
- Patinando (step forward – lunge)
- Balestra (jump forward – lunge)
- "Saber fleche" or "flunge."

4.1.1 General considerations

Saber fencers should start learning their footwork exercises independently of weapon training in order to avoid learning wrong habits. This is not a permanent requirement, however; and at the advanced training level, footwork exercises take place with weapon in hand, especially during individual lessons.

4.1.2 Some of the special features of modern saber:
- Although the forward and backward steps are similar in foil, epee and saber, the character of the step backward, i.e. in defense, differs importantly. A saber fencer can rapidly increase the speed and range of the rear leg movements only by loading the front leg. It allows him or her to fully control distance and shift quickly to an offensive action.
- Parries are often preceded by feints of stop-hits and a simultaneous increase of distance. This requires full coordination between the sword arm and the front leg and maximum foot mobility.
- The footwork in offensive actions relies on jumps forward, rhythmic steps and short glides. One of the most pronounced footwork elements is a series of glides followed by jumps forward. A typical attack used by top saber fencers is a short glide with a jump forward and patinando (step forward – lunge).
- It should be noted that in modern saber, attacks often finish at the end of the piste, having covered about 7 – 8 meters. This is why many footwork combinations are prepare particular lunges, patinandos or balestras.

Fencers and their coaches should remember two important things. First, all the footwork elements should be practiced in harmony and with a proper rhythm in order to avoid, for instance, opponent's counter-attacks. Second, fencers must be aware of the flexibility of saber footwork, which is important during rapidly changing tactical situations and movement directions on the strip.

4.1.3 Elements of footwork
The fencing posture of modern saber fencers is different than those of foilists and epeeists.

- The feet are placed at an acute rather than right angle, i.e. the toe of the rear foot points forward

- The body (and the hips) lean forward, which increases the loading of the front foot. This slight shift of the center of gravity toward the front leg is the main characteristic feature of the saber fencer's position and footwork.

- **LUNGE.** The lunge is part of saber's basic offensive footwork. Traditionally, it started with the arm movement; however, in modern saber this canon has been altered: now it usually commences with the front foot or with the front foot and sword arm simultaneously. The front foot lands first with the heel, then with the instep and the

Fig 4.1: Step Forward (left to right)

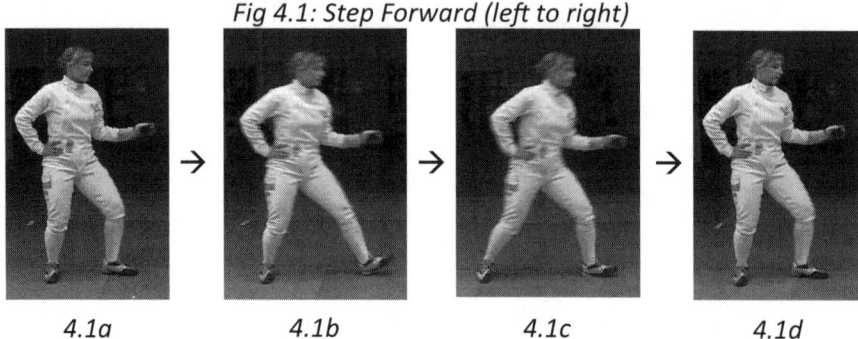

4.1a   4.1b   4.1c   4.1d

In 4.1a, from the on-guard position, the front toe begins to lift. In 4.1b, the fencer strides forward to the front heel. The center of gravity is held somewhat back. In 4.1c, the fencer's front heel has landed and the center of gravity is shifting forward. In 4.1d, the fencer has finished the advance and returned to guard. Both feet have moved an equal distance.

Fig 4.2: Step Backward (right to left)

4.2c   4.2b   4.2a

From on guard, 4.2a (right), The fencer reaches backward with the rear toe, 4.2b (center), keeping the center of gravity somewhat forward. As the sole of the back foot lands, the fencer pushes off the heel of the front foot, and returns to the on-guard position, 4.2c (left), both feet having moved an equal distance.

Fig. 4.3: Jump Forward (l. to r.); Jump Backward (r. to l.)

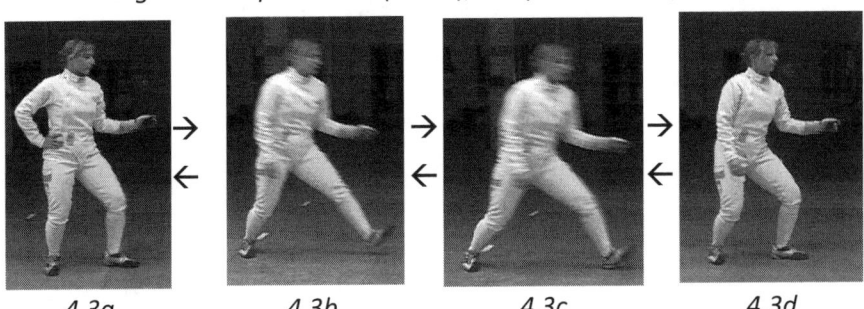

        4.3a   4.3b   4.3c   4.3d

JUMP FORWARD: From the on-guard position, 4.3a, the toe is raised and the front leg is extended, reaching forward with the heel close to the piste, 4.3b. The front foot lands on the heel, 4.3c, and is followed closely by the back foot as the fencer lands in on-guard position 4.3d.

NOTE: In the classic jump forward, both feet land at the same time, which requires the front foot to land on the instep while the back foot moves rapidly forward. In modern saber, as illustrated below, this is not necessary when the jump forward is used to cover distance and change rhythm. It remains necessary when executing a balestra.

JUMP BACKWARD: The jump backward is the reverse of the jump forward, with the rear leg reaching farther backward than in a retreat. The two feet land in close succession. The fencer lands on the rear instep and reassumes the on-guard position.

Fig 4.4: Slide

Slide: The slide is a combination of two steps from on-guard position (*4.4*a): 1) A step forward (*4.4*b), with the rear foot landing close behind the front foot (*4.4*c), is immediately followed by 2) the front foot sliding forward (*4.4*d) and the back foot advancing to finish in the on-guard position (*4.4*e).

toes. The rear foot slides forward slightly. The 90 degrees angle between the thigh and the shin is conventional; it is combined with a wider knee bend, which then makes the transition to further actions much smoother.

Traditionally, saber lunges are divided into:

Accelerating lunge, *Explosive* lunge, and *Waiting* lunge

Although the explosive and waiting lunges are the most common lunges during real fencing bouts, the **ACCELERATING LUNGE** (Fig.4.6) constitutes the starting point for footwork training. It is used in sim-

Fig. 4.5: Lunge (left to right)

4.5a   4.5b   4.5c

LUNGE: From on-guard position (*4.5*a), the toe of the front foot lifts and the front leg is strongly extended (*4.5*b). The front heel lands; the rear foot slides forward; and the front leg is bent at an angle of 90° (*4.5*c). An *explosive lunge* is illustrated.

ple attacks, compound attacks, and attacks with unknown final. An accelerating lunge should be executed lightly, with a slow start and high final acceleration that would take the opponent by surprise.

The **EXPLOSIVE LUNGE** (Fig. *4.8*) is used in simple attacks of first intention at a short distance with maximum speed. It is often applied in a tactical situation of simultaneous attacks as a surprise factor or as the first movement against an opponent's feinted attack.

The **WAITING LUNGE** (Fig. 4.7) is used in attacks of second intention and in counter-time. It contains a waiting phase, which allows the fencer to choose an appropriate reaction against the opponent's counter-attack or, in a multi-feinted attack, forces the opponent to commit an error, cut in false time, or take a premature parry.

Generally, the efficacy of lunges depends on the type of action and accurate choice of distance. In offensive actions of first intention, e.g. cut over to forearm, very short lunges are sufficient. On the other hand, in the final part of a multi-feint attack against an opponent effectively defending himself by retreat, the lunge should be the longest.

Fig. 4.6: Accelerating Lunge

ACCELERATING LUNGE: In this example, note that the attacker (r.) has begun the action with the front foot. The weapon arm is held back, preparing for an explosive finish.

Figs. 4.7 (top to bottom): Waiting Lunge

WAITING LUNGE:

At left we see the slow start of a waiting lunge by the attacker, right. The front foot has started later than in the accelerating lunge in Fig. 4.6 above.

At left, we see that the foot action has progressed considerably, but the arm is still held back as the attacker waits to deal with either of two options from the opponent. If opponent counter-attack, attacker will finish and hit with priority; if opponent parries, attacker will hit the target that opens.

Fig 4.8. (top to bottom): Explosive lunge

EXPLOSIVE LUNGE

Top right: the beginning of an explosive lunge to the head. Note that the arm and leg are more synchronized than in the accelerating or the waiting lunges.

Bottom right: the explosive lunge nears its finish. The arm and leg "explode" forward with maximum speed. As with all these lunges, the attack has landed before (or just as) the front foot hits the piste.

PATINANDO (ADVANCE-LUNGE)

Advance patinando lunge is the second most significant footwork element after the lunge. It is taught after a fencer has mastered sufficiently the technique of steps and lunges. A patinando lunge combines an advance and lunge into a single flow of movement. The training of this element includes three parts: a step forward with one foot, moving forward the rear foot and the actual lunge. The heel and toes of the front foot and the heel of the rear foot tap out the patinando rhythm. A great advantage of the patinando is the possibility of making a prolonged and surprising attack. Moreover, the initial movement of the patinando is like a preparatory action. The opening is relatively slow; the finish is fast and surprising. The attacking fencer is able to change his intention and by forcing the opponent to take a defense position, perform a stop cut or continue the attack with a balestra-lunge. The patinando cannot be illustrated statically; the reader is advised to study the footwork portions of the DVD.

BALESTRA (JUMP FORWARD-LUNGE) (Fig. 4.9)) is statistically the most frequent footwork element in saber fencing. From the methodological standpoint it is a more difficult element than the patinando advance lunge and should be practiced only after all other elements have been mastered. The balestra relies on a very smooth combination of a jump forward and a lunge. Fencers should be taught to avoid such potential errors as jumps upwards (instead of forward) and landing the jump with feet together. This enables correct and effective execution of the entire action. The sword arm-front leg coordination follows the same principles as the patinando advance-lunge.

The fleche in its traditional form consists of transferring the body weight from the front leg to the rear leg by means of a long cross-step. Since current regulations prohibit cross-steps, the fleche may not be used in saber (unlike in foil and epee).

It should be mentioned here that the fleche used to be a very popular action in saber, being almost symbolic of the beauty of this particular fencing event. The image of a saber fencer performing the fleche had

Fig. 4.9a, 4.9b (top to bottom): Balestra

BALESTRA WITH HEAD CUT

At left, the first phase of the balestra, the jump forward. It is forward, rather than upward; the feet land in the on-guard position, and they must land simultaneously so that the action is not simply a weak patinando.

At left, the beginning of the final phase of the balestra, the lunge. The attack will arrive before the front foot lands.

a firm place in popular culture. Many saber enthusiasts claim today that the removal of the fleche seriously impoverished saber fencing. The fleche as a footwork element in saber became popularized in the 1940's by Hungarian fencers. It had been used sporadically by some saber fencers before World War Two. After the war, Polish fencers developed a flying fleche that was almost an art form and became a symbol of the sport (Fig. 4.10). The US Fencing Association still uses a variant of this fleche as its logo, despite the fact that the action has long been illegal.

However, the fleche functioned in the 100-year history of sport saber for only half a century. Looking further back into fencing history, the fleche had never played a part in any of the leading schools of swordsmanship. It was regarded as too dangerous an action in duels and even in competitions. The new changes in saber fencing regulations may be paradoxically perceived as a return to the roots.

Despite the restrictions, saber tactics, speed and the nature of saber as a thrusting and cutting weapon have forced saber fencers to adopt a substitute for the classic fleche – the so-called "saber fleche". This begins like a traditional fleche, but to avoid a cross-over step, the landing is made with the front foot (Fig. 4.11). The "saber fleche" can be very effective, especially in combination with a double-step, balestra or short lunge.

Fig. 4.10: The Polish Fleche, c. 1950.
Wojciech Zablocki fleches; Leszek Suski parries

Chapter 4. Modern Saber Technique 57

Fig 4.11 (top to bottom): The Modern Saber Fleche

4.11a: Attacker shifts the center of gravity forward & loads front foot

4.11b: Attacker is almost falling forward as the attack develops.

4.11c: Attacker hops forward on front leg and hits; rear leg still in air

Part II. The Saber

4.2.1   The parts of the saber (Fig. 4.12)

The saber is constructed in much the same way as the military weapons of the nineteenth century illustrated in Fig. 2.2, but the blade is straight, has an "I" or "Y" cross-section, and is much lighter (the maximum permissible weight being 500g, or just over a pound). The tip is folded over so as not to cut or tear. The rear portion of the blade, called the tang, passes through the guard, which has a knuckle bow to protect the hand. The tang of a modern saber is threaded; and the whole weapon his held together by the pommel nut, which also serves as a counterweight.

4.2.2   Holding the saber (Fig. 4.13)

The proper way of holding the saber has not changed for decades. The saber grip (handle) is held between the thumb and the first joint of the index finger, with the thumb on top, while the other fingers are secondary. Unlike foil and epee, saber uses only one type of grip: the so-called orthopedic or pistol grip has never caught on. The speed of saber bouts requires a very delicate, but at the same time very flexible, hold on the weapon. Parries, beats, binds and – in particular – stop-hits require a firmer grip; whereas attacks with feints and counter-attacks require a looser one. Saber fencers tend to hold the hilt close to the guard, which enables a much greater range of offensive and defensive movements by offering better control of the weapon.

It is very important to be aware that the precise grip of the weapon is not only ensured by the fingers, but also the wrist, elbow and the arm. They constitute a sort of kinematic line determining the entire blade work coordination. Even at the most advanced level, the most common technical errors include excessive stiffening of the shoulder and the elbow. Therefore, during individual fencing lessons, the coach's role is to constantly remind the fencers to loosen up the shoulder, elbow, and wrist. This also prevents overtraining, especially of the shoulder joint. A recommended exercise is to switch weapon arms during weapon training, which does not entail a change in the body position. This also prevents excessive muscle growth on one side of the body and spinal curvatures. Finally, the wrist and elbow should be loose for a very practical reason: the wrist and the elbow are also parts of the valid target area, and a stiff arm and insufficiently flex-

Chapter 4. Modern Saber Technique

Fig. 4.12: Parts of the Saber

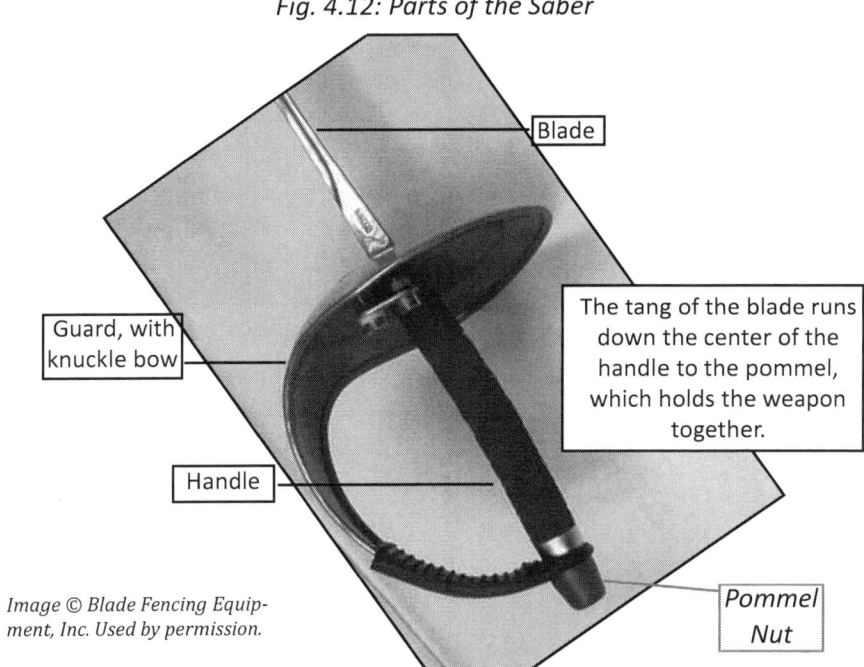

Blade

Guard, with knuckle bow

The tang of the blade runs down the center of the handle to the pommel, which holds the weapon together.

Handle

Image © Blade Fencing Equipment, Inc. Used by permission.

Pommel Nut

Fig. 4.13: Holding the Saber (adapted from Crosnier 1954
"The proper way of holding the saber has not changed for decades."

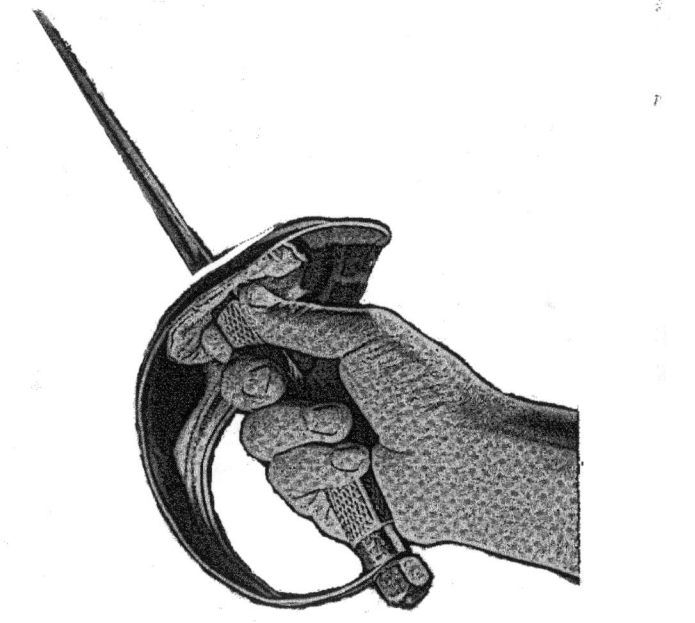

ible grip on the hilt expose the fencer to frequent counter-attacks on the forearm.

4.2.3 The saber target (Fig. 4.14)

Fencing manuals often used to debate just what the saber target was. Early manuals often limited it to the fencer's torso. For decades, the target area was defined very precisely as the head, the arms and torso to a bent line between the iliac spines marking the edge of the classic fencing attire. This definition was intended to avoid debatable calls by referees, but often failed in its purpose. Since the introduction of electronic scoring, the definition of the valid target area in saber is unmistakable. It consists of

1) A metallic jacket made of metallic fabric known as lamé, which covers both arms (but not the hands), the torso from the shoulders to the waist, and the back;
2) A manchette (saber cuff), made of the same metallic lamé as the metallic jacket, which covers the forearm and the back of the weapon hand, but not the palm or the fingers;
3) An electrically conductive mask connected to the metallic jacket by a wire.

If a weapon strikes any part of this conductive target, a hit is registered. A hit striking anything else has no effect.

Fig. 4.14: The Saber Target, from the official rulebook of the International Fencing Federatiion (FIE)
Valid target areas are in white; invalid areas in black.

The conductive target and the weapon communicate with the scoring apparatus. Until recently, this was done by means of a retractable cable, but a wireless scoring apparatus seems to be in the near future.

Fig. 4.15 : Electric Saber Grar

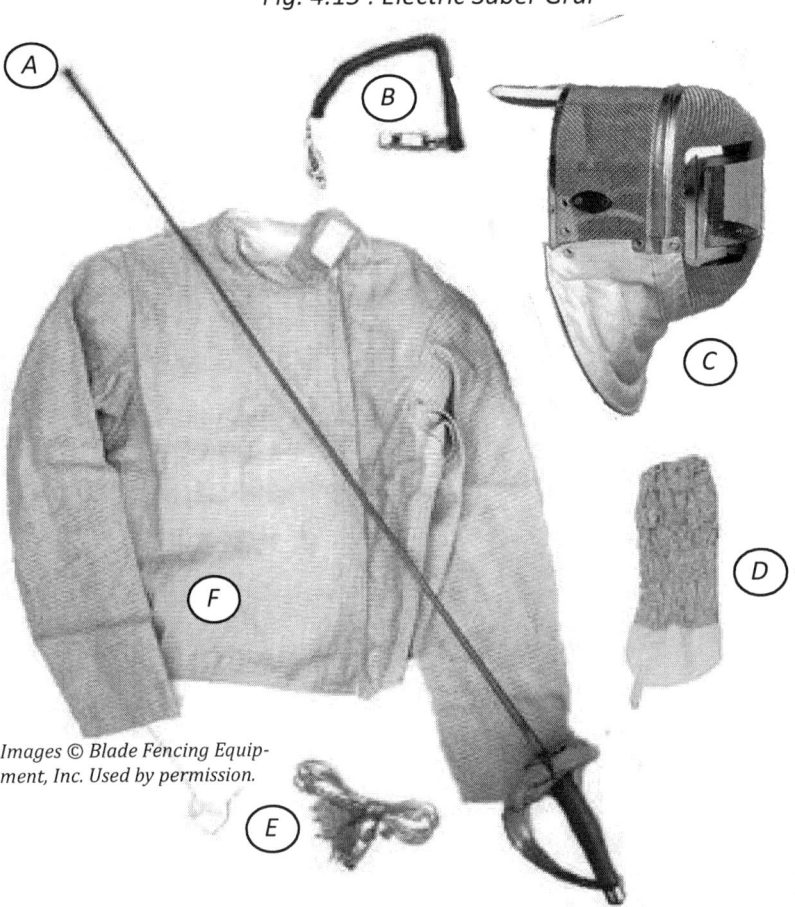

Images © Blade Fencing Equipment, Inc. Used by permission.

Fig.4.15 Electric Saber Gear. Clockwise from top left: A) Saber, B) Mask to Metallic Vest Connector, C) Mask, D) Manchette or Cuff, E) Body Cord, F) Metallic Vest or Lamé. The lamé is worn over a standard fencing jacket. The body cord runs under the sleeve and connects the saber to the scoring apparatus by means of a cable reel. The manchette or cuff is worn over the sleeve of the lamé. Lamé, cuff, and mask constitute the valid target area of modern saber.

Part III. Basic Fencing Positions

4.3.1 Initial position: Point in line. Varying senses of "line."

The traditional **INITIAL POSITION** in saber bouts, is the **POINT IN LINE** position. It is a ceremonial position, a preface to the salute, and is taken by the fencers at the start of the bout before the fencing salute and after the completion of the bout (Fig. 4.16). The point in line position is also used in both offense and defense (It is an "offensive-defensive" action.)

Fig. 4.16: Point in Line
Both fencers have assumed the point in line position in preparation for a salute.

"Line" is also used in the sense of **"LINE OF ATTACK OR DEFENSE."** In this sense it has to do with the relation of the opponents' weapons, whether in contact or not.

In this sense, the lines can be **HIGH OR LOW,** as well as **INSIDE OR OUTSIDE,** defined in relation to the fencer's hand. Above the hand his high; below it is low. Toward the chest (toward the left side of a right-handed fencer) is inside; toward the back (to the right of a right-handed fencer) is outside. These definitions are important in the introductory stage of technical training and remain useful in describing actions. The inside high lines of attack can also be called (inside) **CHEEK** and **CHEST**. The inside low line can be called **BELLY**. The outside high lines can be called (outside) **CHEEK**, and (upper) **ARM**, while the outside low line can be called FLANK. Finally, the forearm and wrist are targets of attack, and the final important target (and the object of many attacks in training) is the HEAD.

4.3.2 Basic position – On guard (Fig. 4.17)

Highly significant from the standpoint of saber fencing training is the position popularly known as BASIC POSITION – ON GUARD

The classic on-guard position fulfills the following criteria:
- The knuckle guard and the blade turn outward at a 45^0 angle to protect the outside target area (forearm, arm, cheek).
- The forearm of the weapon hand is parallel to the ground, the elbow two hands-breadths from the hip, the point slightly above the opponent's eyes,
- The leading foot points towards the opponent, the rear foot is turned at an angle of 90 degrees, knees slightly bent, heels one foot and a half apart.

Fig. 4.17: Classic On-guard position, front and side views

However, we have already noted in the section on footwork that *this basic position is modified for modern saber:* the feet do not form a 90^0 angle, but an acute angle: the rear foot points slightly forward, and the trunk and hips incline forward slightly, loading the front leg.

In addition, all of the above criteria are merely theoretical standards. In practice, some changes may occur because of fencers' individual preferences or their body type and structure. The coach's task is to teach the fencer the proper fencing position so that the latter can assume it correctly and automatically at any stage of a fencing bout.

It should be noted, however, that following the above technical standards makes the training process more uniform and prevents chaos in fencing instruction. Fencers who have been taught similarly can work with many different coaches who may follow different fencing schools and habits in other respects.

The terminology of weapon positions is closely linked to the Hungarian school of swordsmanship, and it was discussed in a detailed way in the famous fencing manual by Szabo (1998 [1977]). His description of weapon positions, however, reminds us of the tremendous evolution of saber fencing technique. Today, the significance of many of these descriptions is mostly theoretical. Szabo divides the weapon positions into free (on-guard position, point in line, invitations) and bind (binds, engagements).

4.3.3 Invitations

The term INVITATION has two meanings. First, an invitation is the position of the weapon in space before an action. The most common saber actions such as a feint of cut to head or a cut to flank are executed from invitations of seconde or quarte (see below) in order to explicitly signal the intention of hitting the opponent's head, in order to induce the opponent to take a parry quinte and expose his or her flank. Secondly, from the tactical standpoint, invitations can be used to trap an opponent: the defending fencer, by exposing a given part of the target area, "invites" the opponent to attack in that direction. He or she can then parry the attack or perform a counter-attack to the arm.

In classical theory, an invitation invites an attack, while a parry blocks or deflects it. It should be stressed, however, that the term "invitation" is rarely used in present-day saber fencing. Fencing coaches have often identified invitations with parries. This remains highly debatable and might be an oversimplification. It is true that an invitation as a weapon position is similar to and marked in the same way as a parry, e.g. parry seconde looks much like invitation of seconde. But an invitation is more like an imitation of an unfinished parry movement. In practice, a fencer who is aware of this subtle difference, uses the point of the weapon and performs the initial stages of feint attacks more accurately. Certainly, fencing coaches, during individual lessons and pair exercises should introduce a number of technical elements, including binds and engagements.

4.4.4 Positions of the hand and blade

PRIME (FIRST, ONE). The position or parry that protects the inside target except for the head, taken with the point lower than the hand, the thumb down and the fingernails facing away from the body, and the forward edge of the blade facing left (for a right-handed fencer) (See Fig. 4.18).

SECONDE (SECOND, TWO): The position or parry that protects the outside target (chest, belly) except for the head and arm, taken with the point lower than the hand, the thumb pointing diagonally downward and the forward edge of the blade facing right (for a right-handed fencer) (See Fig. 4.19).

TIERCE (THIRD, THREE): The position or parry that protects the outside target (flank, upper arm, cheek) including the head, taken with the point higher than the hand, the thumb pointing upward and the blade facing right (for a right-handed fencer) (See Figure 4.20).

QUARTE (FOURTH, FOUR): The position or parry that protects the inside target (chest, belly, cheek) including the head, taken with the point higher than the hand, the thumb pointing upward, and the forward edge of the blade facing left (for a right-handed fencer) (See Fig. 4.21).

QUINTE (FIFTH, FIVE): In saber, the position or parry that protects the head and shoulders from cuts from above, The hand is raised and pushed forward, the blade more or less horizontal or the point slightly higher than the hand, the palm facing forward (pronated), and the forward edge of the blade facing upward (See Fig. 4.22).

[SIXTE (SIXTH, SIX) AND SEPTIME (SEVENTH, SEVEN) are rare in competitive saber today. Sixte protects the head and shoulders from cuts from above. It is a kind of mirror image of quinte, with the hand raised to the left (inside) of the face, the palm facing backward (su-

Fig. 4.18: Position and Parry Prime

Fig. 4.18a: Parry Prime, Front View (Fencer at rear)

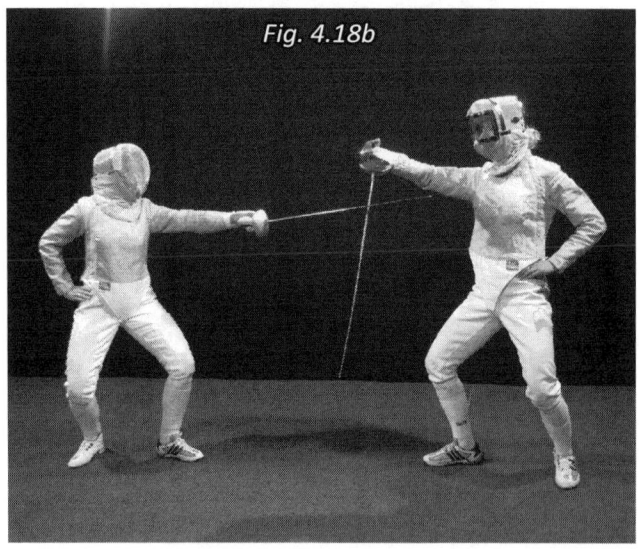

Fig. 4.18b: Parry Prime, Side View (Fencer on right)

Fig. 4.19: Position and Parry Seconde

Fig. 4.19a: Seconde in action   *Fig. 4.19b: Seconde*

Fig. 4.20: Position and Parry Tierce

 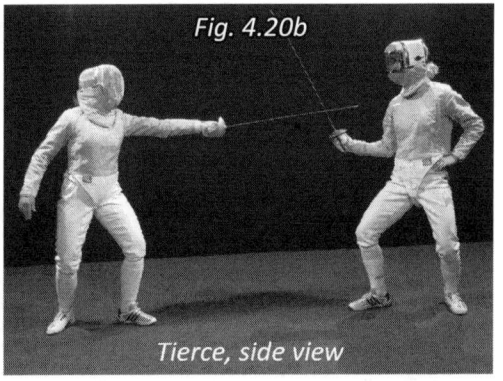

Tierce in action   *Tierce, side view*

Fig. 4.21: Position and Parry Quarte

Fig. 4.21a: Quarte performed left-handed;

Fig. 4.21b: Quarte performed right-handed

Fig. 4.22: Position and Parry Quinte (front and side views)

pinated), and the blade pointing upward and to the right (outside). Septime protects the outside cheek and flank from cuts from the outside. From quinte, the hand is rotated 90 degrees counterclockwise and the thumb pointed downward.]

4.3.5 Actions on the blade: Engagements, beats, binds

Actions on the blade involve contact with of various kinds with the opponent's blade made on the fencer's own initiative, as distinct from the parries, which react to the opponent's attack. They can be defensive or offensive in purpose. They include beats, binds, engagements and changes of engagement, and presses. Actions on the blade are generally more frequent in the thrusting weapons, foil and epee, than they are in saber.

ENGAGEMENT is blade contact that does not displace the opponent's blade. The purpose is to sense the opponent's intentions and create opportunities for later actions. Engagements are also important in the learning process, since they develop the feel of the blade, or sentiment du fer, which the theory of motor skills, is called a proprioceptive feeling (here, the sense of movement and body position).

CHANGE OF ENGAGEMENT involves changing the point of contact with the opponent's blade from one side to another.

A BEAT (Fig. 4.23) is a short, sharp striking of the opponent's blade. The contact should not involve the sliding of one blade along the other; the contact should be momentary. In modern saber, the beats in actual use are (seconde, tierce (and circular tierce), quarte (and circular quarte) and quinte.) Classically, beats were delivered with the front edge of the blade or the first third of the back edge. In modern saber, common variants of beats include blade contacts with the outside or inside flat.

The BIND (Fig. 4.24) is an action consisting of a change of weapon positions that displaces an opponent's blade. Unlike a beat, the contact in a bind is continuous. The bind can be a final action resulting in a hit, a preparation of a final action, or a tactical action with one of several purposes: to draw an attack from an opponent that can be answered by counter-time, or by a retreat out of distance that facilitates one's own attack. To ensure full control over the opponent's blade, binds are made with the pressure of the fencer's forte (strong) or middle on the opponent's foible (weak).

Fig. 4.23a

Fig. 4.23b

Fig. 4.23:
Seconde beat (or bind)
and head cut;

The difference between a beat and a bind cannot be illustrated in still photographs.

A beat is executed with a sharp striking action that makes only momentary, "dry" contact as it drives the opponent's blade out of position.

A bind makes continuous contact as it pushes the opponent's blade out of position.

Note that this terminology is based on the Italo-Hungarian school and not the French, in which the word translated as "bind" has a different meaning.

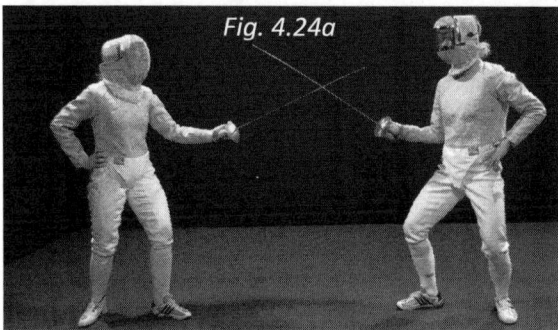

Fig. 4.24a

Fig. 4.24b

Fig. 4.24:
Tierce bind (or beat)
and head cut.

In the opinion of top saber fencing coaches, the most effective binds in modern saber fencing – that is, the most useful in training – are two circular binds: tierce to tierce and quarte to quarte; and bind of seconde for left-handed fencers. Bind of prime, due to the long movement involved, is rather difficult to apply in a real bout. Simple binds: tierce, (Figure 4.24), quarte and quinte are rarely applied in actual bouts, but should be rather considered for technical drills.

PART IV. BASIC FENCING ACTIONS

Any discussion of basic fencing actions should begin with the classification proposed by Czajkowski in 1968 and still widely accepted by fencers, theorists, and coaches. The distinguished Russian coach David Tyshler (1995) agrees that this classification covers the vast range of actions used by modern fencers and is both logical and coherent).

Czajkowski divides fencing actions into real (final) and preparatory actions. This chapter focuses on the real actions, whereas the preparatory actions are discussed in the chapter on tactics. The real fencing actions can be subdivided into **offensive actions** (*attacks, ripostes* and *counter-ripostes*, varieties of *renewed offensive actions*, and *counter-time*), **offensive-defensive actions** (*point in line, counter-attacks*) and **defensive actions** (*parries, evasions, retreats*). During the evolution of saber fencing, only evasions have diminished in practical importance in fencing practice, although they are still important applicable in foil and epee.

4.4.1 Hits

Hits in saber can be made with cuts (lateral movements with the point, flat, edge, or back edge) and thrusts with the point. Classic hits are made on head, chest, trunk, flank, and sword forearm. The cuts can be also made to the cheeks and arms. Valid hits are those arriving on the target (see Fig. 4.14). Only valid hits can score.

4.4.2 Offensive actions

The **ATTACK** is an action on the fencer's initiative which is designed to hit the opponent. (Defensive actions are designed to negate the opponent's offensive action and prepare for one's own.)

Attacks and other actions can be *simple* (executed with a single movement) and *compound* (executed with two or more movements).

Attacks are also classified as attacks of *first intention* or *second intention*. A first intention attack attempts to score despite any defensive action by the opponent. A second intention attack attempts to provoke the opponent's parry-riposte or counter-attack, then to counteract it, e.g. by one's own parry and counter-riposte. Second intention attacks are usually fully planned in advance, but they may also be partly planned, "open eyes" attacks (see below).

Fig. 4.25: Cuts to head and flank from seconde

Fig. 4.25a: Attacker (r.) in seconde

Fig. 4.25b: Cut to head with lunge

Fig. 4.25c: Cut to flank with lunge

Simple attacks can be divided into
- *Direct attacks* (single movement and hit in the same line),
- *Disengagements* (single movement but hit in a new line, passing around the opponent's guard)
- *Counter-disengagements* (single movement and hit in the same line but following a circular movement, e.g. circular parry or circular bind)

Figs. 4.26 : Patinando (advance lunge) attack to flank

a) On-guard position low and close to the attacker's thigh.

b) Arm extends as the final of the attack begins

c) Attack to flank (upper arm) arrives before front foot hits.

- *Coupés/cut-overs* (single movement, hit in a new line by passing the blade around the opponent's point)

A typical simple attack might be a cut to head with lunge (Fig. 4.25b), or a cut to the flank with lunge (Fig. 4.25c), from the position of seconde.

The attack is made with a simultaneous turn of the wrist and fingers bringing the hilt forward. The sword arm and the front leg begin the attack together. Coordination between footwork and weapon arm movement is crucial. In the final stage of the attacking movement, the arm should be ahead of the leg, so that the attack arrives a moment before the foot touches the ground.

Because modern saber employs an increased percentage of hits to the arm and the forearm, coaches need to revise certain traditional approaches to training of offensive actions. First of all, saber fencers should practice more hits on the closest parts of the valid target area, i.e. the upper arm and forearm. Second, at the onset of an attack the attacker's weapon hand should be held closer to the body to avoid possible counter-attacks. A good example of such an exercise is an attack with the edge on the chest from the position of seconde.

Generally, a low on-guard position, even close to the fencer's thigh, is preferable when practicing offensive actions. This can be illustrated in Fig. 4.26, a patinando (advance – lunge) attack to flank.

COMPOUND ATTACKS are attacks made with more than one movement. They include *feint attacks, attacks with actions on the blade* ("attacks on the blade") and *feint attacks with action on the blade.*

FEINT ATTACKS begins with a *feint,* i.e. an imitation thrust or cut with the aim of provoking the opponent's parry, which the fencer will deceive and score a hit on the exposed part of the target.

A typical compound attack is feint cut to head – cut to flank. This feint is made with the point, with the weapon arm still bent at the elbow. The weapon arm extends only in the final stage of the action, and the heel of the front foot touches the floor a moment after the touch.

Such actions are usually the final parts of multi-feint attacks, e.g. an attack preceded by a double feint flank-chest-flank with a step forward — lunge (patinando), as shown in Fig. 4.27.

Fig. 4.27:
Double feint attack, flank – chest – flank, with patinando

a. The first feint is made toward the flank (upper arm), using the point, with the arm well bent.

b. The beginning of the second feint toward the chest is made with the arm still bent.

c. The final is delivered with the back edge of the saber.

ATTACKS WITH ACTIONS ON THE BLADE are actions in which the final hit is preceded by an action on the blade, e.g. beat, pressure, bind, or transfer. There are various types of beats and binds: simple, changing, circular and transferred. Actions on the blade are generally more frequent in thrusting weapons than in modern saber.

In **FEINT ATTACKS WITH ACTION ON THE BLADE,** the feint is preceded by an action on the blade – beat or bind – intended to make the opponent react more quickly to the feint. For example: quarte bind with step forward, followed by feint cut to head — cut to flank with lunge.

According to theory, compound actions can include all actions on the blade, i.e. beats and binds. In modern saber practice, analysis of actual bouts shows that the most common beats are quarte (especially with the inside flat), quinte, and seconde. The most popular binds are the counter-tierce bind and, currently dominant, the counter-quarte bind.

4.4.3 Ripostes and counter-ripostes

A **RIPOSTE** is an immediate offensive action following a successful parry. Ripostes can be simple or compound. In a bout, a parry-

Fig. 4.28:
Parry quinte – riposte to flank against a left-handed opponent

Fig. 4.28. It is often necessary to riposte by coupé (cut-over), as in this illustration, riposting to flank from quinte against an opposite-handed opponent, or when riposting to head from quinte against a same-handed opponent. The riposter's point is brought backward to circle the attacker's point and deliver the riposte.

riposte constitutes a technical – tactical unit in which the parry is a defensive, and the riposte an offensive action. An immediate simple riposte is particularly effective. If, however, the fencer knows that his opponent intends to *counter-riposte* (second intention), the fencer's riposte should be indirect, hitting the opponent in an area opened by his attempt at a counter-parry, after briefly holding the riposte.

Fig. 4.29:
Circular tierce parry and cut to head with counter-time "saber fleche"

a. Attacker (r.) has begun an attack and is met with a stop thrust from defender.

b. Attacker has taken tierce parry against the stop thrust and begun a counter-time attack.

c. Attacker finishes counter-time attack with cut to head with "saber fleche," avoiding a cross-over by landing on the right foot.

A **Counter-riposte** is an immediate offensive action following the parry of any riposte. The most effective is the foreseen (planned) counter-riposte as an action of second intention.

These two classic definitions are not really precise, since with the growing significance of footwork in saber fencing bouts, referees will call a riposte without any preceding parry, e.g. when a fencer with skillful footwork forces the opponent's attack to fall short, thus gaining the right of way.

Like attacks, ripostes and counter-ripostes can be simple or compound. A typical example of a simple riposte is parry- quinte riposte to flank (Fig. 4.28).

4.4.4   Counter-time

Counter-time is defined as any offensive action in response to the opponent's counter-attack (for counter-attacks, see below). Counter-time is made with parry-riposte, beat-cut, and cut or thrust with opposition, e.g. on the opponent's stop-hit, the fencer makes a circular sixte parry and cuts to head with counter time with a "saber fleche," known colloquially in the U.S. as a "flunge." (Fig.4.29).

Covert counter-time, is characteristic of modern saber. The fencer approaches from long distance and feints an attack with extension. This provokes the opponent to counter-attack the extended arm, but the attacker then changes the position of his sword arm and blade, avoids the opponent's cut, and scores a touch.

Note: A feint attack into the opponent's attack that is meant to draw the opponent's parry remains an attack and not a counter-attack, although their execution is similar. A fencer performing this feint must make it with an extended arm, e.g. a chest-forearm feint with lunge, in order to provoke the opponent to take a parry, which he then deceives.

4.4.5   Renewed offensive actions

The renewed offensive actions traditionally include remise, redoublement, and reprise of the attack.

The **Remise** is an immediate, direct replacement of a failed attack without withdrawing the sword arm. A characteristic example of remise is an attack by a left-handed fencer with a cut to the opponent's guard followed by an immediate cut with the edge on the manchette before the opponent's riposte.

Fig 4.30:
Renewed attack (redoublement) after a parried cut

a: The fencer (r) cuts to the opponent's tierce guard with lunge, beginning a second intention attack.

b: Fencer renews the attack, recovering forward, with a quarte beat and begins to lunge.

c: Fencer completes her second intention attack with cut to the head.

REDOUBLEMENT is a renewed attack, aimed at a new line, made after the opponent has negated one's attack by parrying or retreating. A frequent and very effective action in saber is the following second intention attack: cut to the opponent's parry tierce — renewal of the attack by quarte beat and cut to head with lunge. (Fig. 4.30).

The **REPRISE** (retaking the attack) is a simple or compound attack made immediately after reassuming the on-guard position after an initial action.

Practicing reprises in saber teaches the fencer vigilance and tactical initiative as well as gaining distance. However, it should be noted that in modern saber, each interrupted attack leads immediately to counter-time. Thus attempts at reprise of the attack are correctly interpreted by the referees as actions "out of time," i.e. mistaken). If the

Fig. 4.31:
Attacker holding point in line (4.31a) hits by derobement (4.31b)

a. Attacker (r) is maintaining point in line, arm level, fully extended, threatening opponent's target. Opponent is attempting to take attacker's blade counter-tierce

b. By passing the point under the opponent's, using a v-shaped motion of the tip without altering the line of the arm, attacker has deceived the attempt to take the blade and scores by advance with derobement.

opponent parries successfully but delays a riposte or makes a compound riposte, then the attacker's remise or reprise has priority.

4.4.6 Offensive-defensive actions

The offensive-defensive actions are the *point-in-line* (see also earlier discussion) and the *counter-attack*.

POINT IN LINE is a position in which the fencer's arm is extended, with the point constantly threatening the target. Point in line takes priority over all other actions, just as an attack has priority over an out-of-time counter-attack or an immediate riposte has priority over a remise. From the tactical standpoint, the point in line prevents the opponent from developing compound actions since he or she is forced to beat it. The great speed of modern saber bouts makes a valid touch with a simple point in line extremely difficult and therefore rare. However, the point in line can be effective when the fencer deceives the opponent's attempt to take the blade . (Fig. 4.31).

DEROBEMENT is the name given to this evassion of the opponent's point in line, which causes the attacker to lose right of way (FIE rule t.77b).

A new application of point in line in modern saber has appeared in recent years: a preparatory action for a stop-hit consisting of an attempt of feinted attack followed by the defender's simple or compound counter-attacks and landing a hit, sometimes by way of a beat-cut.

The multiple uses of the point in line should be used for teaching tactics during individual lessons.

Back in the 1970's when the Hungarian attacks — which were extremely hard to parry — were very common in saber bouts, the point in line was a defensive action frequently *overused* by saber fencers. It

Fig. 4.32: Stop cut

Fig. 4.32: Stop cut in time: Attacker (r) is feinting an attack by stepping forward with the arm still bent. Counter-attacker (l.) cuts her forearm with the edge of her blade. Her attack has right of way, even if attacker finishes by hitting.

led to a number of controversial decisions by the referees and made a saber bout a boring and one-sided spectacle.

4.4.7 Counter-attacks

Counter-attacks are attacks, simple or compound, made during an opponent's attack (attacking "into" the attack). In saber, as in foil, a counter-attack does not have the right-of-way against the opponent's initiated attack. Therefore, the touch is not automatically scored by the first fencer to hit, since he may be the counter-attacker. Thus the referee's decision when the apparatus registers lights for both sides depends on his judgment. He must decide whether the attacker performed the attack in a one smooth phrase, giving him the right of way, or perhaps hesitated or bent his arm, giving the right of way to the counter-attacker.

Traditionally, SIMPLE COUNTER-ATTACKS are divided into:

Fig. 4.33: Counter-attack by cut-over to the forearm

a. Counter-attacker has hit by cut-over, passing the point over the attacker's point.

b. Counter-attacker follows her attempt to hit with a radical lift of the weapon hand and a strong step backward. (The action is sometimes called a "sky-hook.")

- *Counter-attacks with right-of-way ("in time")*, using the sense of timing (surprise) to hit during the opponent's preparation or on the first movement of his compound attack; e.g. the stop-hit to forearm illustrated in Fig. 4.32.
- *Counter-attacks by derobement* (deception) of an opponent's action on the blade, consisting of a disengagement or disengagement and bind, followed by a valid touch
- *Counter-attacks with opposition*: opposing the opponent's line of attack with one's blade while making one's own hit. These do not have right of way and are valid only if the apparatus registers only one light!

An example of a highly efficient counter-attack frequently used in modern saber is counter-attack to forearm by cut-over (Fig. 4.33).

In the final stage of a feint attack the counter-attacker reduces the distance by executing a cut over. Usually, such hits are clear touches, since the scoring apparatus registers only one light.

COMPOUND COUNTER-ATTACKS are made with more than one movement. They are classified into:
- Feint counter-attacks, most often in response to a second intention parry-riposte: Fencer A attacks and Fencer B parries and begins his riposte with a feint. Fencer A, having planned second intention, attempts to parry but is deceived and hit.
- Counter-attack with a feint before or after an action on the opponent's blade
- Feint with derobement: deception of an attempt to take one's blade, followed by feint attack, rather than direct hit.
- [NOTE: As noted before, a feint attack into the opponent's attack intended to draw his parry is technically an attack, not a counter-attack. The opponent loses his attack at the moment he attempts to parry.]
- Counter-attack by beat of quinte–cut to chest with a lunge (Fig. 4.34).

Statistics show a growing significance of counter-attacks in modern saber. They are estimated to constitute about 30% of all actions during tournament bouts. Thus it can be proposed that about one third of the

Fig. 4.34:
Compound counter-attack on the blade

a: Opponent (l) puts out point in line. Fencer (r) begins to advance, searching for the blade.

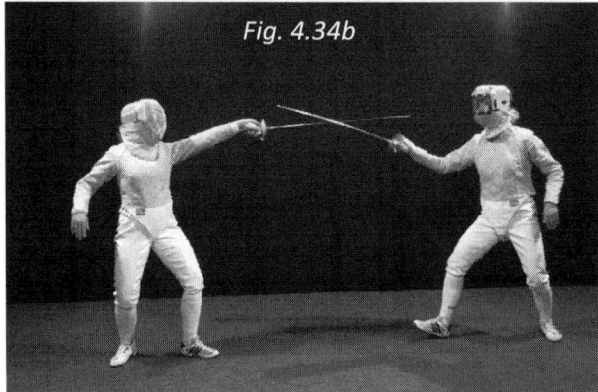

b: Fencer beats quinte

c: ... and cuts to chest with a lunge.

time of individual lessons could be devoted to practicing counter-attacks. Obviously, due to individual predispositions some fencers will use counter-attacks more frequently than others; however, it is important that counter-attacks are included into different tactical variants, such as counter-attacks on the opponent's compound feints, including actions on the blade, and counter-attacks followed by parries.

4.4.8 Defensive actions

A **parry** is a block or deflection of the opponent's blade performed with a movement of the guard or blade. A parry is the most basic and effective defensive action.

Parries are classified:
1) according to the parts of the target area they cover, into prime, seconde, tierce, quarte, quinte (see *positions*, above);
2) according to the blade movement into security, lateral, circular, semi-circular, diagonal, and contracted parries, as well as systems of parries;
3) according to the manner of execution, into removing parry, beating parry, beat/removing parry, and flying parry.

The systems of defense in saber fencing have evolved significantly throughout the decades. Currently seven parries are used: tierce, quarte, and quinte (Hungarian system) as well as some circular parries, mainly counter-tierce and counter-quarte. [Parries sixte and septime are not used in present-day saber.]

The basic parry positions have been illustrated and explained above, under *positions*.

Depending on where the saber position is held and the blade movement, saber parries can be classified as *security parries (guard positions), lateral (simple) parries, circular parries* and *systems of parries*.

Security parries are identical to the basic positions of the weapon which guard a given part of the target area without motion. If, for instance, a saber fencer assumes a parry of tierce, he cannot be hit on the flank.

A **Lateral parry** is a movement of the blade from an outside to an inside line, or vice versa, in the same line, e.g. from tierce to quarte or quarte to tierce.

A **Circular parry** is a parry that moves in a circle away from the line of attack to end up in the same position in which it started, trapping the opponent's blade, e.g. counter-tierce, counter-quarte.

A **System of parries** employs a quick and effective execution of two or three parries, e.g. tierce, counter-tierce or counter-tierce – seconde. It is used against the opponent's feint attack and in situations when the opponent's line of attack cannot be precisely determined.

Depending on the manner of their execution, parries can be divided into *removing parries, beat parries, beat-removing parries, opposition parries,* and *parry-riposte combinations.*

A **Removing parry** moves the opponent's blade to the side, e.g. from tierce to quarte, totally covering the target area. Parry training should start with removing parries.

A **Beat parry** deflects an incoming attack with a sharp striking motion, with the middle part of one's own blade against the opponent's foible or middle part of the blade. Beat parries are used when the opponent's movement is identified very early and the incoming attack can be cut.

Due to the enormous speed of technical actions in modern saber, the beat parries have lost their significance. Their role, in fact, is played by *defensive beats*, whose percentage in the overall number of effective hits has been on the increase. A defensive beat is made with the middle of the blade or the foible (the "weak" part near the tip); its purpose is to take over the offensive before the opponent's attack becomes a threat. It is called defensive because it is made in response to the opponent's initiative.

In the 1960's and 1970's the counterparts of beat parries were the so-called flying parries, e.g. flying quinte, a parry and riposte made as a single movement.

A **Beat-removing parry** removes the opponent's blade as in a removing parry, but with a sharp beat at the end.

An **Opposition parry** is a simple removing parry that does not lose contact with the opponent's blade from an initial engagement. Opposition parries are rarely used in modern saber.

A **Parry-riposte combination** is a parry and riposte made with a single movement. It is similar to a stop thrust with opposition in the thrusting weapons.

An important issue in modern saber is the way the parries are executed. Slow-motion analyses of footage of fencing bouts show that the most effective are beat-removing parries: At the end of the parry movement a fencer attempts to beat the attacker's cut with his forte by a quick press with the thumb to prevent a light from appearing on the apparatus. The appearance of a light may lead a referee to declare a direct hit for the attacker despite defender's attempted parry, sometimes called a malparé (insufficient parry). (Unfortunately, the apparatus cannot yet decide whether the attack arrived before the parry or whether the attacker's blade whipped around a correctly taken parry.) Therefore, parry practice should emphasize taking parries as far as possible from one's own target area. The photographs in this chapter seem to confirm such observations. On the other hand, a classic removing parry can be highly effective against multi-feint attacks. This matter is very complex, but it seems that the most universal training method is to *learn parries in the most flexible way* in order to prepare fencers for changing situations during a fencing bout. A fencer who *always* takes parries in the front away from his own target area may respond to feints too easily and be exposed to easy hits.

Fencing literature devoted to the development of parrying technique mentions the concept of *systems of parries*. A system of parries occurs when a defending fencer is "sensing" the opponent's blade through a series of consecutive parries in order to take a proper parry in the end. This type of defensive action used to be regarded as a state-of-the-art technique. At present, its efficacy is fairly limited and it seems it has been replaced with a *feint of parry*, where the defender merely indicates the direction of a parry rather than actually assuming the parry position.

Chapter Two shows that parries contribute to almost 20% of systems of ripostes and counter-ripostes. Assuming that parries constitute a major part in counter-time actions (11.7%) it can be concluded that parries are involved in about 30% of all technical actions finished with valid touches.

4.4.9 Defense by retreat

Defense by retreat allows a fencer to avoid a hit without taking any other defensive or offensive-defensive actions. The role of defense by retreat in saber tactics results from the following regulations:

- The length of the piste being limited to 14 meters, so that a fencer can no longer retreat once over the end line and be

placed on guard at 2 meters. Now a fencer backing off the end of the strip gets an immediate touch against,
- The introduction of the electrically conductive jacket (lamé) and the end of stopping the bout for non-valid hits, which now simply do not exist. In modern saber, the defending fencer in a critical situation at the end of the piste keeps only one foot in touch with the strip and avoid hit by leaning backwards, so that hits land on his legs, i.e. an invalid target. Since these cause no light to appear, the fencer can now hit with a "riposte" or new attack.
- The referees' (new) adherence to the classical definition of attack. At present, any bending of the sword arm in the final stage of an attack is treated as an error and therefore a loss of right-of-way. This gives the defender the possibility to riposte despite the appearance of double lights on the scoring apparatus.

The above observations demonstrate that the precise control of distance should be a permanent element in training proper tactical habits, using all types of fencing training forms. In modern saber bouts, controlling distance makes it possible to avoid the opponent's hits, take the initiative and perform one's own offensive-defensive actions. It all depends on the quality of footwork, which should be practiced by fencers during collective and individual lessons.

PART V. OVERVIEW OF TENDENCIES IN MODERN SABER

4.5   The transformation of saber

Electronic scoring has transformed saber. While a number of technical elements have become obsolete, the main changes have taken place in bout tactics and strategy. Today the traditional definition of saber as both a cutting and a thrusting weapon is somewhat dubious, since saber thrusts are becoming increasingly ineffective both as offensive and defensive actions. It is true that the electronic scoring apparatus has made the registration of hits practically error-free and therefore greatly increased the technical effectiveness of point in line actions used as offensive-defensive actions by the fencer in defense. That is, a thrust that lands is much more likely to be awarded than in the days of visual judging. Tactically, however, point in line and derobement (deception of an attack on the blade) have currently become much less effective. To some extent they have been replaced by stop-hits with opposition as in epee. However, opposition stop-hits demand enormous technical skills and can only be used effectively by highly advanced fencers.

By contrast, modern saber has made room for a variety of counter-attacks with the point, flat or edge of the saber with lightning speed, especially when aimed at the opponent's manchette (cuff) behind the guard. As in foil and epee, modern saber fencers use the cut over (ending, of course, with a flat cut rather than a point thrust). Generally, the transformations of modern saber fencing have made fencing bout technique more pragmatic rather than traditionally correct.

The classical saber cut had to be powerful in order to be audible as well as visible to the referees. Today, these powerful cuts are completely outmoded and redundant. The ways of holding the weapon, fencing positions and performance of particular simple and compound actions must meet the high-speed requirements of modern fencing.

Chapter 5.

Modern Saber Training

The introduction of electronic scoring and the reduction of the number of referees to one were significant changes in saber fencing, but not the only ones. Thanks to the introduction of the 14m strip and the elimination of the first warning for going off the end, saber bouts became faster and the fencing speed started to determine fencing phrases. As a result, the preparation of the modern saber fencer must include not only learning and perfecting fencing technique. There is now a need for general fitness training with an emphasis on anaerobic exercises and, later, on specialized endurance training. In addition, effective training to develop saber technique should involve both psychomotor components (reaction time and reaction choice) and psychological elements (concentration of attention, repeatability of actions, resistance to fatigue of the central nervous system).

5.1   Forms of fencing training

Modern fencing training should account for all new developments in the theory of sports training and specific training forms used in fencing for many years. The evolution of modern fencing has made the three fencing weapons highly independent of one another, with separate training forms and means for each weapon. For example:

- After the fleche was prohibited in saber, queue training exercises lost much of their significance in saber training, although, as we shall see, they are still employed.

- Common footwork exercises for all three weapons were also abandoned because of different time and technical requirements.

* Pair exercises are highly effective in saber, but much less in the thrusting weapons.

* Additionally, there are different training requirements for female fencers in all fencing weapons.

* There are also differences in the somatic build (body make-up) between saber fencers, epeeists and foilists. Epee and foil fencers are taller and slimmer (ectomorphic) than saber fencers, who are of a more of athletic type (mesomorphic).

Thus, apart from general fitness training, common exercises for all three weapons are nowadays practically impossible. Nevertheless, it is true that the basic fencing training forms continue to include footwork training, individual lessons, collective lessons (group lessons) and pair exercises.

The theoretical framework of technical-tactical fencing preparation used in this book was proposed by Czajkowski (1995), who distinguished between *technical, technical-tactical* and *tactical* fencing skills, based on motor habits.

TECHNICAL SKILLS are strictly related to the performance of characteristic motor habits of a given sport, For example, a fencer – regardless of the performed type of action, e.g. parry, beat, thrust, feint, bind–must develop multi-sensory perception and be able to "feel the blade" (sentiment du fer), handle the weapon in an accurate manner, adjust the rhythm of movements, coordinate the movement of the sword arm and the leading leg, assess the distance to the opponent, etc.

TECHNICAL-TACTICAL SKILLS are not only related to the performance of different actions (technical motor habits of a given sport) but, first of all, to the application of properly selected actions as learnt sensorimotor responses to changing situations on the strip, e.g. directing a thrust or cut at an exposed part of the opponent's target area; determining the course of an attack; riposte or counter-attack; choosing appropriate footwork depending on the distance between the fencers, the fencer's own actions and opponent's actions; changing intentions during an action; recognizing or prolonging an action; or performing a given action in a completely different tactical context (e.g. a direct thrust can be used as a direct attack, direct riposte, direct counter riposte, stop-hit, remise, feint of attack, etc).

TACTICAL SKILLS concern the performance of foreseen, premeditated actions. The real actions must be, however, preceded by preparatory actions, e.g. reconnoitering the opponent, concealing one's own intentions, conscious misleading the opponent, etc. An important tactical skill is application of carefully selected actions following observation and identification of the opponent's combat style, responses and favorite maneuvers, e.g. a fencer uses a feinted attack against an opponent who responds to feints in a quick and nervous manner.

Considering different ways of making decisions and the use of offensive, offensive-defensive, and defensive fencing actions during a bout, the following classification of fencing actions from the point of view of their practical application in a bout can be suggested:

1. **FORESEEN ACTIONS OF FIRST INTENTION.** A fencer performs a foreseen, premeditated action, e.g. a simple attack, hoping to surprise the opponent with the speed of its execution.

2. **FORESEEN ACTIONS OF SECOND INTENTION.** A fencer executes a foreseen, premeditated action, but his first move (feint, feinted attack) does not intend to hit the opponent but draw a certain action from the him to effectively neutralize it and score a touch.

3. **UNFORESEEN ACTIONS:** actions, usually defensive or offensive-defensive, executed in response to unexpected actions of the opponent. A fencer uses his or her *learned sensori-motor responses* (see discussions in the research chapters later in the book).

4. **OPEN-EYES ACTIONS (PARTLY FORESEEN ACTIONS WITH UNKNOWN FINAL).** A fencer commences an action (usually attack) but does not know how it will end. He or she observes carefully the opponent's behavior and ends the performed movement, depending on the opponent's actions, which he has partially foreseen and prepared for. .For example, a fencer begins an open-eyes waiting lunge, ready to deal with a counter-attack, parry, or retreat. This decision is based on a *choice reaction* (see discussions in the research chapters).

5. **CHANGE OF DECISION** while executing an action. This differs from an open-eyes action because the fencer's first idea is to execute a foreseen action (of first or second intention). During execution of a premeditated action the fencer changes his decision due to the opponent's unforeseen movement, e.g. a fencer intends a direct attack but due to the opponent's parry changes his intention and hits an

exposed target area; or in the previous example, the fencer has begun an open-eyes attack with a waiting lunge, but suddenly sees that the defender has "frozen," enabling him to score with a direct hit. His decision is based on a *switching reaction* (see later discussions).

5.2   The individual fencing lesson

The individual lesson is commonly regarded as the most basic form of fencing training. However, an excessive reliance on individual lessons over other training forms makes the specialized fencer's preparation fairly narrow. Individual lessons should be constituent *parts* of the content and time structure of the overall fencers' preparation.

Individual lessons should follow four general principles:

- Their content should be adjusted to the sports level of trainees in relation to particular training levels: introductory, controlled, specialized and championship;
- Each individual lesson should have a logical structure, in accordance with the sport training theory (introductory part, main part, final part);
- They should correspond to the annual periodization of the training process, i.e. different types of lessons should be held before the main events in the competition period, in the preparatory period and in the transition period;
- Their contents should correspond with the pupils' individual psycho-physical predispositions.

In view of the learning outcomes the following types of individual lessons can be distinguished:

- **INSTRUCTION LESSON** applied during the introductory training period is aimed at teaching the basic fencing actions and theoretical knowledge;
- **PERFECTING LESSON** aimed at perfecting the learnt actions in mutual combinations, e.g. sword arm/footwork coordination;
- **MIXED LESSON** combining learning and perfecting elements, used during advanced training periods;
- **WARM-UP LESSON** used before a major fencing competitions or events; it is aimed at achievement of top physical and mental fitness by the fencer;

- **CORRECTIVE LESSON** aimed at improvement of correctness of motor habits and technical skills after the competition.

Depending on their contents, individual lessons can be divided into:
- Technical lesson: aimed at learning and perfecting fencing technique, correct movements;
- Tactical lesson: aimed at learning and perfecting tactical skills in changing combat situations;
- **TECHNICAL-TACTICAL (COMPLEX) LESSON:** integrating all elements of fencing preparation (techniques, tactics, and mental reactions and processes).

5.3   Outlines of individual lessons

This section includes outlines of individual fencing lessons – two for each training level. These outlines are taken from the author's training registers from the years 1990-1997. The lessons were used in training of fencers at different sports levels: from the introductory to the championship levels (junior and senior Polish national teams).

5.4   The introductory training level

The introductory training level is aimed at teaching basic saber fencing technical habits. In my native Poland, the age range for this level is 10-12 years, and depending on a fencer's progress, it should last from one to two years. The introductory training level prepares pupils for their first fencing competitions in the youth age category (12-13 years).

Weapon specialization should start early. Common fencing training for all types of weapons together has not been practiced for many years. Previously, training methodology required first a two-year general training with basic footwork exercises, followed by weapon-specific training. However, the miniaturization of fencing equipment has made it possible to carry out fencing training at a very early age in play forms. Psychological studies show that suppressing the motivation to choose fencing in young pupils (willingness to compete with their peers) in the beginning of the training process is inadvisable. Respecting the principles of children's biological development and pedagogical conditions is crucial in training of young fencers. The general principle is that the introductory training level should create a springboard for the future sports development of young people.

The introductory level focuses on equipping pupils with the best patterns of saber technique, with tactical training left for the future.

Methodological guidelines for the introductory level
- At this training level lessons should be short to keep pupils focused on the accuracy of action execution;
- A lesson does not have to be divided into parts; weapon training lessons should be preceded by 2-4 weeks of basic footwork training;
- At the introductory training level there is a considerable height difference between the coach and the pupil; practicing cuts to head can be limited to a minimum, whereas the amount of forearm cuts and torso cuts exercises can be increased;
- Short breaks with fencing games are necessary in lessons with children (glove catching, hilt catching, etc.).

Sample Lessons: Introductory Level
Lesson Outline 1 – Instructional lesson – duration: 10 min.
1. Fencing position for the saber fencer
2. Learning to hold and control the weapon.
3. Fencing salute.
4. Cut to head.
5. Steps forwards and backwards, step forward – cut to chest with the edge, lunge – cut to forearm.

Lesson Outline 2 – Mixed lesson – duration: 15 min.
1. Perfecting cut to chest with accelerating lunge.
2. Learning of head-flank feint with an advance lunge (patinando).
3. Cut to forearm, arm, head on the spot, with a step forward, with a lunge.
4. Perfecting parries tierce, quarte, quinte followed by ripostes to opening parts of target.
5. Learning and perfecting counter-attack to forearm.
6. Learning and perfecting thrusts on the spot, with a step forward with a lunge.

6. Learning and perfecting thrusts on the spot – with a step forward – with a lunge.

5.5 The intermediate training level

The aim of the intermediate, or controlled, training level is to form the basis for the pupil's future participation in fencing competitions. At this stage the training should involve correct proportions between general fitness training consisting of development of motor potential, psychological and personality traits of pupils, and specialized training. The controlled training level aims at the age range of 13 – 15 years. In this age category fencers may compete at an international level. Fifteen-year-old fencers (girls in particular) often take part in cadet fencing championships. The main objective of individual lessons is development of technical skills, perfecting basic fencing actions and introduction of technical-tactical and tactical elements.

Methodological guidelines for the intermediate training level
* All the actions taught, with the exception of introductory and concluding technical drills, should be practiced with the greatest possible number of variations of footwork with frequent changes of direction (from defense to attack and vice versa);
* Using his creativity and skills the coach must make the execution of exercises as close to the real bouts as possible;
- In terms of speed training the following sequence is proposed: slow, moderate and maximal speed of exercises. In the general (preparatory) training period, slow or moderate speed of exercises should dominate; in the competition period, the maximum speed should take priority.

Sample Lessons – Intermediate Training Level
Lesson Outline 1 – technical lesson – duration: 20 min.

Introductory part: 7 min.
1. Simple cuts to opening target area on the spot and with steps forward and backward.
2. Series of cuts to forearm and arm no the spot and while maneuvering; parry-ripostes to coach's cuts.

Main part: 10 min.
> 3. On coach's movement the pupil executes a feinted attack to opening part of the target on the spot and while maneuvering.
> 4. The pupil and coach maneuver and the pupil tries to score a hit with a direct attack by lunge. If the coach extends his point in line the pupil executes his attack with a beat and direct cut.
> 5. The coach makes a thrusting motion and causes the pupil to take a parry quarte and make a cut to chest with a jump forward-lunge.

Final part: 3 min.
> 1. Counter-attack to arm – parry – riposte.
> 2. Technical drills – series of cuts head-flank-chest and thrusts.

Lesson Outline 2 – technical-tactical lesson – duration: 30 min.

Introductory part: 10 min.
> 1. Cuts and immediate remises to opening parts of target.
> 2. Two consecutive cuts to forearm and flank with a lunge.
> 3. Feint of the line, parry-riposte.

Main part: 15 min.
> 4. Pupil executes a feint attack to head–cut to flank with a lunge. The coach from time to time retreats, the pupil then executes an advance lunge.
> 5. Teaching foreseen counter-time of second intention. The pupil provokes the coach's counter-attack, executes a parry or beat and scores a hit.

Final Part: 5 min.
> 1. The coach in motion provokes beat of quinte or seconde with a lunge.
> 2. Technical drill – beat-cut to forearm, beat with the back edge and direct thrust.

3. Perfecting parry, riposte and counter-riposte technique – tierce, quarte, quinte.

5.6 Advanced, or specialized training level

In consideration of the biological development of children and youth, the advanced, or specialized training level should start in late pubescence. At that time the training loads can be increased and gradually directed towards specialized training. Since puberty can have different dynamics in individual cases, the contents and loads of individual lessons should be adjusted to the level of psycho-motor development of young fencers. This seems to concern boys to a much greater extent, since girls develop faster. If we assume that the specialized training level commences after 6 or 7 years of training, and fencing training can start at the age of 10, than specialized individual lessons can begin in the cadet age category of 16 – 17 years. In this age range, top fencers in many countries already take active part in international tournaments for cadets (16 – 17 years) and juniors (up to 20 years of age). Thus the contents and loads of an individual lesson at this stage of training should be more of competitive character in order to better prepare the young fencers to compete at the top international level. Such lessons should include a great deal of technical-tactical and tactical exercises as well as psychological resistance training.

Sample Lessons – Advanced Training Level

Lesson Outline 1 – technical-tactical lesson – general (preparatory) training period – duration: 40 min.

Introductory part: 10 min.
1. Simple cuts to opening parts of the target, parries-ripostes.
2. Series of cuts to forearm, arm, shoulder – all cuts with a bent ("flexible") sword arm.
3. Compound attacks: head, flank, chest, parry, thrust with a lunge.
4. Accelerating lunge to head. The coach takes and removes quinte parry to give the drill a proper rhythm.

Main part: 30 min.
5. The pupil executes a preparatory jump forward lunge with a series of feints. If the coach attacks to head, the pupil takes quinte parry and riposte. If the coach retreats the pupil executes an open eyes attack (attack with unknown ending).
6. Attack with a change of intention during its execution. From time to time – but not too early and not too often– the coach executes a counter-attack by derobement on the pupil's attempt to take the blade. The pupil then executes counter-time with a parry-riposte.
7. The pupil initiates a counter-tierce parry with a double step, the coach changes the engagement and provokes a beat of quarte – cut on forearm. The coach alternatively marks the change of the line, the pupil executes a compound attack.

Final part: 10 min.
8. Feint of parry, counter-attack to arm, parry-riposte.
9. Choice reaction: the coach changes the position of his weapon. The pupil chooses and executes an attack with an appropriate beat and cut. From time to time, the coach takes a parry and riposte, the pupil has to parry and score a hit with a counter-riposte.
10. Fencing game. The pupil is standing at the end of the piste with no possibility to retreat. The coach executes a single-feint action with or without a lunge giving a signal to the pupil to initiate an "open eyes" action.

*Lesson Outline 2 – technical-tactical lesson –
competition training period – duration: 20 min.*

Introductory part: 5 min.
1. The pupil remains motionless, the coach changes position from tierce to quarte, the pupil executes a quick series of cuts to chest-belly.
2. Technical drill with footwork. Cut to shoulder – head, long cut to chest, simple cut to flank – head – chest with the edge, parries-ripostes.

Main part: 10 min.
3. Cut to head with a jump forward-lunge, the coach retreats, the pupil continues his attack with a feint flank-head with a "saber fleche".
4. Tactical execution of simultaneous attacks, the coach's attacks, the pupil performs an intuitive parry-riposte. A marked attack is time-countered with a simple cut to head with a lunge.
5. Changes of intention. The pupil executes a foreseen second intention cut to flank, the coach parries and ripostes to head, the pupil takes a parry quinte and executes a counter riposte. Then a foreseen second intention action. From time to time – but not too early – the coach after his parry executes a riposte exposing his forearm, the pupil then hits with remise. From time to time, the coach does not parry but retreats then the pupil executes a renewed "open eyes" attack (attack with unknown ending).

Final part: 5-min.
6. Counter-attack to forearm by cut-over, parry-riposte.
7. Technical drill: beat-cut to forearm with the edge, beat with the back edge – cut to cheek, step backwards, counter-tierce parry, thrust to torso with a lunge.

Methodological guidelines – Advanced level

- Individual exercises should be repeated 8 to 10 times. It is important they are carried out at the maximum pace; the percentage of correct responses should be close to 80-90%. A lower accuracy may be an indication of fatigue and the necessity to limit the number of particular exercises or even to stop the training;
- Some of the tactical exercises should be initiated by the fencers; this will make them feel responsible and confident about the execution of exercises;
- Maintaining real combat distance between the fencers is crucial during exercises;
- During practicing all technical-tactical elements the coach should constantly remind the pupil to relax arm, shoulder and leg muscles.

5.7 Championship training level

The championship training level is primarily related to the fencers' sports level; however it is often identified with the fencers' age and training experience. The example of the American Becca Ward, who was cadet, junior and senior world champion in the same year, shows that it is possible to reach the championship level after a relatively short training period (5 years). The Russian Stanislav Pozdniakov won a team gold medal in saber fencing at the Barcelona Olympic Games in 1992, having already secured the world junior championship.

Thus the differences between the specialized and championship training levels can be fairly small in terms of the range of technical exercises and training loads. There are, however, significant differences in the conceptions of individual lessons in terms of strategy and tactics.

The main idea of the championship training is to choose the proper training means to prepare fencers to excel under the conditions of top level competitions. There are two important aspects of championship training.

- First, practice only those actions which coach and fencer are certain will be useful in real combat.

- Second, select of exercises that are consistent with your chosen tactics and prepare the fencer for the opponent's tactics, i.e. they are based on intelligence about the opponent gathered by the coach.

Sample Lessons – Championship level

Lesson Outline 1 – technical lesson – general (preparatory) period
– duration: 20 min.

Lesson Outline 2 – technical-tactical lesson – competition period
– duration: 30 min.

These lessons closely resemble the lessons at the specialized level. It is not possible to specify their content because the training is highly specific to the individual fencer and his or her most probable opponents.

Methodological-tactical guidelines – championship level

- Each lesson should be preceded with a video recording showing the positive elements of training, to bolster the pupil's confidence, but also to point out to elements requiring further perfecting;
- The coach should put an emphasis on actions which are well-known to the fencer and most frequently chosen in decisive parts of his or her bouts;
- The selected exercises should be applied with mental (imagining) training of those actions which can take the opponent by surprise during the upcoming competition;
- While practicing compound offensive actions the fencer must remember about the changing of the rhythm. Timing and anticipation of the opponent's counter-attacks are the necessary conditions of the effectiveness of one's own intentions, in particular "open eyes" actions.

5.8 Pair exercises

Pair exercises are excellent forms of fencing training, which supplement individual lessons, footwork exercises and queue training. Properly conducted pair exercises constitute a valuable link between individual lessons, free bouts and training tournaments. They combine the perfecting of fencing technique, perceptual processes, tactical skills, initiative and creativity in selecting technical-tactical solutions.

Fencing pair exercises have a number of advantages:
- They offer an excellent opportunity to conduct particular exercises in real bout-like conditions;
- They are a form of rivalry between the trainees, ensure the proper training motivation and prevent fatigue;
- They allow for changing partners in particular bouts and learning different styles of actions; they also constitute constructive educational feedback to both opponents;
- The coach has control over the entire group of fencers, not only the pupil to whom he is giving a lesson;
- On the basis of his observations the coach can select better fencers and motivated them by granting them the privilege of demonstrating proper execution of exercises to the other pupils.

Furthermore, pair exercises can be applied at any level of training, from introductory to championship. At the introductory level, pair exercises must be intermingled with fencing plays and games. Tactical elements, mainly in the form of parts of training bouts, should be included in the controlled level and developed at the specialized and championship levels. Experience shows that even top world fencers prefer interesting and logically selected pair exercises to other training forms. Fencers can practice pair exercises with total concentration up to 45 min. Pair exercises can be conducted as tasks to be executed by fencers accurately and with great movement precision.

Pair exercises lend themselves to another important training form – practicing parts of fencing bouts. Certain premeditated actions which constitute a sort of basis for a given pair exercise are repeated multiple times, then each partner can introduce his or her slightly different variant of execution.

For example, fencer A is performing a feint attack to head – cut to flank with a step forward. Fencer B's may either to open his flank to allow the touch or to take a parry tierce and riposte to head. After establishing this pattern, the variations can begin.

Fencer A can
1) replace the attack head – flank with step forward with an attack by lunge with head – flank – head, or
2) answer B's parry-riposte of tierce with a quinte parry-riposte.

On the other hand, fencer B can
1) increase distance, forcing his partner to make a 2-feint attack, or
2) parry- tierce and riposte to head – flank.

Making any of these four decisions by either fencer is a signal to commence a real "bout piece," that is, the cooperative drill turns into a contest at this point.

While performing these exercises, the fencers can take turns (one attacks the other parries, then they switch roles), or one fencer only can initiate the sequence of actions until, let us say, five hits are scored.

Another interesting pair exercise consists of alternate attacks performed by the two fencers. For example, the fencers attack each other alternately with balestra against parries in a premeditated sequence, most often: tierce – quarte – quinte. At a given moment one fencer breaks the sequence and performs a prolonged jump forward – lunge to head – flank – head, signaling the beginning of a training bout. The defending fencer has two options: he can take an appropriate parry-riposte or, detecting a possible error in attack, executes a stop-hit. This kind of exercise has a special advantage as it forces the fencers to control distance, just like during a real bout. If the fencers are not able to exercise it, the ground can be lost, which in practice gives the defender very little chance to succeed in this given action. By remaining too close to the opponent the defending fencer is exposed to easy hits; on the other hand, however, being too far away he or she has no chance to engage in combat and realize his or her own tactical intentions.

Pair exercises have yet another methodological advantage: they (like individual lessons) can make use of overlearning training. This psychological training method aims at making objectively difficult movements subjectively easy. Pair exercises, owing to their complexity and a high degree of stimulation (real bout-like situations) force the fencers to execute accurate movements and teach them the speed of perception and action. Concentration of attention, resistance to fatigue and the necessity of choosing proper technical-tactical actions in response to changing situations on the strip are very important. A fencer who has mastered even the most complex technical skills should not lower the efficacy of his actions under stress during real fencing bouts.

A Sample Set of Pair Exercises

Introductory training level

1. Both pupils execute false attacks alternatively. From time to time one pupil executes a real fast attack. His opponent must take a parry and riposte. This exercise teaches differentiating between real and false attacks.
2. The pupils make systems of parries tierce-quarte provoking a cut on flank with a step forward. The pupil exposing the target area can increase distance and re-take a parry tierce.
3. One pupil initiates a cut to head with a lunge. Then he accelerates the foible to effectively stop-hit the other fencer's foreseen parry quinte.
4. Both pupils are maneuvering on the strip.
   1) From time to time one of them exposes his forearm. His partner attacks to forearm.
   2) From time to time one of the fencers makes an attack exposing his forearm; his partner tries to execute a stop-hit to forearm.
5. One of the pupils executes multiple attacks: cut beat – cut to chest. From time to time his opponent takes a parry quarte–riposte.
6. The fencers alternatively perform cuts on parries tierce, quarte and quinte with steps forwards and backwards. A designated fencer can surprise the opponent with execution of a simple cut on target with a lunge.

Intermediate training level
(The "bout" marks the transition from an exercise to a contest)

1. One fencer takes a parry quarte and maintains distance with steps forward and back. His

opponent attempts to hit him with a thrust to torso with lunge before he can take parry tierce. The fencer's decision to parry quarte the thrust with the starts the bout.
2. One fencer performs a series of balestra- lunges head – flank. The defender opens the target area retreating a step. The signal for a bout is the defender's taking tierce parry-riposte instead of allowing the hit.
3. The fencer attacks with a balestra-lunge head – flank – head. The partner can start the bout by taking parry quinte – riposte.
4. The fencer performs a series of cuts on chest with a patinando advance-lunge. The defending fencer takes a parry quarte – riposte. The attacker starts the bout by taking an "open-eyes" counter-riposte.
5. While maneuvering, the fencer takes point in line provoking a counter-tierce with a step forward. By disengaging, he provokes a beat of quarte to head with a lunge from the opponent. The bout commences with fencer's answering with parry quinte – riposte.
6. Both partners execute a series of simultaneous attacks. The bout begins when time one of the fencers changes his movement, takes a parry and tries to score a hit by riposte.

Advancedand championship training levels
(The "bout" marks the transition from an exercise to a contest)
1. The fencers alternately perform attacks on parry tierce with a jump forward – lunge. At a given time, the attacker can start the bout by changing the sequence of exercise with short feints and start an "open eyes" attack.
2. The attacker cuts to head and either completes his action or stops it about 30 cm. (about a foot) from the opponent's mask – which provokes the opponent to start the bout. The de-

fending fencer should take a parry-riposte or stop-hit, with a remise to head.
3. The fencers are far apart and alternately perform preparatory actions using rhythmic steps. One fencer provokes an attack to flank-chest by opening the flank of his target area, thus beginning the bout. The attacking fencer tries to execute a prolonged feinted attack, whereas the defending fencer can stop-hit or parry.
4. One of the pupils executes a preparatory lunge at a parry tierce intending a beat of quarte to chest against the opponent's riposte. The opponent can take a parry quarte and counter-riposte, starting the bout.
5. While executing simultaneous attacks, one of the fencers exposes his forearm and provokes a cut over stop cut. The opponent can cut over to forearm or feint the cut over and parry-riposte the attacker with counter-time.
6. One of the fencers executes a false attack with advance and short lunge and then takes a parry against defender's simple riposte.
1) Defender from time to time from time to time executes a feint attack and scores a hit.
2) From time to time, the first partner parries the defender's feint attack and scores a hit with a riposte.

5.9 Queue exercises and fencing dummy training

Queue training is a convenient and popular training form among saber fencers. It can be applied at any training level, controlled and specialized, in particular. It is traditionally implemented during the introductory part of a training session before specialized exercises. Queue training is also useful during competition, when the coach takes care of a numerous group of fencers. Due to changes in the fencing regulations concerning the fleche (once the main element of queue training) queue training has lately diminished in popularity.

The advantages of queue training are:

- All fencers taking part in training can practice directly with the coach; it is important from the pedagogical standpoint, since all fencers, regardless of their sports level, receive attention;
- From the methodological point of view queue training can be effectively used for practicing short attacks, renewals of attacks and counter-time;
- In the competition period, it can be used to develop different types of reactions, e.g. simple and complex reactions;
- Queue training exercises can serve as important psychological aids during training: they bolster the confidence and unite the fencers before team competitions.

The disadvantages of queue training are :
- Insufficient time for full control and correction of technical errors committed by fencers during high-speed exercises;
- Tactical unidirectionality – all exercises are dictated by the coach, thus the fencers tend to drill mechanically, without making use of the surprise factor as an important element of preparatory actions;
- The pace of the drills and possibilities of distracting contact between the fencers ("side conversations") have a negative influence on their concentration and on the precision of their execution of technical actions.

5.10 Exercises with a fencing dummy; mirror fencing

The standard equipment of fencing halls should include fencing dummies and mirrors, which can be used by fencers for perfecting footwork and individual weapon techniques. Both dummy and mirror fencing exercises can be applied at any training level; however they are very useful when conducted under the coach's supervision at the introductory and controlled levels. At the higher training levels (specialized and championship) fencers can exercise on their own.

The construction of fencing dummies is different for particular kinds of fencing weapons. A saber fencing dummy should imitate a saber fencer's figure as close as possible, with a properly adjusted sword arm and the saber blade. A fencing dummy is perfect for practicing basic technical actions, e.g. cuts to arm and actions on the blade. Some modern fencing dummies are equipped with color light switches for practicing simple and complex reactions.

Fencing wall targets are more useful in foil and epee training than they are in saber. Dummy training is aimed to develop the habit of practicing individual technical drills on one's own with different variants of footwork. Mirror fencing exercises teach fencers proper fencing positions, holding the weapon, arm-leg coordination and correct execution of basic technical actions. These drills can be applied in the introductory part of specialized training lessons, the main part of lessons at the controlled training level and in the final part as cooling off after exercise.

5.11 Training cycles and the fencing year

No athlete can train at maximum intensity or maintain peak form 100% of the time. Efforts to do so result in flatness, burnout, injury, frustration, and loss of interest. The athlete and his or her trainers must vary the intensity, volume, and frequency of training as well as the kinds of training exercises chosen; and they must make room as well for rest, recovery, and variety. These considerations led to a system called periodization, or training cycles.

Within each cycle, the training load moves from general preparation to specialized training to highly specific pre-competition work. Fencers must build both an aerobic and anaerobic base, as well as building general and fencing-specific coordination and decision-making. In addition, they must move from perfecting separate fencing techniques to combining these techniques, using them in tactical situations, and finally preparing for specific opponents in situations of high intensity as preparation for the target competition.

Conceptually, the macrocycle is a year in length. However, the competitive demands on modern elite athletes in all sports require peaks that are more frequent. Fencers, for example, may need to peak for Cadet or Junior championships, and World Cups, as well as National, European, or World championships. Thus the year may have to contain actual macrocycles of about 4 months, leading up to major competitions, while the coach must still keep in mind the larger annual macrocycle. The shorter macrocycles divide into mesocycles of about a month, and the macrocycles divide into microcycles of up to a week, followed by a transition or recovery period. Special microcycles called pre-comps I and II precede the year's top events.

A transitional rest and recovery period follows – if time permits. In all cases, the annual macrocycle must include a mesocycle consisting of two or three months of preparation.

Coaches must keep the underlying theory of periodization in mind while adapting it to practical requirements. Coaches should base their work on the objective information they derive from e.g. diagnostic assessments (described later in this book) in order to give each fencer what he or she requires. They must know their students and adjust training cycles to the individual profile, as well as the demands of the fencing schedule.

Here are some practical suggestions for coaches:

In the preparation period of the annual macrocycle, the main physical task is building aerobic endurance, which is the foundation of physical conditioning for the whole season. (This statement is slightly theoretical because the fencer's activity during the whole season builds up an aerobic endurance.) We can use specific fencing footwork, group lessons, individual lessons, pair exercises, free fights and task bouts as well as general conditioning and team sports like soccer and basketball.

As we build the aerobic endurance base, however, we should be aware that in real competition, fencers operate in the anaerobic sphere (heart rate over 170). Fencing is becoming a "speed-endurance" discipline rather than an "endurance-speed" discipline.

In addition to building the physical base in this preparatory period, we should consider new technical actions in order to enhance the fencer's repertoire and to surprise potential opponents.

During the competitive microcycles, we should be aware that participating in many bouts and many competitions – however important they may be– degrades our fencers' technical foundation. Therefore, in the middle microcycles, coaches must instill, rebuild, and refresh technical patterns through exercises executed with slow tempo. In addition, on the Monday that follows a weekend competition, the coach and fencers should analyze the positives and negatives of their own and their opponents' performances.

There is a special role for the pre-comp I and II microcycles that immediately precede important tournaments like National or World Championships. Pre-comp I is a recovery microcycle designed to refresh the fencer after a long competitive season and a buildup of increasing intensity before a top event. The task is to rebuild the fencer's energy level and restore his psychological disposition. In this phase, we avoid technical fencing exercises in order to maintain the fencer's "blade hunger." By contrast, in Pre-comp II, training consists of maximal loading of the usual fencing preparations (lessons, bouts, footwork). The final week features an overall reduction in loading and a return to brief exercises that emphasize speed and intensity.

This fluctuation in loading should bring about the optimal preparation of the fencer's body and mind, which we can call peak or championship form.

5.12 Training sessions

COMPLEX TRAINING SESSIONS, consisting of 2 – 3 selected training methods in proper sequence are very important in fencing training. For instance, during a three-part session the first part may aim to develop coordination skills, the second may focus on teaching basic saber techniques and third may develop tactical skills. The emergence of complex and integrated training sessions has changed the way training is planned.

The following widely accepted arrangement of training tasks derives from the need for rest and recovery.
1. Learning and developing individual technical, tactical, and technical-tactical elements
2. Development of speed and motor coordination
3. Development of speed-strength potential
4. Development of speed endurance

INTEGRATED TRAINING SESSIONS involve concurrent development of 2– 3 motor skills in combination with technique.

In addition, there are:
- Endurance training, which uses long running games to develop the fencers' aerobic and anaerobic capacity with proper intensity and rest periods.
- Specialized training, which develops coordination skills and fencing-specific speed.

Training sessions can be also divided into *learning, reviewing, developing,* and *control (check-up) sessions.*

Fencing-specific training includes individual lessons with the coach. If circumstances require, an individual lesson can occupy the whole training session. Individual fencing lessons remain the only most effective means for learning, perfecting, and correcting fencing technique. During the competition period, some individual lessons may take the form of training bouts featuring very fast bout components. After competitions, lessons aimed at improvement of precision and accuracy of execution of the basic fencing techniques are very useful after competition. This type of corrective lessons can be useful in analyzing the causes of failures in the previous competition and in tactical planning of fencing bouts with particular opponents. Technical lessons are useful at all stages as well. The preponderance of either technical or tactical elements is determined by the fencers' sport level and the ongoing training stage.

5.13 Training loads

During training, the fencer's motor abilities (speed, strength, endurance, coordination) must develop in fencing-specific ways. General fitness training should be coordinated with the specific demands of the sport. For fencing, a key aspect of fencing is that effective development of the fencing technique should take place in conditions of optimal stimulation of the nervous system, which can be achieved in conditions of moderate fatigue of the muscle system and complete readiness of the central nervous system. Depending on the phase of training, general fitness training and specialist training should follow the principles of the repetitive method, proper timing of exercises, the number of repetitions as well as time and profile of rest periods (Ważny 1997).

Execution of a training plan includes adjustment of training volume and intensity of each specific exercise.

Concerning training *volume*, the following elements should factor into planning:
- Amount of exercise per day [hour, minute];
- Total amount of exercise in a given training cycle (number and duration of training sessions);
- Number and level of competitions;
- Characteristics of training means in terms of general and specific training.

Concerning training intensity, the following *arbitrary measures of intensity* may prove useful:
- Average, high and maximal loads;

- Percentage scales;
- Point scales, e.g. 1 to 10 points;
- Ratio between the number of exercises performed with maximum intensity and the total number of exercises.

An interesting alternative can be computer-assisted monitoring of training loads with the use of sports testing apparatus that measure exercise intensity on the basis of heart rate (HR) and blood lactate level (La).

Training in general can be divided into five exercise ranges: from aerobic maintenance exercises to anaerobic exercises of maximum intensity. Three of these are of particular significance for fencers:

- *Aerobic exercises of low intensity*: HR-130-140, La< 2mmol/l,
- *Aerobic-anaerobic (mixed) exercises* of high and submaximal intensity: HR< 180, La =4-6 mmol/l,
- *Anaerobic exercises* at near maximal intensity: HR >190, La= 6-9 mmol/l.

The following effort profiles of selected fencing exercises is the result of long-term training experience with saber fencers at different levels, including members of the Polish national team (Table 5.1):

Table 5.1 Selected fencing exercises according to physiological criteria

EXERCISE	CHARACTERISTICS	MEAN HEART RATE
Developmental footwork exercises with a partner	Moderate pace; no significant acceleration	130 – 145
Speed/coordination exercises with equipment such as mats or boxes	Average and faster paces, significant acceleration and changing frequency of movements	145 – 150
Individual fencing lessons	Variable rhythm and pace, multiple repetitions of sequences of technical-tactical actions.	145 – 180
Footwork drills	Perfecting technique, moderate to maximum intensity	155 – 195
Free fencing, training bouts, sparring	Average and high pace of exercises	*160 – 195*

The above distribution can be used in planning real training loads, taking into account the recorded information (technique, tactics, methodology) and energy expenditure (aerobic, anaerobic and mixed exercises). The above system enables proper assessment and analysis of relationships between training loads and the increase in the level of particular skills.

Certainly, the only objective criterion of effectiveness of applied training loads are fencers' results achieved at the major competitions of the season. In this way, the recording of training loads will be a useful aid to fencing coaches, i.e. a valuable source of information about the course of training. The preparation of fencers in short and long training cycles is multidimensional and must involve many factors.

Particularly important here is perceptual training (decision-making speed, anticipation of one's own and one's opponent's actions, programming sensori-motor responses, development of motor memory and different types of attention, etc.). These perceptual training factors, along with psychological preparation, are integral parts of fencing training. However, due to their complexity, the qualitative and quantitative assessment of the training structure is very difficult. Further progress in development of fencing training can only come from the specific expert knowledge of top fencing coaches.

Table 5.2
A Sample Two-Hour Training Session

The specific content of a fencing session depends on the goal of the exercises. For example, in our chapter 5.2 on the individual lesson, we identified five types of lesson based on learning outcomes and three types based on technical-tactical content, giving eight types of lessons in all.

In addition, the particular content of a training session depends on factors such as:

- The level of the fencers involved in the training session;
- The time in the fencing year;
- The resources available at the time and place of training (for example, at a camp, there might be two training sessions per day.)

The training session that follows is a sample of a possible session at the advanced level:

1. Warm-up (20 min.)
- Stretching,
- Agility exercises,
- PNF (proprioceptive neural facilitation) stretching,
- Sprinting games.

2. Basic part (30 min.) devoted to physical fitness
- Coordination exercises,
- Strength training,
- Speed and psychomotor reactions.
- Endurance exercises.

3. Fencing preparation (20 min): chosen from
- Pair exercises,
- Footwork,
- Queue training,
- Exercises with dummy and mirror

4. Specific Fencing part (50 min.)
- Individual lessons,
- Controlled tactical bouts and free fencing.

Chapter 6.

Nutrition of fencers

Fencing is classified as a speed and endurance sport; that is, fencing is a sport which requires near-maximal expenditure of energy over an extended period of time. Present-day fencing training requires a great deal of anaerobic and mixed metabolism. Since an average fencing competition is usually long, with some competitions taking a full day to complete, endurance training plays a very significant role in fencing. On the other hand, recent changes in fencing rules, dating back to the introduction of fifteen-touch, three-period fencing bouts, require, a great deal of speed training as well. A study of short-time (speed) efficiency in saber fencers from the Polish National Team showed that they achieved a level of phosphagen (ATP) power in their legs similar to other endurance and speed sports athletes (Borysiuk 2006). In terms of long time (endurance) efficiency, the saber fencers' power output was similar to that of soccer players, with a VO_2 max between 55 -65 ml/kg/min. The assessment of saber fencers' efficiency using sport testers reveals that most of a fencing fight takes place in the anaerobic zone, above the anaerobic threshold, with heart rate (HR) between 160 and 190 b.p.m. The fencer's efficiency profile and HR curve indicate short,rises in HR lasting a few seconds, followed by a drop to the anaerobic threshold level. Therefore fencers must expend maximum energy during endurance exercise in short periods of time.

On the average, during a competition, fencers take part in about five or six 5-touch bouts in the round of pools and about four or five 15-touch bouts in the direct eliminations. Additionally, it must be emphasized that speed in fencing – understood as a motor ability – has a clear psycho-motor context and must involve three aspects: speed of movements, time of different reactions and frequency of movements. Thus mental processes are crucial in fencing. As a result, fencers' diet should counteract the fatigue of the central nervous system as well as of the muscles: it must restore the micronutrients and elements, e.g. sodium, potassium, magnesium and calcium, responsible for transmission of nervous impulses.

6.1 The role of nutrition in fencing

As shown in Tables 6.1 and 6.2, the weight ratio of protein to fat and to carbohydrates should amount to 1:0/95/4.2 in fencers; whereas the percentage proportions in kcal (kilocalories, called calories in the US in food labeling) should be 14% proteins, 29% fats and 57% carbohydrates in novice and advanced fencers. It should be kept in mind that in the junior period (pubescence) the final nutrient balance should largely involve energy nutrients and structural support nutrients, mostly proteins.

Carbohydrate

Carbohydrates are of crucial significance in endurance – speed sports such as fencing. They are mostly used to maximize the storage of glycogen in the muscles. The larger the fencer's carbohydrate stores, the greater his or her efficiency. A regimen aimed at building up carbohydrate stores is known in sport nutrition theory as carbohydrate loading. It is particularly useful during the initial period of general preparation, and to some extent, in direct pre-competition training. In athletes on a high-carbohydrate diet the storage of glycogen is two times larger than in athletes on a low-carbohydrate diet. Therefore, each endurance training session should be followed by consumption of a light meal containing from 200 to 250g of carbohydrates. An increased intake of carbohydrates is also recommended immediately after sports competition.

After exercise, the muscles have an increased capability of glycogen re-synthesis. An athlete on a diet rich in carbohydrates can re-supply most of his or her glycogen storage over twenty-four hours, whereas an athlete on a low-carbohydrate diet make take forty-eight hours or more. A high-carbohydrate diet should consist of at least 55% carbohydrates. With particularly heavy training loads, when the diet itself cannot satisfy the body's carbohydrate demands, carbohydrate concentrate intake is recommended. The depletion of carbohydrate storage greatly reduces the athlete's performance and leads to the

Table 6.1 Energy Value and Nutrients in the Two Periods of Fencing Training (Celejowa 2001)				
Nutrient	per 1 kg. of body mass in Kcal/MJ		per 72 kg. of body mass in Kcal/MJ	
	Period 1	Period 2	Period 1	Period 2
Energy in Kcal/MJ	61/0.255	69/0.289	4400/18.42	5000/20.93
Total protein (g)	2.1	2.3	144	166
Fat (g)	2.0	2.2	137	148
Carbohydrates (g)	9	10	648	720
Calcium (g)	0.025	0.055	1.8	4.0
Phosphorus (g)	0.045	0.055	3.2	4.0
Iron (mg)	0.3	0.4	22	29
Vitamin A as retinol and carotene as a derivative of Vitamin A (μg)	42.9 μg	62.5 μg	3090 μg	4500 μg
Vitamin B1 (mg)	0.032	0.052	2.3	3.7
Vitamin B2 (mg)	0.04	0.05	2.9	3.6
Vitamin B3 (mg)	0.4	0.5	29	36
Vitamin C (mg)	1.8	2.6	130	190
Weight ratio protein/fat/carbohydrate – 1 / 0.95 / 4.2				

sudden performance breakdown sometimes called "bonking." Carbohydrate loading is, therefore, particularly recommended before sports competition.

The main sources of carbohydrates are, plant foods such as cereals, legumes and vegetables. They all contain starch, which is the most wholesome carbohydrate, since its consumption does not rapidly increase the blood sugar level.

Fat

Fat is the second most important source of energy for the human body; however, it is less efficient than carbohydrate. The profile of fencers' energy expenditure shows that fats play a significant role in metabolism at 60% of VO_2 max. Satisfying the fat demands of the human body is not difficult. In normal training conditions, the athlete's total fat storage is never depleted, even during long and inten-

Table 6.2 Recommended Daily Intake of Foods During the Two Periods of Fencing Training (Celejowa 2001)		
Foods	Period I	Period II
Cereals (grains) (g.)	340	350
Milk and Dairy Products (g.)	1450	1500
Eggs (g.)	80	100
Fresh or cured meats & fish (g.)	450	470
Butter (g.)	40	45
Other fats (g.)	30	35
Potatoes (g.)	370	380
Fruits and vegetables rich in Vitamin C (g.)	460	460
Vegetables rich in carotene (g.)	230	230
Other vegetables and legumes (g.)	420	420
Sugar and sweets (g.)	170	190

sive physical exercise. The fat serves as a "safety measure" for the athlete's body in case the conditions deteriorate further and energy demand increases. Usually, about 30% of energy from fat is enough to satisfy the energy demands of athletes during a training season. As most people know, excessive fat consumption may lower the athlete's overall efficiency. While body type indices in fencers, BMI in particular, show that some level of adipose tissue is not a negative factor, athletes with a tendency to get fat can achieve better sports results by maintaining strict discipline in reducing the fat tissue, especially in the starting period. An optimal BMI can be reached by athletes who follow a proper fat regimen. About 30% of total fats should be vegetable fats, i.e. containing proper amounts of unsaturated fatty acids responsible for regulation of metabolism and liver functioning. "Healthy" fats can also be found in all fish, which are also highly recommended for a good diet. Fish fat protects the circulatory system against a number of ailments and plays an important role in prophylaxis, especially among advanced athletes.

Protein

Protein is not a prime source of energy for athletes. In normal training conditions, only 15% of the daily value comes from protein. The protein supply in fencing – an endurance and speed sport–is similar to the majority of team games and combat sports and amounts to 2.1 g/kcal. Protein is the basic component of a living cell. Proteins are made of amino acids, some of which can be produced by the human body (endogenous or non-essential amino acids as opposed to essential amino acids that must be supplied in the diet). The essential amino acids include leucine, isoleucine, valine, tryptophan, methionine, aniline, threonine and lysine. These amino acids can be found high-protein animal products such as meat, eggs and milk. Such proteins are called complete proteins. Incomplete proteins come from plant sources. All essential amino acids can be supplied in the diet by combining proteins from animal and plant sources.

Protein should not serve as a source of energy in the athlete's diet because energy metabolism of amino acids (due to insufficient energy supply from carbohydrates) leads to liver and kidney overload. Additionally, excessive consumption of proteins is not recommended because unprocessed proteins are transformed into carbohydrates and fats, which may be conducive to athletes gaining weight. However, too little protein is also harmful. A reduction of protein supply to about 1g/kg of body mass leads to a drastic decline in physical efficiency. It should be also kept in mind that most athletes are still very young and their physical development is still incomplete, so their protein requirements are higher than for adults. Protein dietary values should be established with great care.

6.2   Energy reference values and nutritional requirements

In professional literature on athletes' nutrition, fencing is classified as a sport requiring endurance, speed, strength, and precision of movements, like gymnastics, the modern pentathlon and speedway (motorcycle racing on a flat dirt track on motorcycles with one gear and no breaks) (Czajkowski 2001). Daily energy requirements for an athlete weighing 70kg (154.3 lbs.) are 4800-5300 kcal. The percentages of daily values are 14-15% of proteins, 29-32% of fats and 53-

57% of carbohydrates. Nutritional requirements in fencing per 1kg of body mass are 2.1 – 2.3g of proteins, 2.0 – 2.2g of fats and 9.0 – 10g of carbohydrates, which in total translate into 61-69 net kcal and 255.3-288.8 kJ. The above values are similar to the nutritional requirements for practitioners of combat sports, e.g. boxing, karate, taekwondo; and are much lower than for athletes representing strength sports and strength-endurance sports, e.g. wrestling, canoeing, shot put and decathlon.

Using the data from Celejowa (2001), Tables 8.1 and 8.2 present energy values and nutrients as well as recommended daily intakes in different training periods in fencing.

The complex character of fencing training leads to a great diversity in the amount of energy expenditure. It is estimated that during a fencing event a fencer can expend from 2000 to 3500 kcal. During a training session longer than two hours the amount of energy expenditure can reach 4000-5000 kcal. The double-layer protective fencing clothing, which often must be worn in warm environments, can make a fencer lose between 2 and 3 kg. of body weight (in addition to water loss). All these factors all increases fencers' nutritional requirements for carbohydrates, phosphorus, vitamins A and B and electrolytes.

6.3 Intensity of performance and types of energy sources

During physical exercise, the fencer's body uses different energy sources. Like tennis or soccer, fencing involves periods of maximum and sub-maximum intensity. The former are interrupted by breaks at the end of the 3-minute periods or while referees analyze actions. During some parts of a fencing match, fencers may perform low-intensity footwork at the level of 20-30% VO_2 max, resulting from specific bout tactics or strategy. During such low-intensity movements, the fencer's body is mostly burning fats. Once the exercise intensity increases to 55-65% VO_2 max, energy is taken from carbohydrates as well as fats. An increase beyond 70% VO_2 max causes problems with fat oxidation, thus the metabolic processes start using carbohydrates increasingly. During very intense fencing at the level of 90-95% VO_2 max, usually in the final parts of a bout, the energy comes mainly from glucolysis. According to Eberle (2000) during continuous exercise of moderate intensity lasting up to four hours, energy from fats may constitute up to 70% of the fencer's energy expenditure. Characteristically, the body's ability to release fat reserves depends on the storage of muscular glycogen. Once it is exhausted, fatigue sets in rapidly, and the exercise intensity is greatly reduced. Thus fat storage is significant as long as the body has carbohydrate reserves. If not, they must be supplemented by foods rich in carbohydrates and by isotonic drinks. Fencing, especially saber fencing, has evolved toward the dominance of anaerobic metabolism that is based on the metabolism of simple and complex carbohydrates. The requirements for periodization of fencing training and the necessity to develop endurance during the general preparation period render these processes fairly significant; however, strict application of a high-carbohydrate diet is not absolutely necessary. What is important is the stimulation of fat metabolism as a source of energy through long-lasting physical effort.

A well-balanced diet should take into account the demand for protein which, however, should not exceed the recommended daily intake for physically active youth. Such moderate demand results from the speed requirements in all fencing weapons: saber, epee and foil in boys and girls. Excessive muscle mass is negatively correlated with coordination abilities, properties of the organ of locomotion and speed of movements. Increased amounts of protein are necessary in pubescence, when the bones, joints, and muscles are being formed. A high-protein diet can be recommended for fencers in its low-calorie variants, e.g. fish, milk, cottage cheese and eggs.

6.4   Water and electrolyte balance

Physical exercise in high temperatures causes 20 – 40% of total water loss in the body (2-3 liters an hour). In fencing, this can happen because of the heavy uniforms, and also during indoor competitions where the temperature is high (high-level fencing competitions, including the World Championships and Olympic Games take place in the summer months). After exhausting fencing bouts a significant loss of minerals, especially sodium, has also been observed – from 20 to 30g at a day-long event. Research shows (Szyguła 1997) that water constitutes about 50-60% of human total body mass. Daily water metabolism is estimated at 5% of the bodily water (about 2-2.5 liters).

The smallest daily intake of water necessary to sustain the physiological functions of an adult amounts to 1.5l (including water in foods and water produced during the oxidation process (about 1ml/kcal of energy expenditure):

- 1,500 kcal from carbohydrates = 240g of water
- 1,050 kcal from fat = 125g of water
- 450 kcal from protein = 47g of water

During exercise, only 25% of energy is used to perform work. The remaining amount is made into heat, for which the body compensates with perspiration and evaporation. A fencer, like a soccer player, can secrete about 1.5-2 liters of perspiration during a match, i.e. lose about 7% of body mass. During intense training and competition, thirst is usually a signal for athletes to reach for a drink. Thirst indicates the need to equalize osmotic pressure in the bodily fluids. But thirst in humans often occurs well after the need for rehydration. Research and experience show that athletes should rehydrate continuously during training and competition and also immediately before competition.

The rehydration plan should include not only water but also isotonic drinks to compensate for the loss of electrolytes and other minerals. A 2% reduction of body mass resulting from the loss of water through perspiration leads to a significant (10%) drop in athlete's efficiency. Rehydration and supplementation with minerals should always take place during the regulation breaks and breaks between the bouts.

- Rehydration and electrolyte supplementation allow maintaining physical efficiency at a proper level. Certain rules, however, must be followed.
- Drinking refrigerated liquids is inadvisable.
- Drinks should be consumed in room temperature in small amounts but frequently.
- Drinking at one gulp should be avoided.
- Carbonated beverages should be also avoided during competition.
- Contrary to some opinions, excessive consumption of water is not recommended as water flows through the stomach at the speed of 2.5 liters/min, and even the most dilute glucose solutions reduce the liquid flow speed for about 10%.
- Drinking fruit and vegetable juices or special hypotonic and isotonic drinks containing vitamins and minerals is recommended.

- On the other hand, overhydration, i.e. taking excessive fluids into the body overburdens the circulatory system and weakens the heart.
- Fruit such as bananas and apples and some vegetables, e.g. tomato slices in sandwiches, can be a good alternative.
- Specially prepared beverages also act as "deacidifiers" after training sessions and competitions.
- The remnants of acidic metabolism can be effectively neutralized by drinking milk before going to sleep and mineral (alkaline) water in the morning.

6.5 Nutrition during competition and recovery

Fencing competitions usually last many hours, and fencing championships may even be three-day events. Therefore, drinks containing carbohydrates (glucose, fructose, sucrose and starch), minerals and vitamins are not sufficient in terms of fencers' proper nourishment.

- During the breaks, fencers should also consume high-calorie, low-fat, light meals made of fresh produce.
- In competitive conditions, it is difficult to schedule three main meals a day; thus the most substantial meal should be taken 2-3 hours before the most important phase of the tournament, e.g. the finals.
- Heavy meals containing brown bread, beans, cabbage and potatoes should be avoided. High-calorie and small-volume food products such as honey, jam, sugar and even sweets eaten for breakfast and during competition are preferable.

Proper nutrition is crucial, since once the glycogen storage in the muscles is exhausted, liver glycogen releases glucose, whose rapid depletion leads to hypoglycemia. Continuous carbohydrate supplementation during exercise is an important preventive measure. As in other endurance sports, although the complete depletion of glycogen in fencers is virtually impossible, it is recommended to apply moderate carbohydrate loads, starting three days before competition.

Recent studies have pointed to the so-called post-exercise "carbohydrate window", which enables speedy glycogen recovery, 15 – 30 minutes after exercise. That is, the best way to recover glycogen at would be to consume about 80 – 100g of solid or liquid carbohydrates immediately after the exercise. However, coaching practice shows that fencers do not feel hunger right after the bout. Therefore, development of a habit to take carbohydrate supplements might be difficult for the majority of fencers unless closely monitored.

After a competition, with longer recovery, attention should be paid to rapid replenishment of protein storage and high-calorie phosphorus compounds. Thus the proper diet should include foods rich in protein and phosphorus compounds: meat, cured meat, fish, giblets, milk, cheese and nuts. After particularly exhausting events the necessary dietary items should include glutaminic acid and vegetable oil rich in unsaturated fatty acids necessary to produce phospholipids which greatly facilitate the metabolism of fats burdening the liver. As far as particular carbohydrates are concerned, glucose should be taken immediately after competition, followed by easily assimilable amino acids, which together with insulin take part in protein synthesis. A few hours after competition, taking vitamins C, B1 and B12 ensures normalization of the biochemical processes in the body.

6.6 Doping and stimulants

The effectiveness of a fencing bout depends to a large degree on the balance of mental processes, in particular, the balance between stimulation and inhibition. Excessive stimulation makes the fencer over-reactive, which leads to erroneous assessment of the fencer's or the opponent's tactics, as well as to technical errors. On the other hand, excessive inhibition gives fencers a passive fighting style and lack of initiative.

Numerous fencers have tried and failed to use illegal doping to improve this mental balance. Stimulants may have produced an effect over one or two bouts, but caused a rebound effect over the course of a day-long event, leading to apathy and defeat.

Similarly, anabolic steroids or hormonal doping (testosterone) have been used to build muscle mass. Such doping has failed to bring any success in fencing. Excessive muscle mass lowers the fencer's speed abilities, causes problems with coordination and reduces the time of reaction.

Nevertheless, doping does occur in fencing, especially during intensive training and preparation seasons.

A far more serious problem in fencing is posed by consumption of alcohol by young athletes – especially excessive amounts of beer – as well as of such popular stimulants as tea and coffee. Even the smallest amounts of alcohol reach the central nervous system, negatively affecting psycho-motor ability, perception, motor memory, performance of motor habits and proper functioning of the peripheral nervous system. Fencers occasionally reach for alcohol before competition as an aid in their stress management. The alcohol brings on illusory self-expectations, a reduction in energy, heat loss and disturbances of the body's natural balances. Furthermore, it has been proven that alcohol, especially beer, despite its high energy value, is not an energy source for the muscles. Alcohol should be unconditionally excluded from athlete's diet at any stage of athlete's preparation.

(Tea and coffee are acceptable; however, excessive intake of caffeine or theine causes increased diuresis.)

It must be asserted that doping in fencing – a sensori-motor sport – does not lead to tragic consequences like in such endurance sports as cycling or the marathon. Notwithstanding, the race between pharmacology and physiology to increase athletes' efficiency can be a serious health hazard and cause metabolic disorders and acute poisonings.

It should be kept in mind that doping is always short-term and it only temporarily inhibits the body's natural responses to stress and fatigue.

Chapter 7.

Recent Fencing Research: Concepts and Highlights

Too few fencers and coaches are aware of the results of scientific research in fields that bear on fencing. Findings with important implications are often published in specialized journals that are not primarily focused on fencing. The following chapters present results of some advanced research during the modern saber era including studies by the present author. Because they are frequently technical in nature and draw on diverse areas of knowledge, the present section briefly lists some of the findings of the greatest practical importance and serves as an introduction to the terminology and concepts of the scientific fields involved. However, it is impossible to list all the important findings in this brief and non-technical chapter. The author strongly advises the reader to study the following chapters in their own right, or at least to look at the chief points of emphasis.

7.1 Identifying fencing potential and assessing progress

How does a fencer become a foilist, epeeist, or saber fencer? Formerly, it was considered unwise for fencers to specialize from the beginning. Instead, fencers learned basic foil and genral footwork before choosing (or being chosen for), a weapon of specialization. For many reasons, this is no longer true: fencers very often specialize in a single weapon from the beginning of their careers. Thus, coaches face the problem of identifying potential – that is, which beginner will become a champion? – as well as the problem of identifying which weapon gives each fencer the greatest opportunity. They need tools to assess their students' fitness and progress at every stage of their careers. Coaches need to know what to assess; they need assessment tools that are objective and practical; and they need to know how to apply their findings to the task of developing fencers.

The studies presented in the following chapters show that many physical qualities, as well as conformity to some "championship profile," were of limited importance in predicting fencing success or weapon selection and were of limited usefulness in suiting the training method and lesson style to the individual fencer. A series of practical tests for various abilities that can be used to discover potential and/or monitor progress is given in Chapter 9.

Four areas have predictive ability and practical implications:
- Body type, which is useful primarily in weapon selection, but not necessarily in ultimate fencing success;
- Fundamental aerobic and anaerobic energy use potential – that is, whether the fencer is potentially more of an endurance athlete like a distance runner or a power athlete like a sprinter–which is important for lesson structure as well as for tactical preparation;
- Temperament (personality type), is important for lesson structure and tactical preparation;
- Psychomotor abilities (the ability to learn physical tasks until they become automatic, including visual motor co-ordination, ability to divide attention, focus/concentration, etc. – which together are the basis of learning new movements), are the single area most highly predictive of fencing success. Again: *the main predictor of fencing success is the speed, precision, and durability of acquisition and development of motor habits.*

These play a part at all levels of saber fencers' preparation.

7.2 Body type

The fencer's body type, in particular, body mass index (BMI) / Rohrer's indexand length proportions, is important for selection for particular weapons: a more slender build is much more suitable for the thrusting weapons (epee, foil); whereas an athletic (mesomorphic) build is more useful in saber.

The proportions of the weapon arm can be used in the development of a fencer's combat style. A fencer with a considerable arm span should practice cuts at the nearer target areas, e.g. to the wrist, forearm and arm, with all parts of the blade, using diverse footwork in defense and attack. Fencers with shorter arms should focus on technical-tactical actions based on counter-time aimed at the opponent's entire valid target area.

7.3 Aerobic and anaerobic potential

Modern saber fencing uses mostly anaerobic and mixed exercises, which means that fencing coaches should carry out the tactical parts of fencing lessons with the fencers' heart rate (HR) of over 180 beats per minute (and even higher during the competition training period). Top fencers may also include individuals with high levels of VO_2 max (high cardiovascular efficiency), but top fencers are to be found with a very wide range of VO_2 max. Energy-use potential is not the basis for individualization of technical actions during fencing lessons, but it can be very useful for saber fencing tactics. Fencers with high endurance should use a great number of preparatory actions and extend the duration of fencing exchanges to the maximum. A large number of repetitions should dominate combat lessons during the competition period of fencing training.

7.4 Personality type

Studies of athletes' temperament and personality are also crucial to saber fencing. The fencers' temperament types closely correspond to their technical-tactical profiles. The majority of fencers are extraverts and ambiverts (intermediate between extravert and introvert). However, introverts constitute about 25% of the world's top fencers.

Introvert fencers prefer a defensive combat style and anticipatory tactics. They deliver most hits in defense using counter-attacks, beats, parries and counter-ripostes. Of all the offfensive-defensive actions, they most frequently employ counter-time.

Extraverts, on the other hand, prefer first-intention offensive actions. Their attacks are simple and single-feint actions. In defense, they rely on counter-attacks and engagements of the opponent's blade. Tactically, they always try to force their own combat style on their opponent and tend to reduce the fighting distance to be able to deliver surprise attacks.

Further findings on temperament, using the Strelau Temperament Inventory (STI) and the Eysenck Personality Questionnaire, will be found in Chapters 8 and 9. (It turns out that top fencers are characterized by great agility and intensity of nervous processes correlated with extraversion.)

A coach will eventually ascertain the fencer's personality type informally, by observation over time; he can speed up the process, however, by administering any of several personality tests, including the Eysenck Personality Questionnaire, which are readily available and free on line. (The present study also used the Strelau Temperament Inventory, not currently freely available on the Web.) Coaches can use their knowledge of personality type to develop training schemes for individual fencers and choose technical-tactical actions in accordance with a fencer's personality.

7.5   Psychomotor ability

The study results reveal the high importance of visual-motor coordination, as well as the speed and precision of movements. The glove pinning test described in Chapter 9 is consistently valuable at every level of fencing from beginner to elite. Psychomotor ability is an important discriminating factor among fencers, even those at the most advanced training level. It develops through experience and application of appropriate techniques. Proper exercises should include series of cuts used alternately with thrusts to unusual target areas, e.g. thrusts to cheeks or cut-overs with the flat or the back of the blade. Visual-motor coordination can be effectively developed by practicing actions on the blade, feints, and circular parries (as shown in technical lessons 1 and 2 on the DVD).

7.6   Types of reactions and their application in fencing lessons

Swift and effective reactions are central to fencing success. Coaches need to understand the nature of reaction time and the different kinds of reactions in order to develop them in their lessons.

Fencers' reactions are sensori-motor responses; that is, they involve both the senses and the muscles. Although it is common to speak of "reaction time" as if it were simple, reactions in fact have two phases. The first is the *latency phase* (or *reaction time properly so called*) – the period before movement during which the fencer processes and interprets sensory information and reaches a decision on how to respond. The second is the period during which he actually executes the reaction. This is the *movement phase*. The duration of the two phases can be measured by electromyography, a procedure in which electrodes are attached to the skin to measure the time between the appearance of the stimulus and the measurable beginning of muscle contraction.

(Conceptually, it is clear that there is an additional phase, prior to the appearance of the stimulus, which we may call the *preparatory or anticipatory phase*. During this phase, the fencer is waiting for the stimulus to appear and may react to a subtle signal or to an intuition or probabilistic anticipation of his opponent's action before the action actually occurs. This phase is extremely difficult to measure by means of instruments, since by definition it takes place before the appearance of a measurable stimulus. Nevertheless, aspects of it are discussed in the following chapters.)

In addition to these *phases* of reaction, there are different *kinds* of reaction, which vary in their processing speed. Broadly speaking, these are simple reactions and choice reactions, but it has become increasingly clear (cf. Czajkowski 2005 (1995)) that the situation is more complex. There are

1) **SIMPLE REACTIONS**: a fixed reaction to an anticipated stimulus, e.g. pressing a button when a light flashes, or executing a head cut with lunge when the fencing master gives the invitation, and
2) **COMPLEX REACTIONS**, including
   a) **CHOICE REACTION:** recognizing the stimulus and responding correctly, e.g. pressing "R" when the red light appears and "G" when the green light appears, or recognizing the direction of the attack and choosing the correct parry;
   b) **DIFFERENTIAL REACTION**: differentiating between closely similar stimuli and responding correctly, e.g. distinguishing between an actual attack, which must be parried, and a feint, which can be counterattacked; **SWITCHING REACTION:** a response already begun must be altered because of something unforeseen, e.g. the fencer's riposte is met by an unexpected circular parry instead of an anticipated direct parry.
   c) **INTUITIVE REACTION**: a response based on a "feeling" of what the opponent will do, resulting from the fencer's general experience and his opponent's actions during the bout; as opposed to

d) **ANTICIPATORY REACTION:** a response to a signal given before the "real" stimulus, e.g. the opponent puts extra weight on the rear leg before beginning a lunge;
e) **REACTION TO A MOVING OBJECT,** which fencing self-evidently requires.

The top world saber fencers have never been individuals with long *reaction time* (RT), i.e. slowly processing information, although there have been fencers with longer *movement time* (MT), e.g. Imre Gedovari and Damien Touya. Fencers with both instant reactions and very fast movements were, for instance, Wojciech Zabłocki, Jean Francis Lamour, and Aldo Montano. The most versatile saber fencers included, among others, Jerzy Pawłowski, Stanislav Pozdniakov and Grigorij Kirienko.

The highly instructive novice-expert paradigm – a theory supported by a series of studies across many disciplines and many sports– shows that the superiority of expert fencers grows with the increasing complexity of reactions (choice reactions, anticipatory reactions or even intuitive reactions). The most advanced saber fencers are able to reduce the decision-making phase of reactions, i.e. the latency time (LT) of their responses, which also positively affects their movement time (MT). In addition to the quality, precision and accuracy of techniques (motor habits) perceptual training and anticipation of the opponent's actions are important in the process of learning and developing fencing technique. Fencers at the championship level are able to delay the decision-making phase to anticipate the opponent's intention and execute second-intention actions.

The tests of different types of reactions discussed in Chapter 8 allow better understanding of the learning and development of timing-based motor habits, movement automation, and complex technical actions. The last ones – the complex technical actions – are related to the development of cognitive processes in the changing situations of saber bouts. Saber training should generally start with teaching and refining basic technical actions involving both simple and complex motor habits. Next, technical fencing skills combine with possible tactical situations in actual bouts.

The DVD that accompanies this book presents two of the three quintessential models for training saber reactions (purely technical, technico-tactical, and tactical). The first lesson to study is a technical-tactical lesson, featuring the author and Katarzyna Karpińska, that involves three variants of tactical exercises (Lesson 3,). The second, a pre-competition tactical lesson with the author and Wojciech Marczak, uses four exercise variants (Lesson 9b). Please note! In both models, the coach evokes the fencers' desired reactions in situations requiring alternating execution of single and complex offensive actions, single counter-attacks and actions on the blade or defensive actions, mainly parries. In both models, the lesson begins with the fencing master and the fencer both executing (or feinting) a simultaneous attack, which from the standpoint of tactics is most often used in saber fencing bouts.

The contents of the DVD are more fully discussed in Chapter 12.

Chapter 8.

Fencing talent identification and selection

[The material in this and the following chapter derives from the author's own research conducted in 1997 – 1999, updated with references to later relevant studies by the author and others.]

8.1   Review of previous models of talent Identification

One of the most promoted concepts of talent selection and development in sport was the so-called "sport champion" model, a set of guidelines for long-term training. It was developed with the aid of expert and extrapolative methods (Platonow 1990) on the basis of correlations between morpho-structural and physiological parameters and athletes' sports results (Wazny 1989). In Western countries, the paradigms of sports talent identification were constructed by following identification models of scientists, artists and business managers. Such models were often applied at the institutional level, e.g. national programs of talent identification in the United Kingdom (Williams, Reilly 2000), Canada (Bayli 2004), the United States (Malina, Buchard 1991) and Australia (Gulbin, Jason 2004). Their common characteristic was a complex analysis and diagnosis of all parameters affecting high sports results, such as somatic build, physiology, energy use characteristics, psycho-motorics, and central nervous system function, as well as psychological conditions and the impact of genetic factors on one's sports development.

8.2   Criticism of earlier models and new directions

As far as the so-called sport champion model of talent identification is concerned, coaching practice shows that scientific selection is not always conducive to identification of true talents. The scientific selection system has been known to fail to identify candidates who later achieved the highest sports results, including world championship titles. Thus the system may discriminate against some talented athletes rather than discover new ones. Selection methods based on standardization of certain parameters started to be regarded as promoting unreal models. A similar problem was associated with selection and identification methods based on calculus of probability and other mathematical means (referred to as optimization of the training process) including controlled selection.

The criticism of the above concepts resulted in:
- In predisposition testing, focusing on selecting the most predictive tools specific to a given sport or sport event;
  [A note on the word "predisposition" is in order here. As used in these studies, it means innate or acquired talent or potential.)
- Discontinuing longitudinal studies as ineffective and too long, in favor of comparative studies of novice and advanced (expert) athletes;
- Progression from school programs to national programs of talent identification;
- Discovery of sports talents through talent identification, selection and development;
- Discontinuation of central management and creation of interdisciplinary research teams in particular sports communities, clubs and local associations;
- Individualization and careful, specialized coordination of the process of talent development.

One of the major faults of the aforementioned systems of selection is the negligence of learning of motor habits, and predispositions to develop new motor experiences as the basis of technical and tactical preparation in relation to athletes' psychological profiles and their effectiveness in sports combat. These factors are particularly significant in sports with open motor habits, including fencing. A proper process of selection should be treated as a continuation of the entire process of athlete's talent development from the introductory training stage to at least the stage of junior championship contention.

There are also some reservations about the mentioned national programs of talent identification. These programs focus on the diagnosis of morpho-structural and psychophysiological predispositions, whereas the development of motor learning skills and sports technique is often treated marginally.

8.3 Goals of the present study: identification and assessment of fencing-specific talent

- The present study builds on previous studies of talent identification. These were long-term, complex studies of fencers at all levels of sports development, as described later. The results of these studies can be used as reference points for fencing coaches in their comparative analyses of morpho-structural, physiological, psychomotor and fencing-specific conditioning of novice and advanced fencers. They constitute a useful database for assessment of fencing predispositions but not yet fencing talents.
- To this base the present study adds a thorough analysis of different forms of reactions in the development of individual sports development, made with the aid of surface electromyography (Chapter 9).
- The same chapter also presents the results of an original study by the present author using regression analysis, which allowed identification of the most important factors of saber championship among top Polish saber fencers. These results are accompanied by expert, technical observations of championship bouts between advanced fencers. In consequence, the emphasis of fencers' somatic and psychophysiological spheres and their impact on achievement of a high fencing level has been thoroughly revised.
- Psychomotor components, including choice reaction time and spatial anticipation must be regarded as highly important factors in fencing talent identification
- Additionally, by the use of the *novice-expert paradigm, the present study has* made it possible to evaluate these parameters and the relationships between the speed of information processing and the duration of the motor phases of the fencers' sensori-motor responses. A considerable reduction of decision-making time during execution of complex motor tasks was observed among advanced fencers. Following the opinions of top fencing coaches, the above mentioned

factors were found to be of great significance in learning complex motor habits – as well as in real fencing bouts.

8.4 Conclusions and indications of the present study

Complex studies of fencers carried out by a number of authors (Czajkowski 2001; Tyshler, Tyshler 1996) revealed a limited impact of somatic conditions (body build) on fencers' results. Somatic characteristics are useful only in the selection of fencers for particular fencing events. Tall and slim athletes (leptosomic or ectomorph type) are usually selected for epee and foil; shorter fencers of athletic type (mesomorphs) make the best saber fencers. Physiological parameters assessed with the VO_2 max do not reveal statistically significant differences between advanced and novice fencers. Some predispositions related to anaerobic metabolism, primarily to the phosphagen power of the legs measured with the Wingate test, are also significant. However, the main sphere of predictability of high sports results and fencing talents is a complex of psychomotor conditions such as speed, precision and durability of acquisition and development of motor habits during an athlete's sport ontogenesis [individual development] (Borysiuk 2000).

Undoubtedly, in the majority of sports with open motor habits, e.g. combat sports, martial arts, team games, racquet and ball sports, the athlete's physical abilities depend on the sport's technical and tactical requirements or complement one another. The identification of a sport talent in such sports is immensely difficult, since the process of development of motor skills does not correspond to the process of learning motor habits. Motor learning is a permanent process; and at the advanced level of training, the focus shifts from the sphere of physical predispositions to perfect recreation of motor programs under the changing conditions of sports combat and in accordance with the tactical requirements of competition. Despite numerous efforts, the notions of variability and development of technical skills in the training process have not yet been subject to any thorough analysis, often because of the difficulties in making objective assessment, even with the use of state-of-the-art technology (biomechanical analysis, video recording, telemetry and EMG). It seems that proper understanding of these aspects is impossible without adopting an empirical approach involving painstaking research and experts' opinions (Starkes, Ericcson 2003).

The observations and indications presented here are results of studies of novice and advanced fencers with the aid of a specially designed system of surface electromyography (SEMG), which enabled assessment of reaction time (RT) and movement time (MT) during execution of simple and complex motor tasks, spatial and temporal anticipation, and effectiveness of learning motor habits using muscle tension analysis. For the purpose of talent identification in fencing, these research results were complemented with the opinions of top Polish combat sports coaches. (Borysiuk 2006). They became the basis for the analysis of technical actions performed during fencing competitions by junior and senior saber fencers.

Assuming that talent in fencing is an ability to effectively acquire motor habits (motor programs), the following observations about talent identification in sport can be made:

1. The research results point to the significance of reaction time (choice, differential and anticipatory responses to different types of stimulation). They revealed the definite superiority of advanced players over novice players in this sphere. In addition, a greater rationality of recreation of motor programs (lower values of the EMG signal) was noted among the advanced fencers at the advanced and championship levels. The precise measurement of the speed of information processes (RT and MT) showed that top level fencers reduced the time of their sensori-motor responses in the central stage, i.e. they perceived stimuli and made decisions much faster than novice athletes. This observation can be treated as a proof of the influence of specialized training on the effectiveness of perception processes in advanced fencers.

2. In terms of precision, accuracy and repeatability of sensori-motor responses, the results of specialist and motor hybrid tests (visual-motor coordination, spatial orientation, precision and speed of reaction) revealed significant differences between novice and advanced fencers, and much better parameters in advanced fencers. In the analysis of different types of reactions, the advanced fencers displayed high indices of repeatability of the results. Moreover, the tests

carried out prior to fencing competitions pointed to a high correlation between the subjects' results and sport fitness.

3. The analysis of the timing of reaction assessed with the athlete's ability to perform motor programs showed that responses of advanced fencers were significantly faster than responses of the novice ones. Similar results were obtained in tests of anticipation to a moving object. It can be concluded that advanced athletes process signals at the early stage of the perception process using long-time memory, whereas the novice athletes' perception is delayed and based on short-time memory.

4. Statistical analyses and coaching experience point to a relationship between the variety of performed actions (the number of different technical actions they perform) and the ranking position of individual players, at high-level fencing events. Thanks to optimal stimulation fencing champions can effectively utilize their arsenal of technical actions despite enormous psychological pressure. This is one of the main factors differentiating between novice and experienced fencers. It also indicates that high training effectiveness, e.g. of junior fencers, does not have to be related to their final results in a competition.

8.5   Selection in fencing

Probability mathematics shows that the number of outstandingly talented athletes in human population is very small and ranges from one to a few hundred thousand. Certainly, the small proportion of naturally talented players does not make sport coaches give up traditional methods of recruitment such as spontaneous or intuitive selection based on the coach's experience and community and family traditions. Small sports clubs with meager resources are often cradles of highly talented athletes who, by developing their predispositions, can find their way into a junior or senior national team.

In fencing, as in any sport, the the recruitment process can work in any of three ways: a rigorously "scientific" method, based on test results; a "natural" or intuitive method without any scientific testing; and some mixture of the coach's intuition, the student's desire, and the results of testing and sports science. Every coach has the choice of which way is optimal, but everybody can profit from the wide spectrum of diagnostic possibilities presented here.

Candidate selection in fencing features two parallel tendencies. On the one hand, young candidates are selected featuring the best traits necessary for development of pure fencing skills. On the other hand, candidates must be selected for the particular fencing disciplines: saber, epee and foil. In coaching practice, this is accomplished in two ways. The first way stipulates that training at the introductory stage should start with foil as the most basic weapon; the other method of selection of fencers emphasizes starting training in a particular weapon of choice. For instance, at the time of this study (1997 – 1999), due to the relatively short history of women's saber fencing, most of the present-day top female saber fencers had begun their careers as foilists. Contrary to possible expectations, this was beneficial for the female fencers' development, since foil and saber are both conventional, right-of-way weapons.

For a long time the process of selection of fencers was based on regular motor tests examining strength, power, speed, agility and endurance; however, the ultimate results of such selection procedures were not satisfactory. Very often the candidates with the best test results turned out to be mediocre fencers, and, on the contrary, athletes with low test results became successful fencers, even competing at the international level. Because of all these problems, a number of new and original methods of selection for individual fencing events has emerged, aimed at development of accurate diagnostic tools.

One example of such diagnostic problems was the procedure designed by Wężowski (1976), who used a variety of tests for measurement of motor docility. One of the most frequently applied tests in the 1970's had been the Iowa-Brace test, which contained 21 tasks and could be effectively combined depending on the candidates' sex and age. Wężowski's innovation was to supplement this procedure by evaluating the pre-screened candidates by way of direct, round robin, "first-hit" fencing bouts between the candidates. This type of selection was considered to be extremely reliable and accurate. It was to be confirmed by the correlations between results of individual tournaments and sport results achieved during training. Research studies and fencing practice verified the effectiveness of the above methods. However, some candidates, regarded as outstandingly talented, failed to develop their skills any further and others, who initially held no promise, achieved outstanding successes later on. In fact, one rejected fencer, Dariusz Wodke, eventually became world champion! Evidently this "direct selection" method did not work for everyone.

8.5.1 Somatic determinants

The process of fencers' selection starts with the measurement of candidates' morphological build following detailed medical examination. A four-year study of foil, epee and saber fencers at their introductory and advanced training stages, carried out by the Department of Anthropology of the Academy of Physical Education in Warsaw, showed that fencers featured a characteristic body build. The research was conducted on a group of 207 boys and was aimed at determination of somatic changes related to puberty and fencing training. Thirteen somatic parameters were analyzed (armspan, leg and arm length, forearm length, right and left ankle width and shoulder width; shoulder, forearm, thigh and calf circumference; height and weight. The control group consisted of young people from Warsaw at the same age as the studied fencers. The study covered morphological characteristics most representative for fencers and most useful from the standpoint of technical requirements and fencing training specificity.

The study identified characteristics that were particularly prognostic in the process of fencers' selection. The studied athletes were elite junior fencers and won junior national championships. This was important, since only the top fencers – who have gone through intensive selection and are adapted to heavy training loads – are likely to possess the anthropological parameters that are most useful in a given sport. The analysis of morpho-structural profiles of young saber fencers, epeeists and foilists showed that the saber fencers differed significantly in height from the foilists and epeeists. The epee fencers featured predominantly a leptosomic (ectomorphic) type of body build, similar to that of basketball players. They had longer arms and legs and elongated muscle venters. The saber fencers had a shorter armspan and shorter legs, but wider shoulders and greater forearm circumference that the other two groups; and greater calf circumference that the foilists. Their somatotype was predominantly athletic (mesomorphic).

This muscle development in saber fencers is determined by the specific tactical requirements of saber fencing, such as maintenance of distance between the fencers during a bout and saber-specific maneuverability. The analysis of the increments of the studied parameters and the fencers' maturation showed that epee fencers developed physically much faster than the young foilists and saber fencers. Their growth dynamics was simply faster. The study also showed that specialized saber fencing and the type of speed-endurance training that accompanies saber training do not cause excessive muscle growth. During puberty, these young fencers develop their muscles naturally rather than due to their adaptation to training.

The above observations can be used for the purpose of diagnosis of morpho-structural predispositions of young fencers. First, young fencers, with the exception of saber fencers, as opposed to their non-training counterparts, feature a leptosomic body build, in particular longer arms and higher slenderness index. Second, the analysis of increments of morphological parameters revealed no significant deviations from the accepted development norms. Thus fencing training at the introductory stage does not induce any disorders in the young athletes' physical development. Third, it was observed that parameters such as length of body parts and forearm circumference were important in the selection process as they could be affected by training only to some degree. Fourth, the analysis of the saber, epee and foil fencers' somatotypes points to the necessity of early specialization in particular fencing weapons.

8.5.2 Physical capacity parameters

As discussed in Chapter 2, the somatic profile and exercise abilities of saber fencers became even more diversified in comparison with epeeists and foilists following the introduction of electronic scoring apparatus into saber fencing. These changes were confirmed in my study of saber fencers from the Silesia region in Poland (Borysiuk 2005). Besides the somatic parameters, the body mass index (BMI) was used in the study, assessed with bioimpedance analysis; and Rohrer's index, calculated as body weight in grams times 100 divided by the cube of height in centimeters. The physiological indices included VO_2 max using the Monark cycloergometer and the indirect Astrand method, peak power in Wingate test (PP), lactate threshold

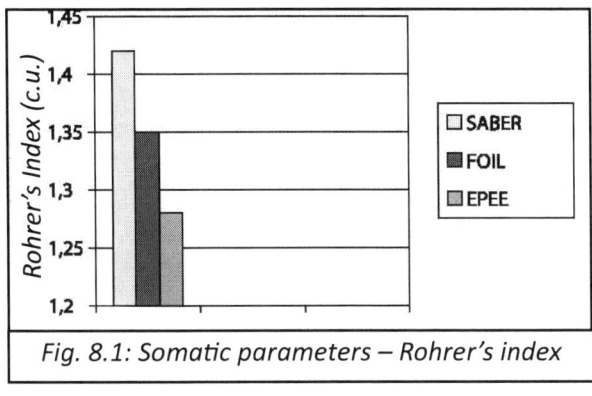

Fig. 8.1: Somatic parameters – Rohrer's index

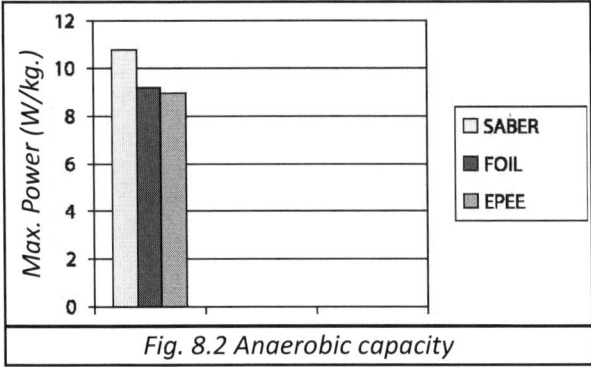

Fig. 8.2 Anaerobic capacity

power (LTP) and the heart rate during the lactate threshold (HRLT) with the Conconi test.

The study results showed that junior saber fencers featured a higher Rohrer's index than foil and epee fencers. The saber fencers' somatotype was more athletic, which was related to the dynamic style of saber combat. This type of body build is most correlated with predispositions to perform anaerobic and anaerobic/aerobic exercises. The saber fencers featured the highest peak power and lactate threshold power values. The VO_2 max and HRLT values during training bouts revealed no significant differences between the three groups of fencers (Figures. 8.1 and 8.2).

It can be concluded that the effort profile of saber fencers predisposes them to perform anaerobic exercise and is closely related to their body build. These observations should be taken into account in the process of selection of fencers of all weapons and in development of individual training plans. Coaches' observations and complex studies of factors affecting fencing results point to the fact that

Table 8.1. Tests measuring fencing predispositions.
[Highly predictive tests are emphasized by
boldface and italics and marked with an asterisk]

Parameters	Test	Diagnostic tool
1. Somatic	***Forearm length****	Anthropometric measuring instrument
2. Motor abilities	Johnson-Metheny test	J-M exercise mat
3. Psychological predispositions	***Temperament test****	Strelau test modified by Wjatkin
4. Psychomotor abilities	***Visual-motor coordination**** complex reaction test	Computer-assisted cross apparatus
5. Running speed	5, 10, and 15m test	Photo finish
6. Anaerobic capacity	Wingate test	Monark cycloergometer

the process of selection in fencing also involves a number of sport talent areas, different than the aforementioned somatic and physical capacity parameters. Certainly, an interesting area of fencing talent research is assessment of motor abilities such as speed, permanence and accuracy of learning new motor tasks. The research of motor abilities was developed with the aid of statistical methods such as factor analysis and regression analysis. Thanks to these methods, it became possible to determine the factors responsible for the effectiveness of training. Wężowski's study mentioned above pointed to the fact that coaches were intuitively aware of the shortcomings of the so-called tests of motor traits, which merely assessed the subject's energy potential without evaluation of coordination predispositions and motor abilities in combination with psychological properties.

Long-term studies on a large number of subjects, using optimization techniques and appropriate statistical methods, show that fencing talent involves four spheres:
- morpho-structural predispositions,
- psychomotor predispositions,
- physical capacity parameters
- motor abilities.

A high sports level in fencing is determined by (in order of importance): visual-motor coordination, height as a somatic parameter, intensity of stimulation processes as a temperamental trait, peak anaerobic power, and low number of errors in complex reaction time.

The psychomotor determinants include visual-motor coordination and the number of errors in choice reaction time; physical capacity parameters – peak anaerobic power; psychomotor predispositions – temperament level; and somatic parameters – height.

8.5.3 Tools for assessment of fencing predispositions

Considering the above research results and opinions about different methods of selection in fencing, a set of tests for recruitment of prospective fencers can be proposed (Table 8.1).

The test results were calculated using ranking points after each trial. To make the differences between particular fencers more accurate, the ranking points of the most predictive tests (emphasized by boldface and italics and marked with an asterisk] were multiplied by 1.5.

The tests can be carried out by any fencing coach. Some diagnostic tools may not be available; however, they can be alternatively replaced with other simpler research tools.

1. Forearm length is measured with an anthropometric instrument. It should be kept in mind that the length proportions of the legs and arms are strongly correlated with one another, therefore the measurement of other somatic parameters, e.g. lower leg length, hand length can also be diagnostically useful.
2. Motor abilities were assessed with a simplified version of the Johnson-Metheny test. The exercise mat was smaller, the number of exercises was limited to 4 for boys and 3 for girls, and the entire test duration was shorter, following the description in Wężowski's study (1976).
3. Temperament was assessed with K.T. Strelau test as modified by Wjatkin. Stawowska (1989) made a very accurate adaptation of this test with a questionnaire and age adjustment tools. The test measures four parameters altogether: intensity of stimulation processes, intensity of inhibition processes, agility of nervous processes and balance of nervous processes; it is suggested the last two parameters be given priority.
4. The psychomotor tests are fully described in Chapter 9. The COS Warszawa has published [in Polish] computer-assisted tests on CDs which emulate the cross apparatus

and include choice reaction tests with registration of errors. These tests have proven extremely useful in many research studies.
5. The 15m running test with time measured after 5 and 10 m was carried out indoors with the aid of computer-assisted photo cells. The trial began with a "flying start" 1 m from the first set of photo cells. The test reflects components of footwork characteristic of real fencing bouts.
6. The Wingate test of anaerobic capacity (30 sec.) with a Monark cycloergometer measures a number of parameters. The two most useful for diagnostic purposes are peak power [W/kg] and power drop [%] indices. If the latter reaches low percentage values, it can be interpreted as a predisposition to perform mixed (aerobic/anaerobic) exercises.
7. The obstacle course test is supposed to reflect coordination abilities, in particular, adaptability to new motor tasks. The test is illustrated in Chapter 9 (Figure 9.3). The test consists of going through the obstacles two times as fast as possible.

Due to the limited capacities of average fencing clubs or sports schools, the cycloergometer in the Wingate test can be replaced with a standing long jump test, which is an equivalent measure of maximal anaerobic power. Similarly, the photo cells in Test 5 can be replaced by an electronic stopwatch.

As far as the psychological tests are concerned, it should be remembered that the intensity of stimulation processes is significantly correlated with extraversion, i.e. a fundamental index of personality. Thus, a useful alternative diagnostic tool for psychological measurements can be the Eysenck questionnaire of personality or the Myers – Briggs Type Indicator, free interactive versions of which are available on the Web.

In the case of young candidates before or during early pubescence the process of their selection for fencing must involve additional anthropometric measurements to determine their biological age. It must be also noted that the process of fencers' selection involves gradual or immediate weapon-specific training.

The most significant diagnostic tests in the selection process seem to be anthropometric measurements and physical capacity parameters. In the case of selection of saber fencers, a greater forearm circumference and predispositions to perform anaerobic and mixed exercises are also significant but not decisive factors.

The above tests should be treated as resources for fencing coaches and their usability can be verified during fencing weapon training. A key element, which is very difficult to assess, are predispositions to fight conventional bouts in saber and foil, whose tactics, unlike those of epee, are based on the right-of-way rules. Coaching practice and experience show that some trainee fencers fail to adapt mentally to the conventions in foil and saber, and despite weaker physical predispositions, choose the epee as a weapon which is more comprehensible from the standpoint of combat tactics.

Chapter 9.

Diagnostic tools in fencing research

As we have seen in the previous chapter, a complex approach to assessment of the sports level of athletes at all stages of development is strongly emphasized in contemporary practice relating to diagnostic tests. Diagnostic tests in fencing involve a number of factors affecting sport combat, such as psychomotor conditions, personality traits, motor abilities, and fencing-specific predispositions. All these complex parameters constitute a fencer's sports level during individual sports events. As Szopa (1989) writes, an athlete's sport level should be assessed not only with the exclusive use of motor tests but also with instruments measuring morpho-structural, energy, coordination and psychological predispositions in combination with sport-specific motor skills.

In practice, assessment tests in sport are used for continuous monitoring of all aspects of sport preparation of athletes, including team selection and evaluation of form before important competitions. For years, fencing studies have been increasingly concerned with the considerable influence of psychomotor and psychological factors on the efficiency of sport combat. However important these factors may be in determining fencing success, other factors, especially somatic and physiological parameters, remain significant. Due to recent rules changes and the increasing dynamism of fencing bouts in all three weapons – especially in saber – the impact of the body's energetic processes on fencing results is becoming more and more palpable. The author's own long-term research has also yielded some valid conclusions. The results of the tests are presented below in table form. They can be used for comparison or as reference ranges for individual sports levels. They were obtained in the course of extensive research carried out between 1997 and 1999 on a sample of 118 senior Polish female and male fencers (representing all three weapons) from the Polish Olympic Team and a group of junior fencers from the Silesia province in Poland (Table 9.1). They have been supplemented with updated research results where applicable.

All diagnostic procedures should satisfy the following preconditions:

1. They should avoid so-called "information noise;" that is, they should select the one or two most predictive assessment methods for a particular area.
2. They should use only research methods that produce results immediately, e.g. on-line. This provides athletes with the necessary motivation.
3. They should be synchronized with the appropriate periods of the training cycle in order to ensure diagnostic accuracy.

A number of the diagnostic tools discussed below are in many ways innovative. Others, such as the ones for physiological assessment, are commonly used in studies of motor function.

Table 9.1 Profile of Groups of Subjects

Subjects	Height (cm)	Weight (kg)	Rohrer's Index (pts)	Body Mass Index [%]	Age
Olympic squad (men)	181.82	76.60	1.32	23.9	23.28
Olympic squad (women)	172.20	60.20	1.18	26.3	22.52
Junior Group	171.72	66.96	1.31	21.20	18.65

9.1 Assessment of somatic and physiological predispositions; Significance of subjects' age.

In recent years, fencing, especially saber, has experienced a rapid evolution of the demands on fencers' morphostructural (body build) parameters and energy processes. The body build of modern fencers, especially modern saber fencers, is of athletic (mesomorphic) type, as indicated by athletes' body mass index and lean body mass values. This tendency is also observed in some other sports, e.g. tennis. It is no longer true that athletes with a low level of physical fitness and low aerobic and anaerobic capacity can be successful fencers. Numerous studies (Borysiuk 2002) show that fencers must possess excellent physical fitness parameters as well as great psychomotor abilities and stress resistance. Until recently, fencing has been defined as a speed-endurance sport with an emphasis on a variety of reactions with different speeds and fencing-specific endurance. Research results show that from the standpoint of physiology, fencing must be classified as a sport determined by the quality of anaerobic processes and based on general endurance of aerobic and mixed character. The fencing coaching community (coaches and instructors) should therefore include into their array of diagnostic means assessment methods of somatic and physiological predispositions (Table 9.2).

Table 9.2. Mean values and standard deviation of somatic and physiological parameters of senior fencers (N=28).

Variable	Mean	Standard Deviation
Height	181.821	5.445
Anaerobic capacity (J/kg)	12.82	5.466
Rohrer's index (pts)	1.322	0.068
BMI (%)	23.90	8.289
VO_2 max [ml/kg min]	54.8	4.325

9.1.1 Measurement tools for assessment of somatic and coordination parameters

- Height and weight measured with Rohrer's index according to the formula: height $[cm]^3$ / body weight $[g]$ x 100;
- Body mass index (BMI) measured using the BIA-101/S.C. impedance analyzer. This computer-assisted device samples tissue resistance (Rx) and tissue reactance (Xc) values as well as tissue volume (Xc), and then calculates the percentage of lean body mass;
- Aerobic capacity measured with a computer-assisted Monark cycloergometer. After processing athlete's personal data and body weight, the computer calculates loads for consecutive test levels as well as heart rate (HR), pedaling velocity (V) and power (P). On the basis of the functional correlation between P, HR and PWC, the value of the PWC index is calculated in the subsequent stages of the test. Next, the maximal oxygen uptake (VO_2 max) is measured according to the formula: VO_2 max = 1.7 + PWC170 + 1240 (VO_2

max – maximal oxygen uptake (ml/kg min); 1.7, 1240 – constant quantities)
- Anaerobic capacity measured with a 10-second or 30-second test using the computer-assisted Monark cycloergometer. During a 10-second exercise with appropriate training loads matched with the athlete's body weight the following indices were calculated:

  - peak anaerobic power [W/kg] – Pmax,
  - attaining peak power [s],
  - maintaining peak power [s],

The test was preceded by a 5-minute warm-up with 1W/kg body mass load.

The above measurements were carried out by the author in cooperation with fencing coaches of the Polish National Team and from various Polish sports clubs. Most of the tests were conducted between 1997 and 1998 during training camps for the senior and junior national teams and at the fencing camps for regional teams. The tests of senior fencers discussed below were carried out before the World Championships in Cape Town in 1997 with the use of computer-assisted indirect measurement of aerobic capacity.

9.1.2 Somatic examination results

The profile of subject groups (Table 9.1) as well as an analysis of correlation reveal a statistically significant influence of somatic indices (height, in particular) on fencing results. This is an important finding, because for a number of fencing coaches and for a long time, somatic differences were no obstacle in the process of fencers' selection.

Height

Height, which was not considered important before, proved to be an especially significant factor. The study results as well as observations of top world fencing competitions show that men fencers below 170cm (5' 7") and women fencers below 160cm (5' 3") of height stand virtually no chance of making the Olympic team. Even in saber, regarded until recently as a weapon in which impressive physical

Table 4.3. Results of maximal work capacity and 5m speed tests. June 14, 1997, Wisła, Poland.

	Name	Year of birth	Body weight	5m test	VO2max
1.	Sobczak R.	1967	77,1	-	68,4
2.	Kurowski B.	1974	85,9	0,97	63,2
3.	Gilman D.	1973	72,9	1,08	62,7
4.	Jędryś Marek	1974	73,0	1,07	61,5
5.	Kiełpikowski P.	1962	79,0	1,05	61,2
6.	Krzesiński A.	1965	94,0	1,08	62,7
7.	Felusiak K.	1973	50,8	1,20	59,5
8.	Maciejewska M.	1970	69,3	-	59,2
9.	Cygan O.	1980	60,0	1,09	57,5
10.	Jeziorowska M.	1970	51,7	1,10	54,8
11.	Szklarski T.	1971	88,5	1,09	53,8
12.	Walka K.	1975	75,5	1,00	53,6
13.	Stokłosa A.	1973	66,2	1,08	50,8
14.	Sobala M.	1972	97,0	0,97	50,6
15.	Piguła T.	1975	91,0	0,98	50,5
16.	Budkiewicz D.	1974	64,0	1,17	49,0
17.	Rybicka A.	1977	61,0	1,20	47,5
18.	Mocek S.	1976	84,8	0,97	44,6
19.	Ciszewska B.	1974	58,0	1,04	40,0
20.	Kryczało A.	1981	84,7	1,11	37,0

parameters were not that important (unlike in epee and foil), a great number of fencers are currently taller than 185cm (6'). The statistical significance of height can be explained by the existence of an obvious correlation between the effectiveness of some tactical actions (counter-attacks) and the length of the sword arm. The mean height of the Olympic fencers: 181.821 (5'11.5") in the men's team (N = 28) and 172.200 (5' 7.8") in the women's team (N = 20) confirms the above observations. It should be mentioned, however, that the elite fencers from the four-member Polish national fencing teams, e.g. men's foil and saber, are on the average as much as 5 cm taller.

Lean Body Mass

As opposed to height, no significant correlation was noted between the fencers' lean body mass (LBM) and effectiveness of fencing performance. The range of fat tissue percentage (17.9% to 33.1%) and Rohrer's index values (1.32 – men and 1.12 – women) can be an indication that the body mass and composition have a marginal effect of the fencers' sport level. In terms of the percentage of adipose tissue, fencers are similar to team hand ball players and soccer players. The mean content of adipose tissue in the men's Olympic team amounted to 23.9%, as compared with 23.0% in first league soccer players, and 10% in world elite sprinters.

Age

The question of subjects' age deserves special attention as the common interpretation: the higher athlete's age, the higher athlete's sports level, is clearly too simplistic and erroneous. In modern fencing the top performance age span falls between 25 and 29 years in men; it is a bit lower in women. Many of the world's best senior women fencers are currently teenagers, e.g. the 2004 Olympic medalists in women's saber. The study shows that the top men and women fencers in all weapons have become younger. Fencers over 30 years of age are rare among world championships medalists. In all likelihood, the age of 30 can be regarded in fencing as an upper limit, above which the level of sport performance decreases gradually.

Certainly, however, there are significant differences in the age at which one ends one's fencing career, depending on the age at which one began. For many fencers who took up fencing at the age of 10, the age span between 25 and 30 years is actually the end of their career.

However, athletes who started fencing later should not be discouraged from continuing their careers past that age. A perfect case in point is Laura Flessel, Olympic champion from Atlanta and bronze medalist from Sydney, who reached the Olympic title at the age of 25 after 6 years of training, and achieved a bronze medal in the World championships ten years later. Then there is Luan Jujie, who began fencing at the age of 17, won a silver medal in World Junior Women's Foil 3 years later, won Olympic gold in 1984…and won her first-round bout at the 2008 Beijing Olympics at the age of 50! It can be concluded that a relatively short competitive experience might condition a high sports performance level, even above the mentioned upper age limit.

9.1.3 Physiological examination results

Vo_2 max

The mean VO_2 max (maximal oxygen uptake) of the best Polish fencers amounted to 54.8 ml/kg min, with two subjects reaching values close to 70 ml/kg min, and five (including four women) below 50 ml/kg min. These results are close to those achieved by first-league soccer players. It seems, therefore, that elite fencers possess significant aerobic capacity, which most certainly can be developed through specific fencing training (Table 4.3).

Similar correlations were observed between the results of junior fencers from the Silesia province and those of athletes representing other sports. The young fencers achieved similar VO_2 max to other endurance athletes, e.g. swimmers. It shows that fencers undergoing special training preparation, participating in controlled training bouts and tournaments reach a high level of aerobic endurance. On the other hand, statistical analyses do not seem to confirm that aerobic capacity is a predictor of the fencers' sport level.

Anaerobic power

The 10-second test measured peak anaerobic power (based on ATP and phosphocreatine concentration) as well as the time of attaining and maintaining Pmax in W/kg. The Olympic fencers achieved the mean peak power at 12.82 in 2.33 seconds and maintained it for 2.03 seconds. This was an indication of their high level of adaptability to anaerobic exercise. The obtained results are similar to those reached by strength-sport athletes.

Rapid attainment of peak power is indicative of the high level of preparation of fencers' leg muscles for dynamic work. The time of peak power attainment is significantly correlated with the results of the 15-meter speed tests with photo cells positioned after each 5 meters. The first 5 meters from a flying start were covered by the Olympic team fencers in 0.97 – 0.99 seconds. These results are truly significant for fencers, since the "spurt" exercises over a short distance are very characteristic of fencing footwork. Statistical analyses show that anaerobic capacity can be classified as one of the five factors affecting fencing results.

Some interesting test results were also obtained during training bouts of saber fencers from the Polish National Team. These tests were carried out with the aid of sport-scientific instruments. The obtained HR values during bouts revealed a progression from 140-160 to 180-190 beats/min. Thus, from the physiological point of view, a typical fencing bout is fought alternately in the aerobic and anaerobic exercise zones, and it crosses the anaerobic threshold back and forth. It seems that the HR reaches maximal values usually in the most decisive stages of the fencing bout.

The mean peak anaerobic power (12,82 J/kg) achieved by the Olympic fencers (Table 9.2) as well as other factors affecting fencers' predispositions to make anaerobic efforts point to a great impact of anaerobic capacity on fencing results. It can be assumed that new regulation changes (e.g. limitation of bout length) will be conducive to the increasing role of predispositions or abilities to perform anaerobic exercise in fencing. For example, in a modern 15-touch saber bout the average combat action time amounts to 50-60 seconds. This means that in a bout with a final score of 15:14, a fencer needs an average of less that 2 seconds to execute each hit. Such dynamic bouts require from modern fencers tremendous releases (and recovery) of their anaerobic energy resources. Fencing coaches should realize that certain parts of individual lessons and footwork training should be of high intensity and short duration, especially, immediately before competition.

As we have just seen, anaerobic capacity is significant in fencing training; however, the problems related to exercise energy processes are far more complex. What must be taken into account is the fact that an average fencing competition lasts two or even three days, if we include the team events at the Olympic Games or World Champion-

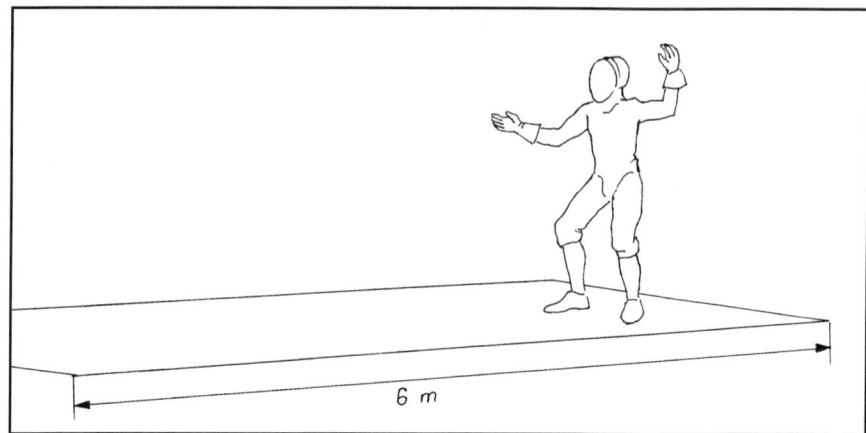

Fig. 9.1: Fencing Endurance Test

Fig. 9.2: Glove Pinning Test

Chapter 9. Diagnostic Tools in Fencing Research   157

Fig. 9.3: Speed of fencing-specific actions with complex coordination

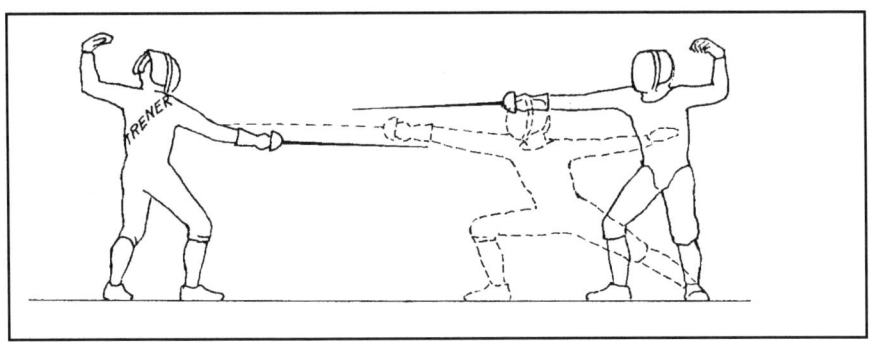

Fig. 9.4: Motor adaptability ("obstacle course") test

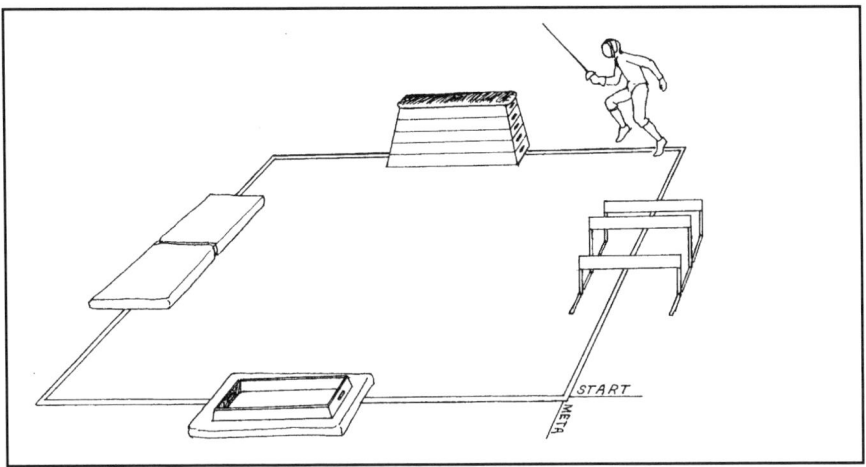

Fig. 9.5: Ability to perform high-frequency movements (Zuchora's test).

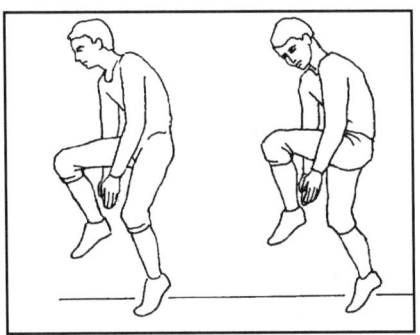

ships. There is no doubt that the most optimal preparation of fencers must also involve aerobic exercises. The study results showed that the men's Olympic group achieved significant mean VO_2 max values (54.8ml/ kg min). Proper fencing fitness training should be based on synchronization of aerobic and anaerobic training loads while taking individual characteristics into consideration.

The issue of anaerobic and aerobic training in fencing still requires detailed research, using a computer-assisted telemetry capable of full monitoring of fencers' physiological parameters during competition bouts.

9.2 Practical tools and for assessing fencing preparation

On the basis of long coaching practice and experience from many Polish fencing clubs, five tests measuring special preparation of fencers were selected. These tests were simple enough to be carried out in any fencing hall and can be used by fencers at all levels of training experience.

1. *Fencing endurance* test consisting of moving back and forth 16 times along the distance of 6m in the on-guard position.
2. *Accuracy and spatial orientation* "glove pinning" test in three five-series trials. The test was performed using a bench propped against the wall bars at a standard angle (70 cm from the wall). The "pinning zone" corresponded to the saber target area (torso) marked with two tapes placed on the bench at 100 cm and 170 cm (3' 3.4" and 5' 7") from the ground. The test results were given in points, i.e. number of successful hits.
3. *Speed of movements with complex coordination*. Test of a combination of three fencing actions, electronically measured. The test started with a forward lunge, assuming the on-guard position – step backward, feinting attack sideways and return to the on-guard position. The combination was used as a form of coach-assisted exercise.
4. *Motor adaptability and agility*. The test consists of completing a square obstacle course (9 x 9m) twice while holding the fencing weapon. The obstacles are placed on each side of the square (three track hurdles, vaulting box, two landing

Table 9.2.1: Statistical analysis of indices of special preparation of senior fencers (N = 28).

Variable	Mean X	SD S
1. Fencing endurance test [s]	38.57	1.69
2. Combination of three fencing actions [s]	4.20	0.40
3. "Glove pinning" [pts]	10.96	1.82
4. "Obstacle course" [s]	34.72	2.31
5. Zuchora's test - 15s [pts]	47.28	4.32

Table 9.2.2: Statistical analysis of indices of special preparation of junior fencers (N = 50).

Variable	Mean X	SD S
1. Fencing endurance test [s]	42.22	3.09
2. Combination of three fencing actions [s]	4.37	0.46
3. "Glove pinning" [pts]	5.94	3.11
4. "Obstacle course" [s]	40.46	6.27
5. Zuchora's test – 15s [pts]	46.56	5.89

mats, the bottom section of the vaulting box). Fencers must overcome the obstacles as quick as possible.
5. Test of *ability to perform movements with great frequency* developed by K. Zuchora (1965). The test consists of skipping and clapping hands below the knees as fast as possible within 15 seconds. The test score is the number of the registered correctly performed hand-claps.

The measurements of fencing-specific preparation should be taken in conditions as close as possible to real competition, in fencing halls with metallic pistes. The combination of three fencing actions and glove pinning tests should be carried out by subjects in full fencing gear. The fencing endurance test (distance of 6m to be covered 16 times back and forth) can be carried out in any sportswear, as during footwork training. The most important requirement is that the tests be performed on a standardized piste to ensure the accuracy of measurement. The obstacle course test can be carried out in a regular gym with the usual exercise equipment: hurdles, vaulting boxes, landing mats. All test results must be measured electronically with a resolution of 0.01 seconds.

9.2.1 Fencing preparation assessment results

The study yielded reference values for women and men fencers in the senior and junior age categories. The mean values of the obtained test results and standard deviation are presented in Tables 9.2.1 and 9.2.2.

These reference values can be used for prospective ranking of young fencers depending on their test scores. Furthermore, a factor analysis of the obtained results was conducted to compile a ranking list of indices and measurement tests (Table 9.2.3).

The factor analysis revealed the fencing endurance test to be the most predictive (marked with an asterisk). It perfectly reflects the specificity, variability and technique of fencing footwork as well as endurance (40 seconds of intense work on the average).

The second most predictive test was the obstacle course, which originally measured fencing-specific motor preparation by requiring subjects to overcome the obstacles holding the fencing weapon all the time and use their own wit and creativeness. The research shows that this test is significantly correlated with fencers' sports level. It often happens that motorically weaker fencers compensate for their lesser speed and agility with creativity in overcoming obstacles, which allows them to achieve better results than fencers with a higher fitness level.

The third most important test was the "glove pinning" test measuring movement speed and precision. Some experts emphasize its extra assessment of spatial orientation. It is an extremely reliable research tool and should be applied in fencing training. The advantages of this test were confirmed by the study of junior and senior saber fencers from the Polish National Team. The glove pinning test is accurate and can even differentiate between fencers from such homogenous groups as the national teams.

The combination of three fencing actions is slightly less significant for achievement of fencing results. It is a coach-supervised test with the weapon, close to real fencing actions. Its lower ranking position is not, however, due to its inaccuracy. Many studies showed that fencers who wanted to perform the test the best way possible, often sidelined movement technique in favor of speed. To make the test more accurate, its results should be completed with an expert's assessment of the fencer's performance on a three-point scale.

The fifth test in terms of its significance for fencing results was the test of ability to perform movements with great frequency. This was the simplest test, consisting of skipping and clapping hands below the knees as fast as possible within 15 seconds. Its results revealed a moderate correlation with specific fencing skills, and due to its its convenience of application (it requires no complex assessment tools) it can be performed in any conditions. Requirements of technical correctness of movements and coordination of skipping and clapping additionally increase its reliability.

The above set of five tests fully reflects the specificity of fencing preparation and can be used in fencing coaching at any level of fencers' sport experience. A comparison of the obtained reference values (Tables 9.2.1., 9.2.2.) with study results by other authors [Czajkowski (1991) and Brol (1989)] shows a high level of predictiveness for three tests; the fencing endurance test, the "obstacle course" and the combination of three fencing actions. In this context, the well-known sport theory rule is confirmed: specialized and psychological predispositions become more significant with the length of training development. At the early stages of sport training, the decisive elements are motor abilities, general fitness and somatic parameters. Thus, the presented set of tests can be used, even for examination of the most advanced fencers.

9.3 Assessment of psychomotor predispositions

Apart from specialized preparation, a significant role in fencing training is played by psychomotor predispositions. Modern theories of motorics underline different reaction times in combination with spatial orientation abilities and visual-motor coordination skills, which are usually associated with coordination predispositions. Undoubtedly, psychomotor predispositions have a significant influence on the development of fencing technique as well as tactical and psychical preparation of individual fencers.

A number of authors have discussed the problem of assessment of the individual constituent elements of psychomotor abilities in fencing, e.g. Keller, Tyshler (1970), Czajkowski (1975, 1984) and Korfanty (1983). The common characteristic of these studies was emphasis of two reaction times: simple reaction time and choice reaction time. All these authors claimed that comprehensive analyses of reaction times constituted the main source of information on prediction of future sports results and assessment of the current competition form. In recent years great progress has been made in the area of diagnosis of psychomotor predispositions because of the emergence of new and highly accurate computer-assisted assessment methods and tools.

At present, reaction time, understood as the interval between the appearance of a visual stimulus and completion of movement, is just one of many measurable elements. Thanks to electromyography, it has become possible to precisely distinguish between reaction time (based on information processing) and movement time, understood as the interval between the appearance of bioelectric tension in muscle (EMG signal) and completion time. A number of popular and useful computer tests have been developed by different research centers. The psychomotor tests discussed together with comparable data in this work were designed in the chair of Sport Theory of the University School of Physical Education in Katowice, Poland (Ryguła 1993). It should be mentioned that computer tests can emulate different assessment tools, however due to still insufficient level of IT education, traditional tools such as cross apparatus or Piórkowski's apparatus are used more appropriately at the present writing.

Table 9.3.1. Mean values and standard deviation of psychomotor indices of senior fencers (N = 28)

Variable	Mean X	SD S
1. Simple reaction time [s]	0.18	0.01
2. Number of errors in simple reaction test [pts]	0.50	0.90
3. Choice reaction time	0.37	0.03
4. Number of errors in choice reaction test [pts]	4.00	3.50
5. Cross apparatus test [pts]	99.92	22.55

Table 9.3.2. Mean values and standard deviation of psychomotor indices of junior fencers (N = 50)

Variable	Mean X	SD S
1. Simple reaction time [s]	0,20	0,03
2. Number of errors in simple reaction test [pts]	1,62	0,51
3. Choice reaction]	0,45	0,03
4. Number of errors in choice reaction test [pts]	6,44	3,91
5. Cross apparatus test [pts]	56,92	30,54

9.3.1 Methods and tools of assessment of psychomotor predispositions

1. Simple reaction time, calculated using a computer program generating 30 light impulses at various intervals. The total test result consisted of the mean reaction speed and, what is also important, the number of errors, i.e. missed stimuli or premature reactions (measured electronically with a resolution of 0.01 second).

2. Choice reaction time. The subjects were to promptly respond with their left or right hand to respective light signals. Different sequences of 40 stimuli used signals in two colors. The program recorded the mean reaction time with the accuracy of 0.01 s. as well as the number of errors.
   In both tests of reaction time, i.e. simple and choice, the registration of errors was regarded as an indicator of concentration of attention.

3. Visual motor coordination measured using the cross apparatus in default mode. The subjects were to press buttons on a coordinate axis to activate respective lights. The test was carried out three times at the set pace of 50, 70 and 90 impulses per minute. Each time, the apparatus emits the same number of impulses, i.e. 49. The test result was calculated as a total of received stimuli in three consecutive trials.

The cross apparatus used for measuring visual motor coordination is commonly applied for testing drivers and athletes representing different sports. According to experts in human motor function the cross apparatus, as well as the equally popular Piorkowski apparatus can also measure spatial orientation. The above study employed the cross apparatus as a more useful tool in fencing. In the author's opinion, the cross apparatus reflects sensori-motor coordination in a much more detailed way. Besides, the attention of fencers during a bout is more focused than, for example, that of team players. Thus, the cross apparatus is a complex diagnostic tool. It measures visual-motor coordination, complex reaction time and spatial orientation

Fig. 9.3.1: Cross Apparatus

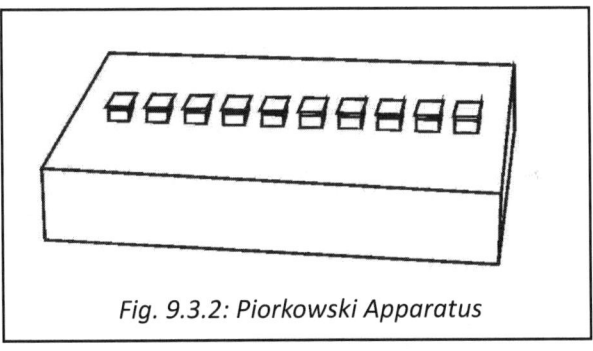

Fig. 9.3.2: Piorkowski Apparatus

as three components of a single entity. The tests can be carried out at a set or a forced pace. In the first case, the apparatus emits impulses with a programmed speed, and the subject's reaction time has no effect on the pace at which signals are emitted. In the case of forced pace the emission of signals depends on the subject's speed of pressing the buttons. The former relies on the number of received stimuli within a fixed period of time; the latter on registering all 49 responses.

9.3.2 Psychomotor examination results

The collective psychomotor test results of the junior and senior fencers are presented in Tables 9.3.1 and 9.3.2. They can serve as reference ranges for comparative analyses.

The presented results show that the senior fencers achieved higher indices than the junior fencers in all psychomotor tests. However, due to significant age differences in both groups of subjects the impact of reaction time tests on the subjects' sport level is certainly limited. More statistically significant differences between junior and senior fencers can be noted in the cross apparatus test results and in the number of errors in reaction time tests. The differences in simple reaction time (seniors – 0.18, juniors – 0.20) and in choice reaction time (seniors – 0.37, juniors – 0.45) show that the process of selection or training at the championship level brings rather moderate achievements in terms of simple and choice reaction times. It can be observed, however, that senior fencers commit 50 percent fewer errors in the simple reaction time test and significantly fewer errors in the choice reaction test. This fact can indicate that advanced fencers differ from juniors not so much in their times of simple and choice reactions as in more complex psychical parameters (concentration of attention, maintenance of reaction, endurance of long-lasting and recurring stimuli).

Of all the psychomotor predispositions affecting the sports level in fencing the most crucial is visual-motor coordination measured with the cross apparatus. Here the senior fencers achieved much better results that the juniors. This demonstrates that this particular predisposition can be significantly developed through training. Moreover, visual-motor coordination is a highly congenital trait, which, means that it can be effectively utilized in the process of fencers' selection. Research results also point to the application of the cross apparatus as an excellent tool for measuring the current form (training level) of advanced fencers.

Optionally, fencers' reaction times in combination with information processes at the level of the central nervous system can be effectively assessed with the aid of electromyography (EMG). During an EMG test, the subject's reaction and movement times during execution of various motor tasks are measured separately via electrodes placed on the subject's hands. The EMG tests can be used to measure simple reaction, choice reaction and right hand-left hand or hand-foot coordination. Interesting results can be also obtained in tests of movement anticipation, during which anticipatory signals are displayed on the computer screen in spatial or temporal modes. As real-world practice shows, most reactions in real bouts are anticipatory responses; thus the anticipatory tests can be particularly useful in fencing training.

Figure 9.3.3 presents the results of a sample EMG test. In the simple reaction test to light signals, the subjects' reaction time amounted to 150 – 180 milliseconds and their movement time to 100 – 120 ms. In the anticipatory reaction tests these times are significantly shorter: 80 – 110 ms in reaction time and 20 – 50 ms in movement time. It should be noted, however, that the timing factors enhance the test results more than visual signals.

Many experts have confirmed the significant role of psychomotor predispositions in fencing, e.g. Salczenko (1980) and Czajkowski (1995). They make the following observations:
- There is a positive correlation between reaction speed and fencing results (the shorter reaction time, the better results);
- Improvement of reaction time decreases with the length of training experience;
- Low class fencers tend to improve their speed by limiting movement (action) time with the use of technical skills;
- Top class fencers with excellent technique improve their speed by limiting reaction time;
- According to American authors (Keele, Hawkins 1982) success in combat sports and team games is determined by reaction time, movement time, perception speed and attention divisibility, and, above all, by alternating attention.

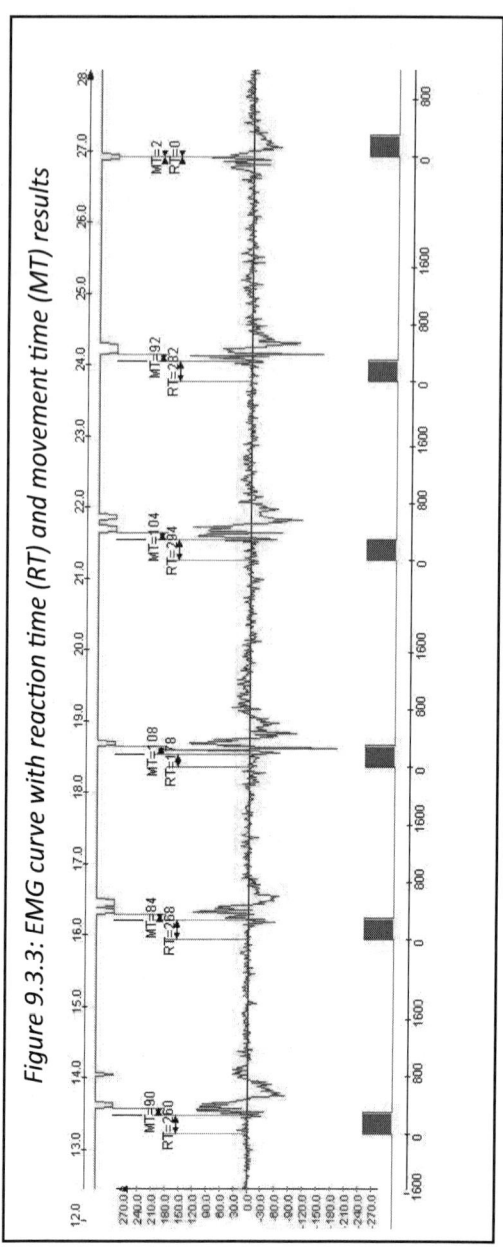

Figure 9.3.3: EMG curve with reaction time (RT) and movement time (MT) results

The obtained results correspond to a large degree with these observations concerning psychomotor parameters. There are some discrepancies as to the first two observations. It seems that the obtained results do not explicitly indicate a positive correlation between reaction speed and sports level. It can rather be concluded that the results of the reaction time tests point to differences between senior and junior fencers; however, within a team, e.g. Polish national team, their impact on the fencers' sports level is not decisive.

9.4 Assessment of psychological predispositions

An important component of diagnostic research in fencing is comprehensive testing of the variability of fencers' temperament and personality traits. The problem of correlation between temperament and personality traits and fencing results has been discussed by a number of authors from Poland and abroad, e.g. Czajkowski (1991, 1996), Czajkowski (1991, 1996), Kłodecka-Różalska (1993), Bandach (1997), Cashen (1977), Heroux (1979) and Szabo (1997 [1977]).

The analysis of professional literature reveals four main research tendencies with regard to fencers' psychological predispositions:

1. From the perspective of cognitive psychology, the areas of emotions and sensitivity, including temperament and personality, are emphasized; from this point of view, fencing is a sport in which the effects of psychological factors on sport success are the greatest;

2. "Seeking the master's model" – developing a set of different personality traits and dimensions as a specific pattern of fencing success;

3. Development of practical methodological guidelines accounting for individual differences and individualization of fencing training.;

4. Determination of intensity of stimulation and inhibition processes as an indicator of psychological predispositions.

In consideration of its strong correlations with nervous resistance, motivation, stress, anxiety neurosis, the last research tendency accompanied with personality analysis is a particularly promising assessment tool in fencing studies. Two psychological tests were used:

Table 9.4.1. Mean values and standard deviation of psychological indices of senior fencers (N=28).

Variable	Mean X	SD S
1. Strelau – agility of nervous processes [pts]	55.500	11.633
2. Eysenck – neuroticism level [pts]	17.000	8.190
3. Eysenck – extraversion level [pts]	35.000	3.919
4. Eysenck – lying level [pts]	7.286	3.544
5. Strelau – intensity of stimulation processes [pts]	44.071	8.984
6. Strelau – intensity of inhibition processes [pts]	40.071	8.289
7. Strelau – equilibrium of nervous processes [pts]	0.162	0.381

Table 9.4.2. Mean values and standard deviation of psychological indices of junior fencers (N=50)

Variable	Mean X	SD S
1. Strelau – agility of nervous processes [pts]	45.840	9.764
2. Eysenck – neuroticism level [pts]	23.440	9.349
3. Eysenck – extraversion level [pts]	26.860	7.313
4. Eysenck – lying level [pts]	7.040	3.549
5. Strelau – intensity of stimulation processes [pts]	34.570	10.528
6. Strelau – intensity of inhibition processes [pts]	39.720	11.433
7. Strelau – equilibrium of nervous processes [pts]	0.929	0.341

the Strelau Questionnaire of Temperament and the Eysenck Personality Questionnaire. Many researchers, e.g. Stawowska (1989), have indicated a significant influence of temperament and personality traits on athletes' sports level. Stawowska found that top fencers are characterized by great agility and intensity of nervous processes combined with extraversion. Unstable introvert fencers are very hard to find. These observations point to the crucial role played by psychological examination in modern fencing. Without psychological evaluation, Stawowska concluded, proper control of fencers' selection and training is impossible.

However, a very comprehensive psychological study of the Polish national men's foil fencing team was by carried out by Bandach in 1997. His application of the EPQ showed that out of 17 studied fencers 12 were extroverts (including 3 neurotic extroverts), 1 was ambivert (emotionally stable) and 4 were introverts (including 3 emotionally unstable). Bandach made an analysis of a possible impact of personality traits on the combat style in foil fencing. Using Cattell's 16 Personality Factors he noted a moderate influence of personality and temperament profile on the foilists' combat style. He also observed that certain isolated personality traits are related to particular technical-tactical fencing actions.

It is interesting to compare Stawowska's finding with Bandach's. Both are respected and qualified researchers. Stawowska's work with a much larger sample may be more applicable to the general fencing population, while Bandach's much smaller sample may be more representative of the fencing elite.

Bandach's results revealed a vast range of fencers' temperament and personality traits, although the so-called master's model features a strong nervous system and lack of neurotic inclinations. Certainly, world championship medalists may include fencers with different characteristics, e.g. introverts with intensive inhibition processes. A number of researchers (Czajkowski 1984 as well as John Kane quoted by him) seem to support a proposition that top fencers are becoming more introvert and neurotic. However, Bandach's observations and the results presented below (Tables 9.4.1, 9.4.2), lead to slightly different conclusions, which point to the majority of strong extrovert types with a low level of neuroticism among fencers.

9.4.1 Methods and tools of assessment of psychological predispositions

Temperament traits assessed with the Strelau Questionnaire of Temperament, modified by Wjatkin (1978). The following four parameters were examined:

- Agility of nervous processes
- Intensity of stimulation
- Intensity of inhibition
- Stability of nervous processes as the quotient of the intensity of stimulation and inhibition.

Personality traits were also measured using H.J. Eysenck's Personality Questionnaire (1975). Three parameters were examined:

- Neuroticism
- Extroversion/introversion
- Truthfulness

The study used Strelau's Questionnaire of Temperament in Stawowska's version (1989). Strelau's questionnaire is commonly used for assessment of human psychology in terms of stimulation and inhibition processes as well as agility and stability of nervous processes. The questionnaire includes 80 questions concerning different characteristics of the nervous system. Answers to the questions are given using a three-point scale ("yes" – 2 pts, "I don't know" – 1 pt, "no" – 0 pts.). The time to answer all the questions was limited to 30 minutes. The intensity and agility of nervous processes are assessed using the obtained score. Additionally, an index of stability of nervous processes was calculated for all the subjects, which was a quotient of the value of intensity of stimulation and inhibition processes. All the questionnaire data were computer-processed and adjusted following the "precipitation" of the impact of subjects' age.

Fencers' personality traits were measured with the Eysenck Personality Questionnaire, which is commonly used in psychology for assessment of neuroticism/stability and extraversion/introversion. The questionnaire also used a third scale of "truthfulness" assessing the reliability of the provided answers. The possible answers were "yes", "no" and "I don't know" ("yes" – 2 pts, "I don't know" – 1 pt, "no" – 0 pts.). The intensity of particular variables was calculated using the obtained point scores, which as raw data were computer-processed. Then the factor of subjects' age was removed. The time to answer all 64 questions on the EPQ was 15 minutes.

9.4.2 Psychological assessment results

An analysis of temperament traits from Tables 9.4.1 and 9.4.2 shows that senior (Olympic) fencers found significantly higher levels of agility of nervous processes and intensity of stimulation than the junior fencers (with a similar level of inhibition processes). In all examined parameters men achieved slightly higher results than women.

There is no doubt that intensity and agility of nervous processes constitute the physiological basis for development of personality dimensions: extraversion and introversion. According to Paisey and Mangan (1980) who compared Eysenck's dimensions of personality with the characteristics of the nervous system in the Strelau Questionnaire of Temperament, there are three strongly correlated clusters of personality-temperament traits:

- Extraversion / intensity of stimulation
- Agility, stability / intensity of stimulation
- Agility and intensity of stimulation / control of impulses

It can be assumed that with such strong correlations of factors from the two questionnaires, a comparison of Eysenck personality traits with Strelau temperament traits should yield similar results. The analysis of configurations of the personality dimensions of neuroticism, extraversion/introversion and truthfulness as functions of fencers' sport level and sex sought to check this assumption. The collected data seem to confirm the dominance of extraversion among the top-level fencers from the Olympic group. A comparison of the extraversion level with the intensity of stimulation processes brings interesting results in terms of the fencers' sport level and sex. Intensity of stimulation processes and agility of nervous processes (32.9%), inhibition and stability of nervous processes (-22.2), and low neuroticism-high extraversion are proofs that although fencers are individuals with widely different personality and temperament profiles, mentally strong types predominate. According to Strelau's concept, the significant role of intensity of stimulation processes is indicative of high reactivity, which is a trait characteristic of top-class athletes.

These results correspond to the results obtained by Bandach, who studied the national team of foil fencers in terms of personality dimensions and revealed that only 25% of his subjects were introverts.

The study results discussed above confirm – like similar observations by other authors – the dominance among fencers of extrovert types with high intensity of stimulation processes. This dominance is slightly more visible among male fencers, however, the noted differences between male and female fencers were statistically non-significant. The low level of neuroticism in the Olympic group as compared with the junior fencers is an indication of the impact of this trait on high sports results in fencing. The female fencers featured a higher level of neuroticism.

The above observations correspond to those made by other authors in their studies of fencers' personality, e.g. Litkowska (1983), particularly in terms of the significance of agility and intensity of nervous processes, highly correlated with extraversion. Discrepancies exist in the levels of introversion and neuroticism of top class fencers. The obtained results indicate that top fencers are rarely unstable introverts, i.e. introverts with a high level of neuroticism.

The evaluation of psychological predispositions of novice and advanced fencers is commonly applied in coaching practice, especially in the process of individualization of fencing training. The precise determination of the stimulation level of individual fencers allows proper choice and adjustment of training loads. For example, some technical-tactical actions are most effectively performed with low stimulation, whereas others, e.g. the fleche, with high stimulation. The assessment of psychological predispositions is also crucial in preparation of fencers before competitions and proper timing of pre-comp warm-up.

The precise assessment of temperament and personality traits is, however, not only important for planning of training loads. It can also be used in the development of fencers' sport fitness and training schedule before the main competition. Fencing coaches' in-depth knowledge of their fencers makes it possible to teach those technical skills that can be employed in stress conditions during real fencing bouts. For instance, fencers with a high intensity of stimulation processes should be equipped with a relatively smaller array of technical-tactical actions, which they ought to master with perfection. On the other hand, introvert fencers take longer to learn their techniques, but retain them much better, and in stress conditions, they are able to display a much largerarray of skills.

Undoubtedly, long-term training allows coaches to get to know their fencers' temperament best; however, the aforementioned diagnostic methods, as well as cooperation with a psychologist, will definitely make this knowledge more useful in daily coaching practice. As Stawowska aptly observed: "The greatest successes in sport, not only in fencing, are achieved by choleric persons who can control themselves and phlegmatic persons who can stimulate themselves."

Chapter 10.

Reaction time and movement time. Types of sensori-motor responses. Fencing tempo (the "sense of timing").

The tactical requirements of fencing combat, involving dozens of unexpected situations, force fencers to master a great number of movement patterns. These appear in the form of motor habits, which become highly automated after long-term training, even in complex technical actions. Making quick and right decisions in fencing depends on a combination of such factors as concentration, selective perception of stimuli, and the choice of sensori-motor responses in rapidly changing combat situations. The crucial timing components of individual sensori-motor responses in combat sports are *reaction time* and *movement time*.

The "sense of timing" in fencing is also very significant. Thanks to one's ability to feel the so-called fencing tempo, a fencer can take his or her opponent by surprise at the most convenient moment. Through adjusting the distance to the opponent and the positioning of the weapon, fencers try to achieve tactical superiority by provoking their opponents' uncontrolled reactions. The knowledge of timing and the development of proper movement patterns, as well as the fencing tempo itself, is very important in the training process and affects fencers' individual combat styles.

Timing is also part of a fencer's individual development, since during the course of their sports careers fencers develop different types of reactions and shift the emphasis from strictly movement factors to neuro-psychical factors. A thorough analysis of these processes requires application of research methods from movement control theory as well as research results achieved by top fencing coaches.

10.1 Reaction time and movement time

Measuring the timing of sensori-motor responses is, next to assessment of movement precision, one of the two fundamental ways to evaluate the quality of motor behavior. It is assumed that an athlete who processes information faster is more efficient in different types of motor behavior (Schmidt 1991). Reaction time and movement time in milliseconds are the basic correlated measurements of information processing.

REACTION TIME (RT) is defined as the length of the **LATENCY PHASE**, i.e. the interval between the occurrence of an unexpected stimulus and the beginning of a response.

MOVEMENT TIME (MT) is defined as the interval between the commencement of a response (the end of reaction time) to the completion of a particular movement, e.g. pressing a panel button during a lab test.

The development of fencing technique is, in particular, subject to accurate and quick execution of technical and tactical tasks. (One of the best fencing-specific speed tests is "pinning" a falling fencing glove. It is a hybrid test, since it requires from fencers a combination of such skills as high speed of response, movement precision and spatial anticipation of the dropping spot of the glove.)

During actual competition, combat sports athletes and team players deal all the time with different types of reactions which are hard to measure, since one cannot place the measuring equipment on the athlete's body. Measurements, however, can be carried out during training or in laboratory conditions. Thanks to the use of electromyelography (EMG) in laboratory tests, it is possible to record the reaction time (RT), i.e. the latency phase, and movement time (MT) of sensori-motor responses.

A thorough analysis of reaction time and movement time can yield important information about their variability depending on the type of movement. Latash (1993) noted that fast and dynamic sequential movements should be subject to peripheral rather than central interpretation. It can be thus assumed that fast movements lack the full effect of feedback. In performing difficult, complex movements, the time of information processing is crucial, especially at the stage of response choice. Generally, all studies of RT have been carried out for two important reasons: first, RT is a component of a real motor task to be performed by the subjects; second, it is a measure of mental processes (stimuli processing, decision making and response programming). The obtained study results make it possible to understand the nature of information processes leading to the adoption of appropriate patterns of motor behavior.

In combat sports, the movements take very little time, e.g. a saber fencer's cut to the opponent's head or a karate hit, lasting from about 30 to 50 ms. In saber, a cut following a single feint may be 100 – 120 ms long. Apart from relatively simple actions, fencers or boxers use complex movements in combat, e.g. a series of hits, feinted counters or parries, which can last from a few hundred milliseconds to a few seconds. In laboratory EMG tests consisting of pressing panel buttons with one's hand the MT may be from 40 – 50 ms to 150 – 180 ms; in anticipatory tests it can be reduced to a few dozen ms.

Highly automated movements (boxing and karate hits, fencing cuts and thrusts) are based on a closed-loop control system of M2 type (Schmidt, Wriesberg 2004); that is, they are acquired motor habits that can be controlled with some degree of consciousness at the spinal cord level. In coordination with motor programs learned earlier, the latency phase for M2 responses amounts from 50 to 80 ms. A more complex movement of the M3 type based on complete feedback, e.g. a series of karate hits or feinted attack in fencing lasts from 200 to 350 ms. This type of response features a longer latency phase (80 – 120 ms) than an M2 response. It is susceptible to variations and greatly affected by the learning process.

After multiple repetitions, M3 responses can be transformed into regular, well-learnt and highly automated motor habits. Practical examples of such reactions include a number of daily motor responses following the "wine glass" effect (Johansson & Westling 1984), i.e. the grip force exerted during lifting and holding an object slightly exceeds the minimum amplitude required to prevent the object from slipping. The mechanism of reaction in this case uses the skin receptors which, after receiving the vibrations from the object, evoke a signal to grasp it firmer. This is an unconscious and fully automated response resulting from earlier experience. The source of response in this case are the tactile receptors. An analogous process can be noted in fencing: in reaction to the opponent's attack on the blade, a saber fencer or epeeist instinctively counters the pressure of the blade and while attempting to parry performs a pre-emptive hit.

It should be noted that some fencers and fencing theorists underestimate MT, emphasizing RT instead as the component which determines the quality of a sensori-motor response. This overemphasizes the effect of genetic predispositions on movement time. Movement time also determines the type of feedback-induced corrections and significantly affects the latency phase, i.e. RT, mainly at the stage of sensori-motor response programming. The knowledge of the above relations in combination with the fencers' psychological types as well as the correlation between reaction time and movement time are crucial in fencing training.

Individual characteristics point to significant differences between fencers in terms of the speed of their responses (latency phase) and their movement. Olympic and world saber champions have included individuals with instant responses, fast movements and relatively simple actions based on simple reactions, e.g. Wojciech Zablocki, Felix Becker, Jean Francois Lamour, or Aldo Montano. On the other had, champions such as Pal Gerevich, Imre Gedovari, or Damien Touya display excellent anticipatory capabilities without any extraordinary speed of movements. And fencers like Jerzy Pawlowski, Grigoriy Kirienko, Janusz Olech, or Stanislav Pozdniakov have featured all the above characteristics and also used a number of complex actions with great anticipatory capabilities. Fencers with slow reaction times, i.e. slowly processing information in time, are difficult to find at the championship level.

Fencing coaches with a thorough knowledge of the timing of information processes are able to adjust the training structure to the fencers' individual predispositions, in particular, in terms of development of their technical and tactical skills. This timing of information processing in fencing is strictly related to the concept of sensori-motor responses and development of simple and complex fencing motor habits. It has been known that fencers with capabilities of instant improvisation rely on recreation of simple movement patterns, while more versatile fencers acquire the motor habits through complex, interlinked motor programs. These differences in the ways of learning and developing technical elements in fencing should be considered in relating training methods to fencers' specific capacities to master and execute individual movement patterns in competition. The best forms of training the timing of fencing movement patterns include individual tutorials with the coach and exercising in pairs aimed at the mastery of tactical set pieces of a fencing bout.

10.2 Classification of sensori-motor responses

Different types of reactions correspond with decision-making processes, which have been a subject of extensive research for over one hundred years. The term "reaction time" was coined by the Austrian physiologist Sigmund Exner in 1873. The present-day separation of reaction time from movement time was suggested by E. Bernstein in 1967. The classification of different types of reactions was then developed by Luce (1986) and Sage (1984). Three basic types of sensori-motor responses have usually been distinguished:

- simple reaction – a response to a single unanticipated stimulus;
- choice reaction – a response to stimuli using acquired movement patterns;
- differential reaction – a type of choice reaction consisting in identifying similar stimuli, responding to proper signals and ignoring interfering ones.

However, one of the most interesting and scientifically justified concepts of different types of reactions in sport and motor function was developed by Czajkowski in 2001, who expanded the classic three-fold division of sensori-motor responses to seven. Apart from simple reaction, choice reaction and differential reaction Czajkowski distinguishes:

- reaction to an initial signal of movement;
- reaction to an object in motion;
- switching reaction
- intuitive reaction.

This extended classification has proven very useful at a practical level in fencing training.

SIMPLE REACTION: A great number of motor habits in sport are present in the form of sensori-motor responses. A simple reaction is a response to a stimuli with a well-mastered movement, e.g. a sprinter's or swimmer's starting reaction, or a boxer's straight punch at the coach's signal. A simple reaction in fencing can be a fencer's response to a known stimulus (coach's movement) with a simple thrust or cut. What the fencer does not know is the timing of the coach's signal. This model of simple reaction is the basis for one of the most commonly used training methods in combat sports, i.e. exercising a chosen action in response to an expected trainer's movement (Borysiuk 2000). Accordingly, simple reaction time can be divided into three stages:

1. Preparatory – from the signal of attention to the occurrence of the stimulus;
2. Latency – from the occurrence of the stimulus to the commencement of a movement;
3. Executive (final) – from the beginning to the completion of the movement.

CHOICE REACTION: A choice reaction time is a response to an unknown stimulus with a different action every time. In other words, we know all the answers but we do not know the question. Choice reactions involve a greater deal of information an athlete must process in the latency stage of his or her reaction: stimulus identification, response choice and response programming.

In their laboratory tests on choice reactions Rosenbaum (1989) and Keele (1986) confirmed Hick's well-known law that reaction time increased directly with the number of choices up to 600 ms. Above the limit of 600 ms, the increase in the number of stimuli affects the extension of reaction time insignificantly.

A choice reaction differs from a simple reaction in its prolongedlatency stage consisting of five components:

1. sensory part of the reaction latency stage;
2. isolation of the stimulus from other concurrent stimuli;
3. recognition of the stimulus and its proper classification;
4. differentiation of the stimulus and the choice of response;
5. motor part of the reaction latency stage.

The significance of choice reaction in combat sports derives from the fact that these sports always involve two contestants. A karate fighter, boxer or fencer – even one in possession of valuable information about the opponent – is still not able to anticipate fully all possible moves of the latter. Fencers must recognize their opponents' action and choose an appropriate reaction in a flash – an attack, counter or block (Richman, Rehberg 1986). The changing situations during a bout make fencers constantly adjust their previously learned motor programs.

DIFFERENTIAL REACTION (reaction of recognition):

A differential reaction consists of identification of the correct signal from among many similar stimuli. This reaction type is very common in team games and combat sports and is the foundation for technical and tactical actions (Kurian, Catering, Kulhavy 1993). A feinted throw in basketball followed by a pass to a teammate in a better position on the court, or, in saber, a feint head cut followed by thrust are actions which high-level competitors must recognize immediately. Another type of differential reaction is a motor response in which a competitor reacts to some stimuli and refrains from reacting to others. This type of reaction is important in combat sports tactics as competitors try to conceal their intentions and evoke their opponents' reactions which can be then effectively countered.

REACTION TO AN INITIAL MOVEMENT SIGNAL: This type of reaction is very common in combat sports and team games. It features a longer latency stage than movement stage. Examples of such reactions include goalkeepers' responses in soccer, hockey or team handball. The speed of the ball or the puck moving towards the goal is much higher than the goalkeeper's capacity of information perception and processing (Shestakov, Averkin, Molchanov 2002). The goalkeeper's successful reaction is possible if it commences earlier, following his or her observations of the initial signals of movement. A goalkeeper responds correctly to a "sign" of movement. A study by Salczenko (1980) showed that the most experienced fencers commenced their responses to the opponent's lunge for about 40 ms earlier before the opponent began his or her attack. The time analysis of these reactions was possible thanks to the use of an oscilloscope and surface EMG. It turned out that, despite the commencement of the attack by the fencing hand, in a classic lunge the highest bioelectric tension in muscle is generated in the fencer's rear leg 100 – 120 ms earlier. It was observation of the opponent's rear leg which triggered the fencer's earlier responses. The obtained results were confirmed in the second part of the study, during which the attacker's legs were covered. The defender who could not identify the initial signals of a movement reacted in a regular way, with his or her responses delayed for over

100 ms. The effectiveness of reaction to the initial signals was also found to be statistically correlated with the fencer's sport experience and rank. Champion fencers responded significantly faster and their success was determined by their ability to effectively process the initial signals of the opponent's actions.

REACTION TO AN OBJECT IN MOTION:

According to Borysiuk, Zmarzly (2005) sensori-motor responses to moving objects are objective indices of athletes' abilities and level of training and condition in combat sports. In this type of reaction a competitor perceives a moving object (ball, opponent's blade, etc.), instantly (and subconsciously) anticipates its course and speed and reacts in time by catching or hitting the ball or parrying the opponent's thrust. The reactions to an object in motion, when the distance between the competitors is rather short, are facilitated by the observation of the initial signals of movement, e.g. sweeping arm movement, swinging the body, and not the movement of the fencing hand or weapon. These reactions are effective due to the interaction of spatial anticipation and proper timing of particular movement patterns (fencing techniques).

SWITCHING REACTION (CHANGING INTENTIONS DURING THE ACTION):

A switching reaction occurs when a competitor performs an intended action but due to the opponent's unexpected movement switches the course of his or her action and pursues another movement pattern (Tyshler, Tyshler 1995). Situations involving switching reactions dominate in combat sports (Dryukov, Pavlenko, Shadrina 2003). For instance, a saber fencer who commences a feint attack notices the opponent's intention to counterattack, parries the opponent's blade and executes a head cut. The effectiveness of such responses depends on the reaction time and movement time, but also on movement precision. There have been cases of outstanding saber fencers whose movement stage of the response was relatively slow but compensated with the response speed. On the other hand, faster anticipation of the opponent's intentions gives the fencer's the comfort of longer information processing and responding at the last moment to prevent the opponent's effective defense. This factor, along with movement precision, plays a crucial role in all combat sports, and is inherently connected with reaction time.

Speed of reaction is known to be negatively correlated with movement precision, so switching exercises in actions with unpredictable outcomes should be developed as part of fencing training, along with free exercises involving instant improvisation.

INTUITIVE REACTION:

A number of decisions in sport combat are not made after a thorough analysis of a given situation but on the basis of so-called statistical intuition. If a fencer faces certain situations hundreds or thousands of times, he or she can most likely predict the opponent's movement and action using long time memory and his own experience (Fig.10.1). Experience plays a significant role in making decisions in sport combat.

In real sport combat, intuitive reactions are intermingled with reactions to initial signals of movement. The latter and anticipation can also enhance the intuitive reactions. Planning fencing training on the basis of intuitive reactions is, however, very difficult.

Fig. 10.1: Significance of Experience in Sport

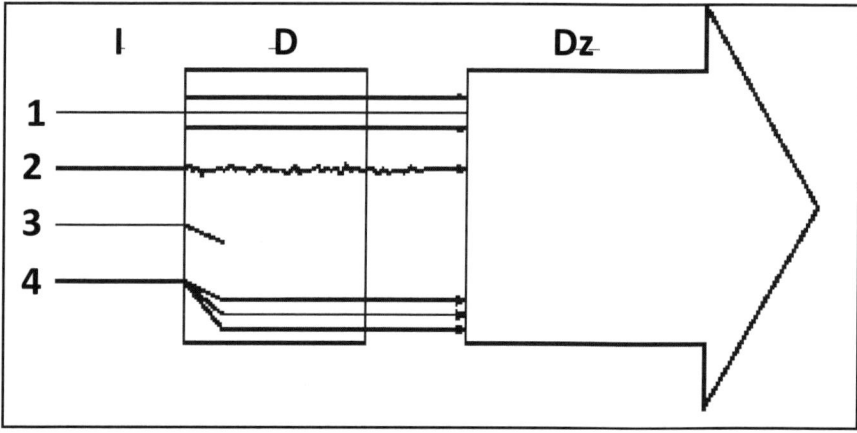

figure 10.1. Significance of experience in sport (Czajkowski 2005).

I. –information,   **D**–experience, **Dz**–action through experience;
1.–information enhanced by experience;
2 – information transformed by experience
3.– information discarded through experience as incorrect or redundant
4. – information creatiing a need for further information.

Fencing exercises aimed at training of this type of reactions were developed by Borsodi (Czajkowski 1970). A fencer is to execute a planned action intuitively anticipating the coach's intentions. To complete such exercises, both the coach and the fencer must play fair and not bluff or hide their real intentions. In this way, parts of a fencing bout are rehearsed in both the coach's and fencer's minds before the actual enactment during exercise. Such fencing exercises are of great methodological and diagnostic value. As has been observed in numerous training sessions, a high level of sport efficiency is correlated with a good sports condition, thus fencers at the championship level achieve the best sports results.

The above classification of sensori-motor responses is a result of experts' competencies and wide coaching experience. It has been accepted by the coaching community and as a concept can be very useful in creative and systematic fencing training. In particular, the reactions to initial signals of a movement, reactions to an object in motion and switching reactions correspond to the scientific concept of anticipatory responses developed and analyzed by Richard Schmidt in his publications.

ANTICIPATORY RESPONSES:

Anticipatory responses are strictly connected with the stage of response choice in information processing. Thanks to anticipatory mechanisms during this stage the reduction of the normal time of information processing becomes possible. According to Rosenbaum and Patashnik (1980) a significant reduction in reaction time (RT) results from a bypass of the stage of response choice followed by the immediate commencement of the stage of response programming.

In laboratory tests of different types of reactions, unexpected stimuli are used in order to avoid the effect of anticipation. This includes also timing tests using randomly emitted signals. The simple and choice reactions are, precisely, responses to *unexpected* stimuli.

A number of sport studies (Ward, Williams, Bennett 2002), (Borysiuk 2007) using EMG and video footage show that athletes at the championship level with a long sport experience greatly benefit from the use of anticipatory responses. They apply anticipatory strategies consisting of concentration on the initial signals, i.e. movements frequently unnoticed by novice athletes, and are able to prepare adequate responses in advance. The process of anticipation can be spatial and/or temporal. The former aims at predicting what will actually happen; the latter, at predicting the time it will happen (Fig. 10.2). In real sport combat, the separation of these two types of anticipation is often impossible. A karate fighter who recognizes a series of the opponent's kicks anticipates the precise timing of the opponent's attack and prepares a block leading to a counterattack. A fencer who identifies the opponent's feint – lunge anticipates the moment of the thrust completion, extends the distance by stepping backwards, prepares a parry and counters with a thrust at an unguarded target area.

In the case of overlapping of spatial and temporal anticipation the latter becomes dominant and decides about the effectiveness of the anticipatory response. These observations have been confirmed by empirical studies and experts' opinions in such sports as karate or fencing. When a contestant is able to use a wide spectrum of techni-

Fig. 10.2: The influence of the type of anticipation on reaction time (Schmidt, Wrisberg 2004).

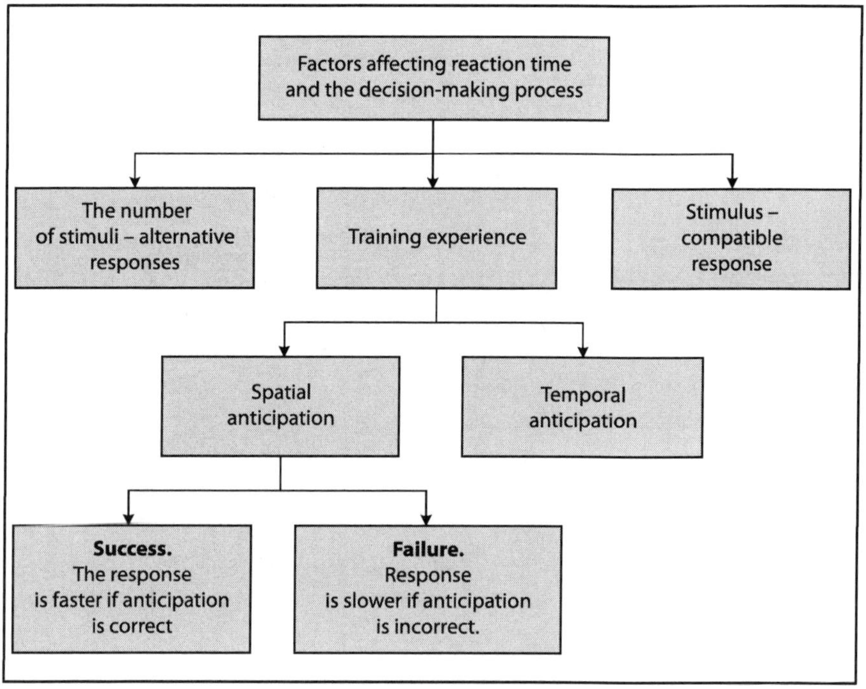

cal skills in attack, it is very difficult for his or her opponent to identify correctly and explicitly the type of attacking technique, but he or she can – to a great extent – anticipate when the attack will finish.

The essence of combat sports is a rivalry of anticipated actions and exchange of anticipatory responses between the contestants. In practice, a great deal of such anticipatory actions are countered by the opponent, which forces the attacker to adjust their original plans. Incorrect anticipatory responses may slow down a contestant's reactions. For instance, a boxer expecting a right hook from his opponent who notices a change in his opponent's intentions adjusts his guard against a left hook and blocks the unexpected attack.

Posner (1978) developed the concept of cost-benefit analysis of erroneous anticipatory responses. He showed that correcting missed anticipatory responses extends the time of motor reaction from 40 to 83 ms. Providing the gains from anticipatory responses amount from 40 to 100 ms, it can be concluded that the time necessary for correction of missed responses is relatively short, comparable with the results of anticipatory responses in general.

It can be stated that, depending on the type of sport, the use of anticipatory responses and their subsequent adjustment can be very effective in the final analysis. A conservative combat style not justified by tactics – simply waiting for the opponent's movements – often results in losing the initiative.

In combat sports featuring great speed of action, three strategies are used. On the one hand, contestants can follow their opponents' initial signals, using anticipatory responses. However, in trying to anticipate the opponent's movements, a contestant risks a belated response in situations in which the adjustment of sensori-motor responses is necessary. On the other hand, it is worth waiting for the opponent's completion of a movement, trying to avoid feints and respond only to real threats. In practice, experienced contestants reduce the negative aspects of these two tactics and use a more versatile combat style combining the two, depending on immediate tactical goals. The above consideration is presented in a diagram illustrating the decision-making process in sport (Fig. 10.3, 10.4, 10.5). It shows that the source of correct anticipatory responses is comprehensive training practice with spatial anticipation as the dominant factor of effectiveness. According to the researchers temporal anticipation is auxiliary, i.e. if a contestant interprets the opponent's action in a wrong way, an appropriate timing will not adjust the incorrect response.

Many studies have also been concerned with movement precision in relation to the duration of motor responses. These studies usually encompass an assessment of the variability of movement time (MT) and precision aiming at an electronic target. The results of these studies show that movement precision is inversely correlated with reaction time (RT). This can be explained by the fact that the improvement of aiming effectiveness is a result of the extension of the stage of programming of a complex response. It also shows that MT is a determinant of reaction time (RT). The author's long-term study of 127 fencers at different levels of sports experience (Borysiuk 2006) revealed that fencers featured extraordinary concurrent movement

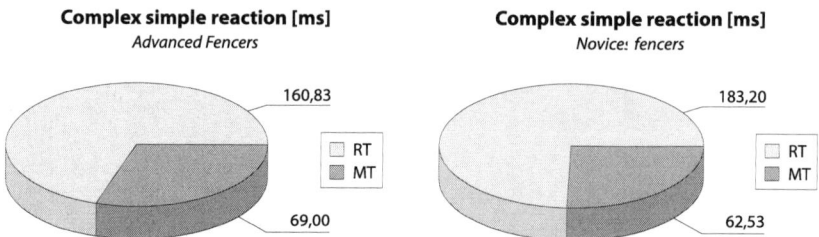

Fig. 10.3. Reaction Time (RT) and Movement Time (MT) in simple reaction test

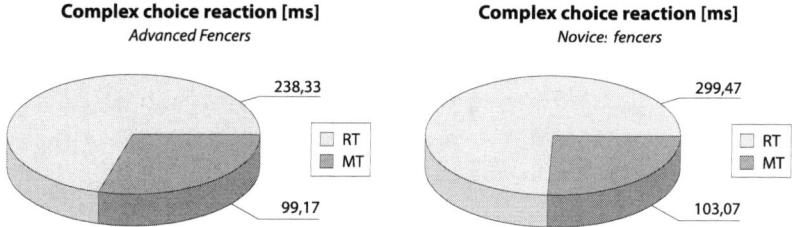

Fig. 10.4. Reaction Time (RT) and Movement Time (MT) in choice reaction test

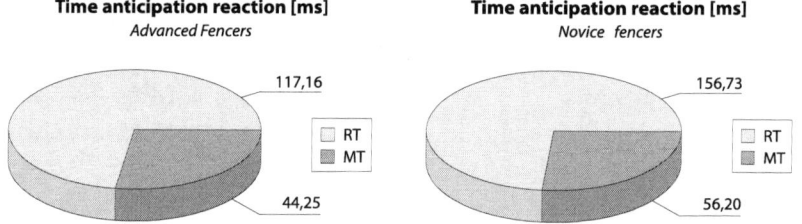

Fig. 10.5. Reaction Time (RT) and Movement Time (MT) in spatial anticipation test

speed and precision as compared with athletes representing other sports. Studies using the Vienna Test System showed that during visual-motor coordination, special orientation and movement precision tests their speed did not affect their precision in a negative way. The fencers displayed much better movement speed and precision parameters than badminton players, gymnasts, soccer players and taekwondo practitioners.

10.3 Novice – expert paradigm

Reaction time and movement time are two components of sensorimotor responses that constitute a valuable source of information about changes during long-term training. The relations between reaction time and movement time are very significant for training, and are best usually examined by way of comparative analysis between novice and advanced fencers. Coaches have extensively pointed out the growing significance of reaction time, i.e. shortening the decision-making time thanks to longer experience. The question remains how big is the gap between the novice and expert fencers. The author helped carry out a study on a sample of 22 novice and 16 advanced fencers representing all the three fencing weapons: epee, saber and foil. The research procedures were selected to test three different types of reaction: simple reaction, choice reaction and spatial anticipation reaction (Fig. 10.3, 10.4, 10.5). The study used an EMG system for testing psychomotor responses, differentiation between the latency stage and movement time of complex sensori-motor responses (Borysiuk, Zmarzly 2005).

1. The study revealed significant differences between the times of simple reaction and choice reaction to visual stimuli as well as the superiority of experienced fencers over the novice ones. The assessment of RT and MT of information processes in simple reaction and choice reaction tests showed that advanced fencers tend to shorten the time of their sensori-motor response, mostly during the central stage, thus they perceive and make decisions much faster than the novice fencers. This tendency should be seen as a constant process of shortening the latency stage of reaction time inherent in the development of sports championship and as the impact of specialized training on the effectiveness of perception processes in advanced fencers.

2. The effectiveness of anticipatory responses to signals of spatial anticipation was far greater among the advanced fencers, who processed the signals at the early stage of signal perception. The system registered premature responses as incorrect.

3. In sports with open motor habits, anticipatory responses based on the identification of the opponent's initial signals of movement are a major feature of champion class competitors as opposed to competitors on an intermediate level. The results of the study point out to a similar distinction between novice and advanced fencers. The effects of anticipatory responses are characteristic of combat sports. They serve as indications that a properly structured perpetual training affects the sensory system and allows for a prompt input into the neuronal representations. Anticipatory information is a pathway for a more speedy and accurate choice of sensori-motor responses. The advanced fencers have a great superiority over the novice fencers in both spatial and temporal anticipation. The obtained lower EMG values also demonstrated that the efficiency and certainty of anticipatory responses were characteristic of the advanced fencers.

The above observations do not explain the entire complexity of the process. The novice-expert research paradigm confirms the reduction in the time of sensori-motor responses, mostly during the latency stage, due to the superiority in training experience of advanced fencers. However, some individual cases show that fencing champions have a tendency to consciously extend the decision-making stage, allowing for the opponent's unexpected actions, in order to gain enough time to correct the response. This tendency was observed in laboratory tests and it shows that a long-term fencing training has an real impact on the timing of movement patterns and makes the RT more flexible. The comparative analysis between advanced and novice fencers showed that the former tended to program their responses longer and then instantly react during the MT stage. This may partially contradict the results obtained above. It might be concluded that this process concerns only the most highly talented fencers, or that fencing champions are so versatile so that they can extend the latency stage depending on the tactical situation.

10.4 Fencing tempo (sense of timing)

For decades, the concept of fencing tempo has been undergoing a number of alterations, even though the most fundamental understanding of fencing tempo remains the same and is still the essence of competition in fencing. The development of fencing training methods and the advent of the electronic scoring apparatus made the fencing intervals much shorter than before in saber and foil, but also in epee. In saber, the lockout times were reduced to necessitate the separation of the parry phase from the riposte stage and to prevent turning on two lights at the same time, which poses interpretation problems for the referees and unprepared spectators. The lockout time in saber fencing is currently 120 ms. This interval reflects the quality of speed training of present-day saber fencers. Thanks to its brevity, simultaneous hits, which can make a bout boring to the spectators, are avoided.

What is stressed by fencing experts is the fact that the mentioned timing is felt better by female saber fencers. This is manifested in girls' bouts with longer fencing times, and more frequent exchanges of parries and counterattacks. In this context, the bouts of female saber fencers are better understood and more exciting to the audience. Perhaps the fencing regulations should account for the sex differences in determining the lockout time, but on the other hand the adjustment of the electronic scoring apparatus in relation to the fencers' sex might lead to a paradox. Research has shown (Borysiuk 2001) that in terms of fencers' psychomotor predispositions sexual dimorphism plays a marginal role in fencing.

The correct interpretation of the concept of fencing tempo in saber and foil is far more complex than in epee. In epee, the scoring apparatus can register double touches, although the touches must be within 40 ms of each other. Hits that are beyond this interval are blocked. Unlike saber and foil, in epee there are no right-of-way rules regarding attacking, i.e. touches are awarded solely on the basis of which fencer makes a touch first. In the event of a double hit in saber, the attack always takes precedence before the counterattack, unless the counterattacks are faster than the lockout time of 120 ms. Belated hits are not considered valid by the referees. In saber, a number of winning actions performed according to the classic saber bout regulations may not be properly registered by the scoring apparatus.

Most frequently two tactical situations can cause this problem. The first is when fencers make technical errors in offensive actions –e.g. starting footwork without appropriate offensive action of the fencing hand–which leads to a loss of the fencing tempo and of the right-of-way. Sometimes fencers complete hits despite losing the tempo, but this results in two simultaneous light signals on the apparatus. Such situations are often controversial in terms of refereeing. The other situation occurs when fencers while performing a parry-riposte produce the effect of two lights on the apparatus, which may result in the referee's erroneous decisions. These two situations reveal the significance of fencing tempo in modern competition and the necessity of its precise definition and understanding.

There is no doubt that the fencing tempo is mostly an abstract concept strictly related to saber tactics and depends on the fencers' age. The classic definition of the fencing tempo is the time required to complete a single fencing action and it works as such for novice fencers. This definition, however, involves flexibility in understanding of the tempo in terms of a fencer's speed of movement. The fencing tempo can be thus different for advanced and novice fencers, although the lockout time on the scoring apparatus is the same all the time, e.g. 120 ms. The referee's interpretations are essential in such situations and consist of perceiving the moment of surprising the opponent, i.e. "gaining" the tempo. In this context the fencing tempo should be trained along with exercises involving elements of surprise.

The above problem is associated with the correct evaluation of technical and tactical actions, including the referee's identification of feints. According to fencing regulations, an offensive action is made by extending the sword arm and continuously threatening the valid target of the opponent. Many fencers feint their attacks, however, in order to obtain the right-of-way.

Training and development of the fencing tempo has a motor context and is related to the concept of sensori-motor responses discussed above. It seems that the training of abilities of choice reaction and spatial and temporal anticipation is truly decisive. The basis of good decision-making is the choice of the response least expected by the opponent, i.e. the surprise factor. Secondly, by identifying initial signals of the opponent's intentions, a fencer can shorten the time of response choice for about 80 – 100 ms, i.e. close to the lockout time in saber.

Chapter 10. Reaction Time & Movement Time. Responses. Fencing Tempo.

The psychological dimension of fencing tempo is also important. During a bout, fencers often experience shifts of concentration owing to fatigue and emotions. Taking advantage of the opponent's moment of low concentration is a surprise factor. It requires careful tactics and patience and great skill to use a situational advantage resulting from imposing one's own style of combat on the opponent. On the other hand, difficult situations and the experience of failure require stimulation, inhibition and maintenance of the psychological function in order to be ready to overcome temporary failures.

A fencer's footwork plays a very significant (but often underestimated) part in development of the sense of fencing tempo. The essence of surprise is to maintain a proper distance from the opponent so as to be close enough to be able to perform an unexpected attack but, at the same time, far enough away to avoid being hit. Effective footwork is based on constant maneuverability, mobility as well as changes of the pace and direction. It is important to use the widest possible spectrum of footwork techniques to pose a constant threat to the opponent. The key methodological activity in tempo training is imposing one's own pace of movement. It creates numerous possibilities of establishing one's superiority and taking the adversary by surprise. The highest level of footwork quality is featured by those fencers who can throw their opponents off balance and decide themselves about the choice of the time of attack. In fencing the most effective is footwork training carried out by the fencing coach using mirrors for correction of technical errors.

Modern saber fencing is extremely dynamic. The average time necessary to complete a single fencing action is merely a few seconds. Practically, saber fencers do not have much time for maneuvering on the piste, thus the margin for errors and their correction is very small. Saber fencers' decisions must be quick and firm. The fencing referees have been recently allowed to record fencing actions and play them back in slow motion. If in doubt a referee can check the video footage before making his or her decision. Such new developments have been aimed at the maximum reduction of referees' errors and enhancement of correct assessment of even the most confusing fencing actions.

Many components of the saber fencing tempo, surprise and the sense of timing should be perfectly trained and automated. Fencers who execute tactical tasks and get to know the opponent's favorite movements do not have to analyze every fencing situation. The effectiveness of some of their actions can be based on anticipation and earlier visualization of a given situation, which would automatically trigger a given motor program.

Modern science and technology can be very useful in fencing tempo training, e.g. fencers can train and develop their sense of timing with the aid of simulators emitting programmed signals corresponding to the intervals of the fencing tempo. Thanks to such devices fencers can develop their motor memory and precisely recreate the timing of movement patterns. New technologies in fencing training will never replace the fencing coach but they could be useful supplements to individual fencing classes and training bouts.

Chapter 11.

Information processes, stimulation and perceptual training

Traditionally, one of the first actions learned by beginning fencers has been an attack on the opponent's torso in the thrusting weapons (foil, epee) or a cut to the opponent's head in saber. In teaching/learning modern Olympic fencing, these actions commence from the contact between the fencer's and the coach's blades. This method of learning this characteristic fencing technique confirms the significance of tactile stimuli in all fencing weapons. It has given rise to the concept of "feeling the blade *(sentiment du fer)*" specific to the attacks au fer or prises de fer. Many responses in saber, epee and foil are produced through the sense of touch and pressure, especially during such actions as parries, engagements or transfers.

In general, learning and development of motor skills and techniques in fencing and other sports with open motor habits are based on perceptual processes involving the senses of vision, touch and hearing. A significant role is also played by proprioceptive mechanisms responsible for static and locomotive balance. The efficacy of technical and tactical actions is affected by the way information is acquired from the environment as well as the different perception speeds of the individual senses.

11.1 Information processes

The significance of tactile stimuli, next to acoustic and visual, as cognitive factors affecting the quality of training motor habits has been subject to numerous studies in the areas of motor function and sport theory. According to Proctor and Dutta (1995), factors which determine the quality of perceptual processes are stages called: *detection* (of a stimulus), *differentiation, recognition and identification.*

The term **DETECTION** has been discussed in a number of studies only in the context of visual stimuli. This stage of perception determines the moment of appearance of a stimulus. Thanks to its diversity, fencing training makes it possible to reduce the stage of perception and to improve individual capabilities of signal detection.

During **DIFFERENTIATION** of the stimuli types, the athlete's task is to assess the force of stimuli and compare their quality, e.g. fencers assess the pressure and the location of the beat, parry, or engagement in order to respond successfully to the opponent's actions.

The **RECOGNITION** stage entails a greater complication of the perception process, i.e. it involves both detection and differentiation of the incoming signals. These learning tasks are of motor character, since at this stage fencers must display an adequate level of trained responses in order to recognize a signal correctly. This type of perception is crucial in most sports with open motor habits and constitutes a prototype of motor skills and sports technique. The ability to recognize signals conditions the linking of movement sequences in order and allows proper coordination of foot and arm work, which plays the key role in fencing.

IDENTIFICATION is the most advanced stage of the perceptual process. It requires specific responses from fencers, depending on a given combat situation. In fencing, the same stimuli can yield defensive or offensive actions, which are strictly related to the tactics and strategy of sport combat as well as fencers' individual preferences. Identification as a perceptual process is linked to motor training and is a process of making constant sensory corrections following the principles of extrinsic feedback (resulting from a coach's corrections and motivational actions) and intrinsic feedback (resulting from the athlete's knowledge and acquired motor habits and skills).

An original concept of the significance and interpretation of perceptual processes based on coaching practice at the highest sport level was suggested by Czajkowski in 2001. According to it, during the learning of new actions and the development of common motor patterns, the most important aspect is the *selectivity of the perception process*. Not only should the athlete's perception of stimuli be selective, but also conscious. The processing of external information should be time-conscious; this is, it should take place before choosing and executing an action or, in some situations, remembering a pattern of response and recreating it later. The process of perception of information allows anticipation of the course of events and proper decision making. The most frequently used information channel is the sense of vision, followed by hearing and touch. One is informed about one's body's movements and position via other senses, kinesthesia and the sense of equilibrium being proprioceptive factors. Therefore, a significant part of training is teaching an athlete *selective perception,* proper understanding and subtle differentiation of stimuli as well as the ignoring of non-significant and false signals, for example discriminating between real actions and feints.

Many other authors (Abernethy 1996; Williams, Grant 1999) have stressed the significance of visual strategy. There have been many studies of visual perception among novice and expert athletes. The latter use strategies based on central vision and imaging of mastered vision patterns, which greatly reduce the duration of the processes of perception. On the other hand, novice athletes begin the process of perception by using peripheral vision, which extends the period of visual perception and causes redundant fixations. Knowledge and experience improve the effectiveness of perception processes through filtering information most appropriate for a given situation. Furthermore, the strategy of choice permits reception of only the most essential amount of stimuli which are of key significance. In the case of novice athletes, this poses serious difficulty.

There has been a strong emphasis on comparisons of perceptual processes between novice and expert athletes in experimental research. Analyses of cognitive processes in young athletes and studies of developmental profiles of novice and experienced athletes constitute at present one of the key research areas in teaching motor control and sports technique. Czajkowski's studies (2005) show that complex information processing (motor memory, concentration, choice of motor programs) is significantly slower in novices than in advanced athletes. However, the peripheral factors related to the speed of dispatching executive commands in novice athletes are close to those of advanced ones.

Cognitive processes should be analyzed from the standpoint of speed of processing information from the environment. Some sports regarded as sensori-motor (golf, bowling) as well as endurance (track and field) do not require fast processing of external signals. It is quite opposite in the case of combat sports and team games in which the speed of processing information is often crucial.

According to Knudson and Morrison (2002), perceptual processes and information processes constitute the basis of all cognitive processes in motor control and training. The continuity of information processing must be emphasized, since identification of stimuli, being the highest stage of perception, is linked to information processes, which precede the choice and programming of sensori-motor responses. These processes require a comprehensive research approach and allow a qualitative diagnostic analysis of motor tasks. The analysis of perceptual processes is an introduction to the description of information processes using the basic indices of information processing speed such as reaction time (RT) and movement time (MT).

According to Luce (1986), the identification stage is a transformation of physical stimulation into biological codes followed by their identification. In sport practice, the most instantaneous recognition of the right stimuli is highly important. In combat sports like boxing or fencing, it is important to discriminate between feints and initial signals of real threat from feints. Sport research and practice show that the efficiency of "recreation" of patterns of stimuli identification is related to long-term experiences in different complex situations of combat sports.

Keller and Tyshler (1970) confirmed the importance of experience in the speed of information processing between the environment and the commencement of motor activity. Both novice and experienced competitors may experience a similar tactical situation and the same set of stimuli. For beginners, the multitude of signals overburdens the perceptual system, and they are not able to control the vast amount of information. Their actions are incorrect and fail to respond to the rapidly changing situations in sports combat. Experienced competitors ignore a great deal of signals, even those anticipated, and focus on stimuli that determine the effectiveness of technical and tactical actions. By choosing a few signals for processing they progress immediately to the decision-making stages of the information process. Salczenko's studies of advanced and novice fencers (1980) consisting of setting blocks against subjects' attacks showed that the novice fencers failed to notice the initial signals from their opponents' foot movements, and their responses were belated. In the case of experienced fencers their perception of an initial signal (muscle tension in the rear leg) triggered a defensive habit consisting of assuming an appropriate block. The difference in reaction time (RT) amounted to about 120 ms between the two groups of subjects. When later during the experiment the attacking fencers' legs were covered, no differences in reaction time between the two groups were observed. The comparative analysis showed that effective anticipation was conducive to the experienced fencers' decision-making as they used signals from these parts of the opponent's body which affected the speed and accuracy of offensive actions. Similar studies of tennis players (Starkes, Ericsson 2001) showed that experienced players identified initial signals by perceiving tensions and movements of the opponent's torso and shoulders, which allowed them to anticipate the opponent's service or plays.

11.2 Stage of response choice

According to Schmidt's classic model of information processes (1991) the identification stage is followed by the *stage of response choice* and the *stage of response programming*

The **STAGE OF RESPONSE CHOICE** is a logical continuation of the stage of identification, during which a complex assessment of information takes place. Such information is recognized as allowing appropriate decisions. The athletes choose the type of response or no response. This stage is a kind of transformation of receptor stimulation into a specific activation in time. Sequences of events evoke appropriate responses in fencers from among the plethora of possible behavior patterns they have acquired during their training. This stage is the process of identification of stimulation associated with motor memory in a given time (Keele, Hawkins 1982). According to ideomotor theory, specific stimuli evoke specific responses from among many potential ones.

In combat sports (fencing, taekwondo, karate, boxing), the changeability of situations evokes simple reactions and choice reactions in competitors in conditions of time deficit. In one type of choice reaction – differential reaction (Czajkowski 2001) – an athlete responds differently to similar stimuli, e.g. a boxer either ducking a hook or countering a hook with a slow swing; or a saber fencer parrying an attack to the head or counterattacking an attack with a bent arm. Another type of differential reaction consists of refraining from actions that are tactical traps.

Empirical data (Borysiuk 2000) show that choice reactions are two-times longer than simple reactions in combat sports athletes (180

– 220 ms and 380 – 410 ms, respectively). Moreover, observations made by coaches seem to confirm that increasing task difficulty by increasing the number of alternatives significantly extends the stage of response choice. In laboratory studies this stage is described using the choice reaction paradigm formulated by Hick (after Keele 1986), which states that the correlation between choice reaction time (RT) and the number of possible responses is linear: In their discussion of different studies on choice reactions, Klapp and Erwin (1976) confirmed that reaction time increased with the number of sent stimuli proportionately to $\log^2(N)$ (where N = the number of extra stimuli) up to about 600 ms. Above this level, an increase in the amount of information affects the extension of reaction time insignificantly. The extra information delayed reaction time from 100 to 150 ms. The great variety of offensive actions in karate or fencing offers a number of technical possibilities, often unpredictable for the defending opponents, who need more time to choose appropriate responses. In sport practice, when reaction time for a punch in boxing or a thrust in fencing is estimated at about 50 ms, an increase in information processing time for more than 100 ms has a distinct negative impact on competitors, who are not prepared to respond so quickly.

Studies examining the effects of motor training (Quesada, Schmidt 1970) demonstrated that multiple repetitions of tasks with four alternatives reduced the time of response choice to that of choosing between only two possibilities. It should be emphasized that in the case of elite athletes, motivation factors are also involved in the process – as shown by Zukowski (1995) in his study of taekwondo practitioners, where in simple reaction and choice reaction tests, Polish Taekwondo National Team competitors achieved similar or slightly worse results. A possible interpretation of these results might be that more difficult tasks were an additional factor motivating them to perform the tests more effectively. Similar conclusions were drawn from the studies of simple and complex reactions of elite and novice Polish epeeists (Borysiuk 2006).

The speed of choice of motor responses is not a matter of individual predisposition, but it is strictly linked to subjects' age. Welford's longitudinal studies (1980) showed that the stage of response choice was greatly reduced over the course of individual development – from puberty to adulthood. In general, the aforementioned authors observed that training determined the speed and effectiveness of perceptual processes in association with information processes in the course of individual development, i.e. that they depended on acquired motor habits and skills. Experience is part of the complex knowledge thanks to which novice athletes develop their anticipatory competencies much faster. Thanks to systematic training, young athletes achieve better results in particular components of the decision-making process than their older colleagues who gave up their active lifestyle.

11.3   Stage of response programming

The choice of a motor response results in an appropriate re-organization of the motor system to ensure efficient and successful execution of a given task. From the neurophysiological standpoint, the key role in this process is played by the brain, which programs a desired movement by stimulating lower levels of the central nervous system, mostly the cerebellum, to effectively control and coordinate the work of skeletal muscles in terms of contraction speed and force. In other words, response programming is the stage of movement initiation, i.e. transition from the stage of an abstract idea to the stage of activation of appropriate muscles. This is a complex process affected by memory mechanisms and the duration of motor responses as illustrated by the course of EMG curves (Borysiuk Zmarzly 2005). Longer motor tasks demand an increase in programming time. Response programming is thus the final stage of information processes, which allows communication with the environment.

Studies on response programming were carried out by Zelaznik, Schmidt, Gielen (1986) and Schmidt, Wriesberg (2004) and concentrated on relations between reaction time (RT) and movement time (MT) as functions of complex motor responses. These authors observed that subjects' time of reaction to the same light signals varied depending on the duration of different complex motor tasks using tennis balls. The RT amounted to 159 ms (first trial with no balls), 195 ms (second trial with catching a ball) and 208 ms (third trial with hitting the ball twice). The MT amounted to 0, 95 and 465 ms, respectively. Similar tests were carried out by Sternberg (1969) who specialized in assessment of the time of reaction (RT) to a number of uttered words and letters set in a designated sequence. A greater number of words and letters resulted in an increase in reaction time and decrease in subjects' typing efficacy. In the aforementioned research cases the obtained results were interpreted as effects of complex responses on reaction time (RT). The increase in reaction time resulted from the necessity to prepare an appropriate motor program, i.e. create a feedback network.

The above cases can be neurologically explained: It can be assumed that increasing the complexity of motor tasks requires more complex commands in order to control a number of movements at different levels of coordination with the central nervous system.

Practicing combat sports involves a direct confrontation with the opponent. In order to take the opponent by surprise it is necessary to constantly vary tactical intentions using appropriate timing. Therefore, the time of motor responses is essential. For instance, a saber fencer feinting an attack to the chest can deceive the opponent's parry and hit him on the flank. The correct programming of the attacker's action makes the defender respond to the feint by assuming the quarte parry with no possibility of effective defense against the flank. This is an illustration of how well-trained competitors can control the opponent's reactions and prevent effective counters. Pashler's laboratory research (1994) which focused on these issues led to the formation of the so-called double-stimulation paradigm. Competitors were able to respond within one second (1000 ms) only two or three times to sequential stimuli. As in the case of the saber fencer above, it can be concluded that in a multi-feint attack, a pre-programmed attack indicated too explicitly may not produce a desired response from the opponent, and that the programmed attack will fail, e.g. hit the defender's parry. Similar situations occur during bouts involving novice fencers, whose reactions are usually belated, opposite, or premature due to excessive stimulation.

One should also be aware that standard responses, which are well-known and described in motor function sciences, do not apply to elite competitors, whose speed of information processing can be truly astonishing. For instance, saber is a conventional weapon in which the referee's decision gives priority to the attack over a counterattack performed at the same time (right-of-way) The electronic scoring equipment only registers hits that arrive within 120 ms of each other, which means that the defending fencer must be ahead of the attacker by at least 120 ms to get a single light on the scoring apparatus; otherwise he is judged as hit. During training, saber fencers learn to differentiate such short time intervals and to be ready to receive stimuli in conditions of time deficit. Long-term training makes a number of motor habits automatic. They are mastered, with limited involvement of awareness processes. Fencing training at the advanced level focuses on vivid changes of situations, which makes it possible to re-program intended movements during their execution.

11.4 Stimulation types (tactile, acoustic, visual, kinesthetic) and time of sensori-motor responses

From the standpoint of the training process, the significance of dominant stimuli in each sport or sport event should be most definitely taken into account. Team games and combat sports generally involve visual and kinesthetic stimulation. In running, swimming and ice-skating, perception and quick identification of acoustic stimuli are of key significance. Some sports (tennis, fencing) feature a wide spectrum of requirements in terms of visual and sensori-motor perception. For instance, in fencing, reactions to tactile stimuli ("feeling the blade") are immensely significant, along with the most obvious reactions to visual stimuli. Similarly, in tennis, "feeling the ball on the racket" is one of the determinants of effectiveness of tennis play. Acoustic stimuli are also important, e.g. the fencer's footwork rhythm allows evaluation of the distance between the fighting opponents, whereas the sound of the tennis ball informs the player about the opponent's hit strength. The time of reaction to kinesthetic, acoustic and visual stimuli has been subject to different studies (Enoka, 2000). All the authors have assumed that the time of simple reaction to (exteroceptive (external) stimulation ranges from 90 to 130 ms. It is longer, from 20 to 50 ms, in the case of acoustic stimuli, and amounts to 180 – 200 ms in the case of visual stimuli. It should be remembered that the expression of all types of stimuli (visual, tactile, acoustic, olfactory) takes place simultaneously (Schmidt, Wrisberg 2004), and after the identification stage choice stages, a program considering only selected "filtered" information is launched (Fig. 11.1.)

In most combat sports, including fencing, the most significant is visual stimulation. Two types of visual stimulation can be distinguished: focal vision and ambient vision (McCormick, Sanders 1982). Focal vision concentrates on registering detailed information about the observed object, mostly with postural balance in a two-dimensional way, and involves static visual acuity (SVA). Ambient vision is responsible for such factors as differentiation of stimuli, contrasts,

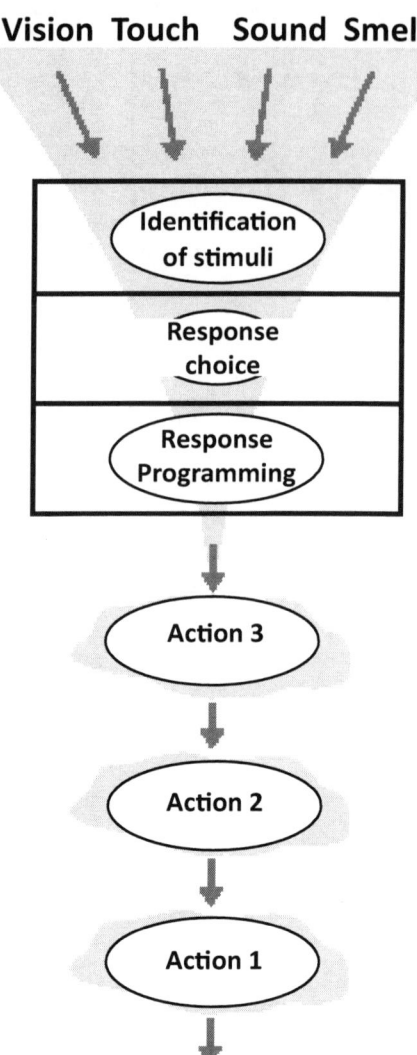

Figure 11.1. Model of expression of sensory stimuli and consecutive responses (Schmidt, Wrisberg 2004, p. 80).

colors, color saturation, movements and time. It is three-dimensional and features dynamic visual acuity (DVA). Both visions interact in the process of stimulus perception; however, in the case of an athlete in motion the DVA is decisive. According to Kluka, (1987) if both opponents are in motion in a combat sport then the time necessary for assessment of the situation (focusing attention on the moving object) decreases rapidly. According to Wood and Abernethy (1997) the dynamic visual acuity decreases from 60 to 70 degrees per second. This can be explained by the fact that the retina is not able to acquire and store a changing image of an object in conditions of increasing time deficit. Moreover, the two kinds of visual perception are only moderately correlated, whereas the development of dynamic visual acuity (DVA) is greatly affected by training. Focal vision identifies the object and it involves an insignificant part of the retina in the process of image reception. It is estimated that a small point on the retina confines the visual angle to merely 3 degrees. Ambient vision locates the object and assesses its motion and distance from the observer. It receives information using the entire retina and it encompasses both central and peripheral vision. The aforementioned authors consider both types of information to be integrated. Their significance and application in motor control encompass the assessment of:
1. Movement speed.;
2. Direction of movement in relation to the observer's position and changes of the object's position;
3. The object's movement in relation to the observer;
4. Time of contact between the object and the observer;

The above information is extremely useful in motor training and development of fencing technique. It allows preparation of an appropriate strategy of perception of the position of the opponent's blade, in particular the point and the bell guard, for one's own offensive actions. Knowledge about the opponent's movements, distance evaluation, visual concentration on the most useful signals provides the fencer and the coach with valuable feedback. It permits a strategy of switching from focal vision to ambient vision and vice versa. It develops concentration, ability to react to initial signals and anticipation of the opponent's actions. It allows recognition of significant signals and rejection of misleading information, e.g. opponent's feints.

Another type of stimulation is acoustic. The author's own study (Borysiuk, Zmarzly 2005) shows the time of reaction to acoustic stimuli is the shortest, ranging between 140 ms to 160 ms. It is commonly thought that the reason for such fast processing of acoustic signals is the quick pace of activation of receptors in both ears, and the very short time of transmission of the afferent signal to the brain along the nervous pathways (8 – 10 ms). In the case of cognitive processes in sports with open motor habits, acoustic perception, as the fastest, can and does enable entire movement structures. Acoustic information includes such aspects as perception of the fencing tempo, movement frequency, timing as well as sound pitch and amplitude. The significance of hearing in sports has been widely discussed in literature. In fencing (Szabo 1988, Evangelista 2000) footwork training is based on the sense of rhythm which is related to the fencing tempo. Losing the tempo during attack in conventional fencing weapons (epee, foil) results in the loss of right-of-way and exposes fencers to hits in individual engagements. The sense of rhythm and movement frequency registered by the organ of hearing determines predisposition towards the feeling of distance between the fencers, and thus the overall effectiveness of offensive and defensive actions.

Similar observations about the speed of information processing (RT) are associated with the sense of touch. However, according to Luce, (1986) the time of reaction to tactile stimuli is 20– 40 ms longer than to acoustic stimuli. The results of my own studies of advanced fencers (Figs. 11.2, 11.3) using an EMG system show that the time of reaction to tactile stimulation is similar or slightly shorter than to acoustic stimuli. The tactile system delivers data gathered by tactile receptors (Meissner's and Ruffini corpuscles) and deep pressure receptors (Pacinian corpuscles). When the stimulation exceeds the activation threshold of the sensory nerves, the signals are activated and transmitted directly to the brain. The pressure receptors have a higher activation threshold than tactile receptors, and that is why tactile reactions are faster than pressure reactions. Therefore, a subtle use of the blade and the point can provide a fencer with a number of technical and tactical possibilities, making the contact with the opponent's blade more effective.

Several of my own laboratory studies dealt with the impact of different types of stimulation on reaction time, movement time and muscle bioelectric tension (EMG). The research sample consisted of 15 novice fencers (at the introductory stage of their training) and 12 advanced fencers. Figure 11.2. shows that fencers from both groups

Chapter 11. Information Processing, Stimulation, and Perceptual Training

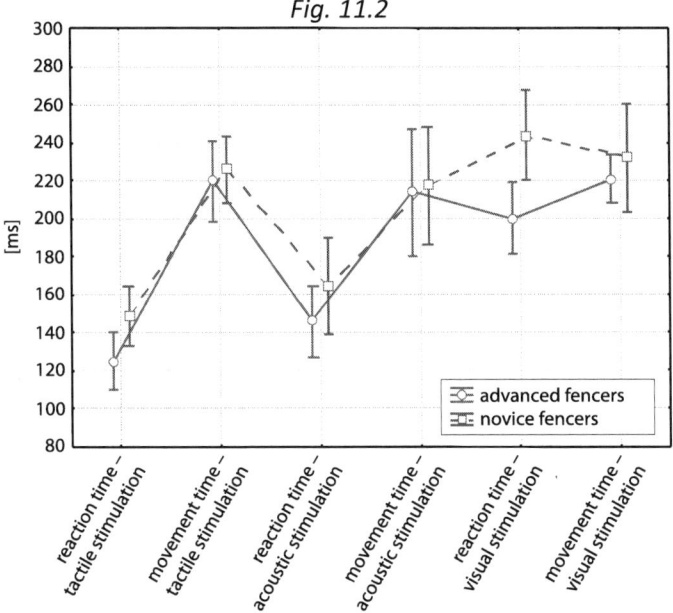

Figure 11.2: Reaction time and movement time to the three types of stimulation by novice and advanced fencers.

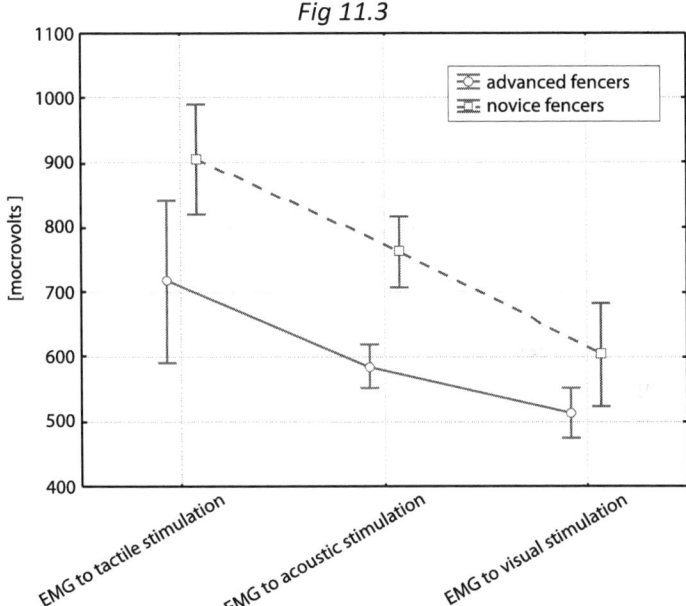

Figure 11.3. The EMG signal in response to the three types of stimulation in novice and advanced fencers.

responded fastest to tactile stimuli, followed by acoustic stimuli and visual stimuli; however, the advanced fencers were faster than the novice fencers in all the studied parameters. The time differences were statistically significant in reaction time (RT), understood as the latency stage of the sensori-motor response without the MT component. Responses to acoustic stimuli failed to produce any significant differences between the two groups of subjects; it can be assumed, therefore, that fencers' responses to tactile and visual, but not necessarily acoustical stimulation can be learnt to a great extent. (On the other hand, novice fencers compensated for their longer latency phases of information processing with MT, which was identical in both groups of subjects in response to acoustic stimulation.)

From a neurophysiological perspective, the above differentiation is related to nerve conduction. The process of triggering responses to visual stimuli seems to be linked to the great number of synaptic connections with the retina. It can be assumed that the significantly faster responses to tactile stimuli are associated with the concentration of about two thousand receptors in the digital pulp as well as with the speed of activation of the sensory cortical areas (Enoka 2000). The effectiveness of the hearing system depends on the receptors in the cochlea, from which the impulses are transmitted along nervous pathways to the temporal lobes of the cerebral cortex. This distance is covered within 10 – 15 ms.

The analysis of the sEMG signal also yielded interesting results. Figure 11.3. shows that the fencers who focused on tactile stimulation generated higher bioelectrical tension than those focusing on acoustic stimulation. In responses to visual stimuli, the EMG signal was the lowest, which may be an indication that the response and sheer anticipation of this type of stimulation reduce the level of muscle tension. The EMG signal was significantly lower in the advanced fencers in all three types of stimulation. This may demonstrate that the psycho-motor superiority of expert fencers results in a reduction of the bioelectrical tension of muscles involved in performing the motor tasks. These correlations confirm results of studies carried out by a number of experts on combat sports (Lukovich 1997, Pitman 1990).

11.5 Integration of data from different senses.

Every coach needs to understand the perception and processing of information from four senses (vision, touch, hearing and kinesthesia) as well as their mutual interactions. Various observations made by coaches confirm that the brain automatically integrates all types of sensory information and gives priority to those stimuli which are significant for a given competition. According to Marino (1982), there is a similarity between the process of linguistic perception and cognitive processes in motor learning. Marino claims that language skills acquisition takes place in two phases: a pre-linguistic introductory phase in which the information is merely registered; and a linguistic-semantic phase in which the information is encoded and put into semantic order. Certainly, the information is processed faster in the introductory phase than in the semantic phase. It is similar in sports. For instance, in direct-contact combat sports (judo, wrestling) tactile information is processed faster, whereas in karate and boxing visual information is followed by acoustic information. It is also similar in individual fencing bouts involving actions on the blade, where tactile stimulation is an integral part of information that must be taken into account by the fencer.

From a cognitive point of view (Seat, Wrisberg 1996), combining different types of sensory information occurs within three categories: detection, spatial stimulation and temporal situation. The reaction time (RT) for particular types of stimulation was discussed above. *It should be emphasized that responses to stimuli from the different senses, with the exception of acoustic stimuli, can be learned in the course of training.* The sequence of stimuli detection depends on their strength, and usually athletes' perception is focused on stronger stimuli. Shiffrar and Freyd (1990) described the phenomenon of inhibition of information with weaker expression. This can be explained psychologically as subject to selective concentration of attention, and physiologically as muscle tension can be detected in some sensory organs and inhibition in others. If initial stimulation is of high intensity, it can inhibit the expression of other sensations. To optimize the different effects of stimulation, sensory expressions should occur simultaneously. That is why synergy and mutual enhancement of muscles of auditory ossicles and papillary muscles have been observed. A similar process can be noticed in the case of mutual synesthesia of the senses of touch and hearing enhanced by the sense of vision. This synesthesia simultaneously broadens and improves the reception of stimuli, as the receiver uses at least two types of stimulation. Moreover, this does not exclude selective processing of information.

Considering spatial stimuli, the dominant sense, according to Rhodes, Courney and Hajduk (2002), is the sense of vision followed by hearing, proprioception and touch. They noted a close interaction between visual and acoustic perceptions in processing spatial information. They also observed differences between the perceptions of acoustic stimuli, which is horizontal, and of visual stimuli, which is vertical as well. Visual perception serves as a sort of framework for acoustic information. In other words, visual memory is a map for acoustic expression in relation to motor proprioception.

In regard to temporal information, in cases when temporal stimuli are emitted in short intervals, acoustic information dominates over tactile and visual. Faster perception of acoustic stimuli makes it possible to process them more slowly. It can be concluded that visual information is complementary to the decision-making process. Coaches taking direct part in training (fencing or boxing tutorials) should during their situation evaluation regard acoustic signals as determining the feedback processes (Tyshler, Tyshler 1995), (Cheris 2002).

11.6 Perceptual training

Perceptual training is – next to physical, technical and tactical training – the main component of preparation of athletes to achieve high sports results (Williams and Grant 1999), (Czajkowski 2005). Perceptual skills enable athletes to respond to important signals in sport competition and ignore disrupting ones which lower the effectiveness of sports combat. Time pressure during sports competition makes it necessary to reduce decision-making time and sensori-motor response time in the motor phase as much as possible. The study results (Figs. 11.2, 3) show that experienced athletes reached decisions much faster than their novice colleagues. Furthermore, the advanced fencers featured better efficiency and economy of their motor actions, which was reflected in lower muscle bioelectric tension to all types of stimuli. It conforms to the main strategy of perceptual training, i.e. gaining maximum benefits at the lowest expense (Williams, Davids, Burwitz, Williams 1992). Quick decision-making is strictly associated with the stimulus detection effectiveness and the re-creation of acquired motor patterns. A successful choice of responses depends on proper assessment of the space-time relationships, which enables anticipation and appropriate decision-making. Highly significant here are the specialized types of perception such as "feeling the blade" as well as spatial-temporal orientation of the fencing hand-weapon position. The organs of perception, mostly vision, can then focus on receiving possible the largest amount of information for immediate processing. Numerous studies have demonstrated that athletes of sports with open motor habits, who follow the target strategy, rely in their perception on the long-term memory (LTM). This strategy, although extending the phase of stimulus detection, in fact reduces the time of information processing. A number of studies of fencers have pointed to significant differences in simple and complex reactions in novice and advanced fencers. They have been concerned with difficult visual tasks and their results correspond to those obtained by Keller, Tyshler (1970) and Salczenko (1980). These observations are also confirmed by the barely significant differences in simple reactions based on short time memory. Out of the two groups of subjects under study, the advanced fencers were not significantly better than their novice counterparts, which can be an indication that at this level of reaction complexity the responses were automatic.

A significant factor in further reduction of the information processing time in the choice phase is perceptual anticipation. Following the opinions of fencing experts (Szabo 1998, Lukovich 1997), the unique anticipatory efficiency of expert fencers is a result of their capabilities of attention splitting. They are 50% more effective in perception of signals which are significant for victory then the novice fencers. Timing effectiveness is crucial. Information acquired at the right time allows making an optimal decision and executing the intended action. This is conditioned by selective perception of stimuli to avoid incorrect or delayed reactions. According to Ericsson, Kilbom, Wiktorin, Winkiel (1991) the key elements of perceptual skills development in sports with open motor habits should include:

- Development of abilities to recall and recreate technical and tactical patterns specific to a given sport;
- Quick detection of temporal-spatial intervals of moving objects, competitors, weapons, etc.;
- Development of the ability to extend visual perception in response to specific signals related to the opponent's postural orientation:

- Application of focal and ambient vision;
- Differentiation of stimuli and selection of information that can be effectively used in sport competition;
- Preservation of sensori-motor patterns and their execution regardless of emotional pressure during sport competition;
- Matching the temporal structure of motor patterns with individual psycho-motor predispositions and combat styles preferred by different temperamental types of fencers.

With regard to perceptual training, a unique problem in fencing is the over-representation of left-handed competitors among the world elite foil fencers, epeeists and saber fencers. Quite interesting results were demonstrated by Borysiuk and Zmarzly (2005) in our study of choice reaction time with regard to ocular dominance, using surface electromyography. The measurement used in the study consisted of two parallel control panels with screens transmitting light signals either directly opposite (compatible reaction) or laterally to the subject's eyes (incompatible reaction). In the former case the subjects needed only 40 ms to make a decision; in the latter the reaction time was 110 ms.

Possible interpretations of these results may contribute to explanation of the phenomenon of the dominance of left-handed competitors in fencing, e.g. Olympic champions Victor Sidjak and Victor Krovopuskov; three Olympic foil champions from the same team Witold Woyda, Lech Koziejowski, Marek Dabrowski; Olympic epee champion Laura Flessel and many others. The Polish National Epee Team – the current European Champions – consists of left-handed fencers only. A student of mine, Dariusz Gilman, Cadet World Champion, Junior European Champion, and Senior Team World Championships bronze medalist is also a left hander. The list could be extended indefinitely; and at the highest levels, the explanation offered for the success of left-handers – right-handers' relative unfamiliarity with them – clearly does not apply.

It appears that the left-handed fencers, who most often compete against their right-handed counterparts, acquire an ability to process compatible signals (directly opposite their eyes) much faster, since their opponent's right weapon arm is the closest target area to them. The dominance of left-handed fencers can be additionally confirmed by the difficulties experienced by right-handed fencers with blade work, blocks and parries in combat with left-handed opponents.

My other studies with the use of surface electromyography produced insignificant effects of functional hand asymmetry, i.e. left-hand or right-hand superiority in terms of reaction time. Observed differences included increased bioelectric tension in the non-dominant arm, sensori-motor facilitation of impulse transmission along nervous pathways and improvement of reaction time of the non-dominant arm following a series of tests using the dominant arm. This can be an indicator of the greater significance of information processes in the speed of information processing than of the effects of functional asymmetry.

A unique aspect of fencing is the fact that the key fencing training is individual coaching lessons. In methodological terms, the fencing coach's task is incorporation of perceptual training (learning responses to all kinds of stimuli) into tactical training and combining it with the development of such psychical properties as concentration, attention divisibility and attention shifting. In order to meet these challenges fencing coaches should be highly skilled in fencing and create training conditions as close as possible to real combat, i.e. fencing tempo, speed, rhythm, quick changes of decisions during performance, as well as providing diverse exercises and multiple repetitions.

With reference to the issue of functional asymmetry the coaches should not only apply asymmetric exercises but also act as left-handed or right-handed opponents, depending on their fencers' handedness. It has been observed that exercises involving both sides of the body not only develop motor habits but may also correct motor habits acquired earlier by the dominant arm. Such exercises improve one's own fencing technique, functional ambidexterity, and – what is also significant – compensate for the osteomuscular system.

Chapter 12

The DVD: Description and Commentary

The main objective of the DVD that accompanies Modern Saber Fencing is to be a useful instructional tool, not only for advanced saber fencers, but also for young fencers, and their parents, instructors and coaches as well. So I have kept two things in mind when selecting the technical and tactical actions that appear here. First, I wanted to illustrate all the traditional saber actions that have been used for decades and more. Even though saber has evolved enormously, I wanted to show the continuity in saber tradition. Secondly, though, I wanted to highlight those technical and tactical actions that are most characteristic of the modern electric saber – the techniques and tactics necessary for top results. The material reflects the real training methodology currently used in fencing clubs throughout Poland and at the training camps of the Polish national fencing team. Furthermore, as I emphasize throughout this book, present-day saber fencing uses electronic scoring equipment and rules interpretation that have redefined the fencing tempo, as well as many other technical and tactical actions.

The central idea was to present the best technical patterns demonstrated by top-level fencers – members of the Polish Women's Saber Olympic Team, plus women juniors as well as junior and senior male sabreurs. All the exercises were carried out by Arkadiusz Roszak – the coach of the Polish National Women's Saber Fencing Team – and by me.

The DVD contains nine parts, illustrating the most important fencing training forms: individual technical, technical-tactical and tactical lessons, footwork training, pair exercises, and queue training.

12.1 Technical lesson [Roszak – Więckowska].
Duration: 4.10 min. Instructor: Arkadiusz Roszak.
Fencer: Irena Więckowska.

1. The fencer performs simple cuts to parts of the target area uncovered by the instructor. This type of training is a classic saber fencing exercise, which follows simple technical patterns. It can also serve as a good warm-up exercise.

2. In the next part of the lesson, the instructor suggests technical actions characteristic of modern saber fencing. The fencer makes cuts to the chest, followed by beats of quarte and cuts to the head or the chest. Then she performs technical attacks to the forearm. The exercise is executed with a slightly bent weapon arm (contrary to the traditional technical canons). It develops the fencer's habit of hitting the closest parts of the opponent's target area, and it also allows extending one's own simple attack into an effective compound attack. The technical routines -- beats, cuts to forearm, and cuts to head -- are all carried out in a similar manner, i.e. with the elbow bent in the initial stage of action. The entire sequence is developed by the instructor while maneuvering (steps forward and backward) and concludes with a lunge. This part of the lesson reveals the great advantages of beginning attacks slowly and with a bent weapon arm.

3. The fencer performs parry-ripostes (tierce, quarte and quinte) as actions of defense. The parry-riposte technique is very important. Their effectiveness is ensured by taking them well forward, away from the body. In modern electric saber parry-ripostes are very similar to beats, unlike in the days of visually-judged saber when parries were taken close to the body. A way of perfecting parries is a feint of counter-attack followed by taking an appropriate parry. The fencer makes a twisting movement with the fingers to mark the feint more explicitly with the weapon point. The stop-hit feint allows the fencer to anticipate the timing of the opponent's final move.

4. The lesson concludes with a series of cuts with a lunge to uncovered parts of the target area. The instructor uncovers his flank or chest to enforce the fencer's correct responses. It should be noted that the fencer often makes the hits to the chest with a classic flat or edge cut -- the latter being more effective in modern electric saber. Cuts with the flat used to be common in dry saber as they were more suggestive and explicit to the referees.

12.2 Technical-tactical lesson [Borysiuk – Wator].
Duration: 7.30 min. instructor: Zbigniew Borysiuk.
Fencer: Marta Wator.

The lesson contains technical elements as well as a number of tactical exercises that might be useful during the preparatory training season. The lesson can be treated as a warm-up, or it can be prolonged to 20-30 minutes. For the purpose of this DVD the duration of the lesson was reduced and many repetitions were dropped.

1. In the beginning the fencer makes a series of simple hits to parts of the target area uncovered by the instructor. Then the instructor changes the distance in order to combine cuts with parry-ripostes. Such lesson organization, if treated as a warm-up before competition, can provide the coach with valuable information about the fencer's speed of reaction and ability to make appropriate choices, i.e. about the fencer's pre-comp form. The instructor increases the exercise difficulty and enforces double hits to the uncovered target area (executed with a bent arm) as well as ripostes and counter-ripostes to the offensive actions by the instructor that follow fencer's cuts. This technical part of the lesson concludes with complex practice of cuts to different parts of the target area, completed with a lunge and a thrust to the torso.

2. Technical-tactical part. The fencer takes parries preceded with a feint of counter-attack and executes ripostes to the uncovered part of the target area. From time to time, the instructor increases the distance, enforcing a riposte with a lunge. The next exercise is of more technical character and consists of a type of feinted attack: feint of cut to the instructor's uncovered target areas – cut to an open target area with a jump forward-lunge. Please notice that the feint is executed with a bent arm, and the final cut with a straight arm, following the principles of traditional fencing saber technique. As part of the technical-tactical exercises the instructor arranges preparatory actions on his blade and then ripostes enforcing a technically accurate exchange with varied distance and footwork.

3. The main tactical component of the lesson consists of a exercise used in a situation of simultaneous attacks. The concepts are very important and effective in modern saber. The fencer and the instructor start toward each other, as if in a common simultaneous attack. The instructor arranges three very common situations found in real

competition circumstances. First, he bends his weapon arm, making his own attack fall short and calling for the fencer to respond with a simple attack with lunge. As a second alternative, he indicates his intention to hit the fencer, calling for an appropriate parry and riposte. Finally, after pretending to start a simultaneous attack, he gives up the attack, calling for the fencer to commence a compound attack.

4. The lesson concludes with a classic dry-saber tactical exercise which is still applicable in modern saber. On the instructor's presentation of the point in line, the fencer executes a preparatory action – binding of counter-tierce with a patinando to an open target area. From time to time, the instructor uses a derobement, which makes the fencer take a parry seconde and land a hit on an open target area. The purpose of this multi-version exercise is developing the habit of developing counter-time skills in fencers, i.e. effective counteracting of all stop-hits, and provoking the opponent's stop-hits to parry them in a correct manner. From the tactical standpoint, these actions have been important in both dry and electric saber and still require constant perfecting.

12.3   Technical-tactical lesson [Borysiuk – Karpińska].
Duration: 12.05 min.
Instructor: Zbigniew Borysiuk. Fencer: Katarzyna Karpińska.

The lesson's aim is to demonstrate traditional technical elements in saber, including many actions shown in Lesson 2, as well as a number of technical-tactical actions considered useful in real competition conditions. In addition, it contains elements specific to electric saber such as different versions of counter-time and cuts with the flat to the forearm. All the elements are set in a logical sequence of a complex individual lesson that can be used during advanced training and in the competition training period of advanced saber fencers.

1. The introductory part of the lesson contains a number of technical actions, including technical routines. In the beginning the fencer executes double cuts to an uncovered target area in combination with parry-ripostes, followed by triple cuts to different parts of the target area, first standing still and then while maneuvering, and finishing the routine sequence with a lunge. Then the fencer practices parry-ripostes preceded by a feint of counterattack – simple thrust to the torso. The instructor carries out a strictly technical exercise of jump

forward lunge with a feint toward an uncovered target area and a cut to an uncovering area. This exercise concludes the preparatory part of the lesson and prepares the fencer to undertake a whole gamut of tactical exercises. A slow motion recording shows very clearly that the first feint is marked to the chest with a short movement of the bent weapon arm, with the point relatively far away from the instructor's target area, to avoid a counterattack with a beat – cut. This set allows a smooth transition from the feint to flank to an extended attack and cut to the chest.

2. The main part of the lesson starts with an exchange of parries concluded with an open eyes jump forward lunge. Next, the fencer carries out multi-version exercises aimed at preparation of a two-step and an action on the instructor's blade – counter-tierce bind – jump forward lunge after a feint to an open area - cut to an opening area or taking a defensive action. Counter-attack to forearm and parry-riposte.

As an action of defense against the instructor's counter-quarte bind, the fencer executes a derobement cut-over to the forearm. It is a very characteristic technical element in electric saber using blade flexibility to ensure the effectiveness of cut-overs to the forearm from the top and the side. Next, the fencer takes a double step forward, provoking the instructor to counterattack, takes an appropriate parry, and ripostes (as counter-time) to the instructor's uncovered target area.

The main component of these tactical exercises is the three-version tactical handling of simultaneous attacks.

    a. Following the instructor's incorrect attack, the fencer takes the initiative and executes an attack with a lunge.
    b. The fencer parries and ripostes the instructor's smooth attack.
    c. Following the instructor's retreat, the fencer commences a compound attack with a prolonged jump forward lunge.

The next exercise is clearly technical: while maneuvering (steps back and forth) the instructor places his blade in three positions to enforce the fencer's appropriate beats: quinte, quarte and seconde in combination with parries and ripostes. The last tactical exercise is the so-called covert counter-time, which is of crucial importance in modern saber. The fencer pretends to make a technical error with a double step forward and feints an attack by extension, provoking the instructor to counter-attack. Then she changes the position of her weapon arm and blade, makes the opponent miss, and scores the touch.

3. The last part of the lesson is purely technical, aimed at correction of the fencer's errors and cooling down. The fencer makes a series of hits with different parts of the edge or the back edge of the blade as derobements of the instructor's blade, and interrupts them with slow and correctly executed parries. There follows a very useful exercise consists of short twisting finger movements of the hilt and the blade, similar to short feints. This exercise allows controlling the weapon during fast movements and improves the timing of feints in offensive actions. Good mastery of this drill helps avoid possible beats. The lesson concludes with slow parry-ripostes.

12.4 Technical-tactical lesson – championship level [Roszak – Więckowska]

Duration: 13.20 min.
Instructor: Arkadiusz Roszak (Polish national fencing team coach).
Fencer: Irena Więckowska.

The lesson demonstrates a set of technical-tactical exercises for championship training of advanced players. The dark backdrop makes all the technical saber features, including the fencer's and instructor's blades, more visible. For example, the dynamics of the offensive actions, the way of holding the blade and the position of weapon arm in the same line as the hip – as well as the specific arm-foot coordination with the weapon in that position -- are very characteristic of modern saber. The lesson mostly includes actions which are highly evolved and are most useful in real combat, e.g. combinations of feints of parries with stop-hits, parry-ripostes, counter-attacks with all parts of the blade, different attacks (including counter-time) and the specific sabreur's fleches with no cross-over. The last tactical action of the lesson is counter-time with a sabreur's fleche. Feeling the timing results in gaining right of way when the opponent attacks incorrectly, bending the arms and shortening the attack. In saber, fencers who feel their timing effectively use counter-time very often.

1. The lesson commences with three types of lunges, the details of which can be studied in slow motion. In the first, a classic accelerat-

ing lunge, a simultaneous weapon arm and front foot action can be noted, followed by a simultaneous simple cut and front foot tap on the floor. The next two exercises are aimed at developing the habit of executing a waiting lunge. The fencer during the waiting stage lands a hit on the forearm and then cuts to the head as the front heel lands. In the third exercise, the waiting stage of the lunge features a series of short feints made with the fingers, followed by a simple attack to the head or flank, just before the front foot touches the floor.

2. The next exercise is a classic offensive counter-time. The fencer starts the action slowly with a bent weapon arm and the blade close to the body, provoking the instructor to a stop-hit which is met by a parry-riposte to an open target area. The common element of the above actions, i.e. lunge and counter-time with a jump forward lunge, uses the slow waiting and commencement of attacks with the blade and the hilt close to the fencer's body. This is diametrically opposed to "dry" saber, where feints were marked immediately to gain right of way. Currently, it takes place in the final stage of a multi-feint attack.

3. The remaining technical-tactical actions were discussed in Lessons 2 and 3: variations on simultaneous attacks, varieties of counter-time, feints of parries with initiation of attacks or stop-hits combined with parries and ripostes and different types of beats. Important differences include the perfection of execution of particular exercises in combination with a larger variety of finishing attacks, with more compound actions. Initiative and creativeness of the top class fencer is an important element. With elite fencers, most preparatory actions should be initiated by the fencer, not only prompted by the instructor. Such an approach develops fencers' initiative and helps them dictate of their own tactical concepts and impose their own combat style on their opponents.

12.5 Group footwork training of the Polish national team

Duration: 6.10 min
Arkadiusz Roszak – national team coach.–
prepares the team for the European Championships,
where they won the gold medal in the team event,
and the Beijing Olympic Games. .

1. The fencers begin their footwork training with steps forward and backward at a variable pace and distance. Some fencers continue footwork training with the weapon in hand, aiming at perfecting the coordination of arm and leg movement, especially during lunges. In this part of the lesson the instructor is passive, and the fencers should treat footwork exercises as a form of ideomotor training, not merely as mechanical repetitions. Steps and other footwork should be executed consciously, following a mental image of a real bout and opponent's anticipated reactions. During these exercises, the instructor measures the speed of individual movement sequences and motivates the fencers to exercise more intensively.

2. The next part of the lesson involves the instructor, who determines the distance of steps and the pace of moving forward and backward. The fencers' objective is to maintain the set distance and respond to visual signals made by the instructor with his hands. The signals, established earlier, should provoke the fencers' immediate responses with lunges, patinandos (advance-lunges), and jump forward lunges. The sequences of exercises include rhythmic interruptions, which in a real bout can mark the opponent's intentions of offensive actions. These exercises are not a novelty in terms of footwork evolution in electric saber, unlike the pair footwork exercises that follow.

3. Pair exercises develop the ability of gaining the right of way. A fencer lets her partner perform a few jump forward lunges. At any moment she increases the distance and in accordance with the convention in saber can gain priority by executing her own offensive action. Next the fencers switch their roles and, maintaining their distance, repeat the exercise.

4. The lesson concludes with footwork exercises with the non-dominant arm. They are important to compensate for the overuse of one side of the body and to remove the negative aspects of functional asymmetry. Moreover, following the rules of transfer, the exercises

provide the instructor with the possibility of correction of small technical errors in terms of feet and body positioning.

12.6   Individual footwork training.
Duration:2:14 min.
Fencer: Izabela Sajewicz from the Polish national saber fencing team, who has trained only saber fencing since the beginning of her career.

Individual footwork training greatly supplements individual lessons and collective footwork training. It is an important component of the warm-up before competition and at the beginning of a fencing training session, including individual lessons and pair exercises. Individual footwork exercises can be carried out under instructor's guidance or with the use of a mirror. The majority or all exercises should be performed with the fencing weapon.

1. The fencer starts the footwork training with a series of steps forward and backward, with jumps forward and glides as preparatory actions for patinandos and jump forward lunges. Two crucial elements must be taken into consideration in terms of arm-leg coordination. In the simple step forward, the movement starts with the arm, whereas a step backwards is made simultaneously with extending the arm forward and moving the rear foot to the back. This habit is important in real bouts, since it constitutes a form of counter-attack while in defense. The fencing posture itself involves the torso leaning forward with a slight tendency to move the hip to the front. As observed earlier, modern saber fencers tend to hold the weapon close to the body, while the elbow remains in the same line with the hip or is even slightly pulled back.

2. The classic accelerating lunge (not waiting or explosive lunges) demonstrated by the fencer features a simultaneous weapon arm and front foot action, followed by an accelerating movement of the arm slightly preceding the tapping of the front foot on the floor.

3. Observation of the patinando and jump forward technique reveals that in the initial stage of the attack the arm and the point of the weapon do not extend forward until the completion of the step or forward jump. Only in the lunging stage does the weapon arm accelerate and precede the front foot.

4. The lesson concludes with dynamic footwork training with occasional fast jump forward lunges, reflecting the real fencing combat conditions.

12.7   Queue training.
Duration: 3.30 min.
Instructor: Zbigniew Borysiuk. Fencers: Wojciech Marczak and Jan Karkosz, members of the Polish national saber fencing team.

Queue training is aimed at inclusion of a greater number of fencers into specialist technical-tactical exercises. The lesson features only two fencers; however, the number of participants in such a training form should be 4 or 6 fencers, which enables the coach to supervise the exercises and monitor their effectiveness, and yet ensures a sufficient number of repetitions of a given exercise for each fencer. Queue exercises are perfect as a warm-up before and during competition before subsequent bouts for an entire fencing team. Queue training usually includes simple technical and tactical exercises with a low number of repetitions. The emphasis is put on the speed and accuracy of execution of individual exercises.

1. The first exercise consists of a series of technical repetitions of cuts to the instructor's uncovered target area (chest, flank, head) in combination with parries and simple ripostes while maneuvering or at a set pace. It should be noted that while making hits to a closer target area, e.g. the forearm, the fencers do not fully extend their weapon arm. They skillfully react to the uncovered torso area, scoring touches with the edge or the flat, as in dry saber.

2. The instructor changes the fencing distance, prompting a feint of counter-attack -- parry-riposte to an open target area. This part of the lesson is carried out with a much faster pace set by the instructor.

3. Another technical routine is a triple cut to the mask (both cheeks, head) and a cut with the flat to the chest, retreating one step and thrust with a lunge to the torso.

4. A technical-tactical exercise: jump forward – lunge with a feint, preceded with rhythmic preparation. It should be noted that the feint itself, after the marking of attack with a double step, is executed with a bent weapon arm, and the energetic feinting movement is initiated by the opponent's point, with quick finger-work of the weapon hand.

5. The next exercise includes two basic beats in a real bout: seconde and quinte, depending on the position of the instructor's blade.

6. The queue training concludes with the most complex exercise. While exchanging parries a fencer executes a jump forward and patinando with a cut to an open target area. This footwork element coordinated with short feints of the blade is the most common form of attack in modern saber. The short jump forward serves as a signal, after which the fencer with right of way lands a hit on an open target area, and precedes the final cut to the flank or the torso with a short fast feint.

12.8 Pair exercises.
Duration: 12.40 min.
Fencers: Wojciech Marczak and Jan Karkosz, members of the Polish national saber fencing team. Instructor: Zbigniew Borysiuk.

Pair exercises are a traditional form of advanced fencing training used for many years. As regards learning technique, they significantly supplement individual lessons with a coach. Pair exercises are often used as a warm-up during competition. They can be applied at any stage of fencers' training. The footage demonstrates an extension of classic forms of learning fencing technique with a partner, using "bout pieces," which are elements of sincere competition set into the technical drills. The fencers decide who plays the role of the fencing master and what action will begin the bout piece. These exercises incorporate elements of rivalry into the process of perfection of technical-tactical skills. Thanks to this, pair exercises are not tiring to the fencers and allow them to maintain stimulation and concentration for a long time.

1. The fencers start the exercise with exchanges of basic engagements: tierce, quarte, quinte, after which the designated attacker tries to hit a selected part of the target area, provoking an appropriate parry-riposte. Then the fencers increase the distance between them, which prompts the fencer executing the action to take the riposte with a step forward.

2. Technical exercise. At a set pace the fencers execute alternately waiting lunges. The partner's role is to begin a parry of quinte, which significantly accelerates the lunging fencer's arm movement and cut to head.

3. As a technical exercise, with a longer distance between the fencers, the starting fencer uncovers a target area provoking his partner to perform a lunge and a hit. From time to time, he takes a parry and ripostes, signaling the start of a "bout piece." The fencer starts with a weapon in line, while his partner follows with a beat – cut to head, which is randomly parried, commencing a possible bout piece.

4. The fencers exchange engagements alternately with the three basic weapon positions, after which a fencer executes a cut to an open target area with a simple lunge. Taking a parry and riposte depends on his partner's decision. In the same manner, the fencers practice simple thrust with a lunge, which can be parried and riposted by one of them and commence a bout piece.

5. A jump forward-lunge, feint to head – cut flank, and an extended attack and a double feint head – flank – head. A parry by one fencer commences a "bout piece."

6. During a bout piece, a fencer takes a quarte to tierce parry provoking his partner to a cut to the chest with a patinando. The fencer's parry quarte and riposte to the head signals the start of the exchange, which should result in the partner's counter-riposte from quinte parry to an open target area.

7. One fencer begins with weapon in line, forcing his partner to remove the blade with a binding of counter-tierce. At a moment of his choosing, the fencer's response is a derobement and commencement of an exchange.

8. The fencers execute alternate attacks on the head with a jump forward lunge. None has right of way. A fencer can start a duel at any moment by parrying the opponent's attack or shorten his own attack and taking a defensive action.

9. Exercise with a similar convention to 8: exchange of parries, jump forward lunges during which a fencer can decide about taking a parry and commence a compound attack.

10. The fencers stand at a long distance from one another. They rhythmically exercise short preparatory actions. One fencer uncovers a target area provoking the opponent's feinted attack, which he then can parry, commencing an exchange. Then the attacks are extended and the patinando is signaled by a jump forward.

11. The fencers practice short jump forward lunges to the head over a short distance. At any moment, one fencer breaks the attack and

makes a stop-hit to the mask. It is a very good exercise for perfecting the sense of fencing tempo. The next exercise consisting of a preparatory attack to tierce guard is in a similar manner. The fencer performs a counter-attack with a beat-cut to head, which can be parried by the partner.

12. The lesson concludes with two types of stop-hits, frequently used in modern saber: counter-attack to the forearm by a cut-over, and stop-hit to the forearm preceded with a feint of parry quinte. The fencers may also try to parry foreseen stop-hits by staging short bout pieces.

12.9 Individual lessons with members of the Polish national men's saber team

Fencers: Jan Karkosz and Wojciech Marczak, members of the Polish national saber team. Instructor: Zbigniew Borysiuk.

12.9.1 Technical lesson (Jan Karkosz)
Duration: 2.40 min.

The aim of the lesson is to re-instill correct technical habits that might have been distorted due to frequent participation in saber tournaments during the competition season. Such lessons are usually called corrective ones and should be implemented following competition or in the early stage of preparation for the main competition of the season. The pace of exercises should be fairly moderate with some slight accelerations. The exercises include:

1. Double cuts with the edge to an uncovered target area in combination with the basic parries and varied directions of steps. A characteristic element in the electric saber is taking parries well forward with a slight twist of the wrist.

2. Technical routines, during which the instructor attempting an engagement to positions tierce, quarte and quinte, corrects the fencer's parries and then executes real cuts on the parry, taking ripostes and responding with counter-ripostes.

3. Classic technical routine: the fencer makes three cuts to the mask (head, cheek, cheek), cut with the flat to the chest, a step backwards and a simple thrust with a lunge to the torso.

4. A compound technical routine: beat of quarte to the forearm, beat with the back edge to the cheek, cut to the chest with the flat, retreat,

thrust with a lunge to the torso in combination with parries-ripostes. The complex of cuts develops the ability to hit with all sides of the blade, which requires great dexterity and fingerwork of the weapon arm.

12.9.2 Tactical lesson before competition (Wojciech Marczak)
Duration: 4.50 min.

The lesson's goal is to prepare the fencer for a tournament by perfecting the choice of the most appropriate technical-tactical routines in the most typical segments of the saber bout. It also develops the choice of fencing tempo, extension of attacks and speed and full arm-foot coordination. The selected set of exercises includes the most representative sequences of tactical actions, which are most appropriate in the context of preparation for competition. To increase the fencer's sport fitness three days before competition, individual lessons should include mostly tactical exercises, be intensive and last only about 15-20 minutes.

1. At a set pace the fencer makes a preparatory double step forward and then retreats to the initial position. When the instructor uncovers a part of the target area, the fencer makes a feint and a cut to the uncovered area. From time to time the instructor increases the distance, enforcing an extended attack with a jump forward and a patinando.

2. On the instructor's presentation of weapon in line, the fencer executes a bind of counter-tierce. The instructor uses two tactical situations: first, his attack with a bent elbow is a signal to make a counter-attack to the forearm and parry-riposte; second, his retreat provokes a simple attack and his extension of distance provokes a compound attack.

3. In a simultaneous-attack exercise, the instructor arranges four tactical situations (not three as in earlier lessons):
    a. Interrupting his own attack provokes the fencer to execute a simple attack with a lunge,
    b. Bending the elbow is a signal to a stop-hit to the arm,
    c. Smoothly developing his own attack and finishing with a cut provokes the fencer to take a parry-riposte,
    d. Pretending to start a simultaneous attack and then retreating invites the fencer's compound offensive action, which

the instructor can parry-riposte, and the fencer can parry and counter-riposte.

4. As above, the instructor shortens his attack giving a signal to the fencer to gain right of way and execute a sabreur's fleche at the instructor's uncovered target area. It should be remembered that according to fencing regulations the fencer executing the "new" sabreur's fleche is not allowed to make a cross-over step with his rear foot; in the final stage of the fleche the front foot is the one landing on the piste.

References

Abernethy B., 1996. Training the visual-perceptual skills of athletes: Insights from the study of motor expertise. "American Journal of Sport Medicine" 24. 589-592.
Bandach L., 1997. Osobowościowe uwarunkowania stylu walki w szermierce na florety. Sport Wyczynowy 3-4.
Bandach L., 1998. Fencer's Style of Fighting. Sport Wyczynowy. Warsaw, 7-8. 44-47.
Barbasetti L., 1900, Das Stossfechten. Wien.
Bayli I., 2004. Naturally Enhancing Life. Performance and Healing. healingsearch.com
Bernstein N., 1967.The Coordination and Regulations of Movements. Oxford. Pergamon.
Borysiuk Z., 1996. Kierunki rozwoju szermierki. Szabla wychodzi z kryzysu. Sport Wyczynowy 1-2. 64-70.
Borysiuk Z., 2000. Factors Determining Sport Performance Level for Fencers at the Preliminary and Championship Stages of their Training. ECSS Conference, Jyvaskyla.
Borysiuk Z., 2001. Psychomotor and Personality-Related Aspects of Sexual Dimorphism – an Example of the Polish National Fencing Team. 15th ECSS Conference, Cologne, 524.
Borysiuk Z., 2001. Somatyczne, wysiłkowe i koordynacyjne determinanty mistrzostwa sportowego w szermierce. Sport Wyczynowy 1-2. 11-17.
Borysiuk Z., 2002. Psychomotoryczne i osobowościowe uwarunkowania poziomu mistrzowskiego w szermierce. Politechnika Opolska, Opole.
Borysiuk Z., 2005. Współczesna szermierka na szable. COS. Warszawa.
Borysiuk Z., 2006. Complex evaluation of fencers predisposition in three stages of sport development. Biology of Sport 1. 41-55.
Borysiuk Z., 2007. Time and spatial aspects of movement anticipation. Biology of Sport 24, 3. 285-295.

Borysiuk Z., Zmarzły D., 2005. Surface electromyography (sEMG) as a research tool of psychomotor reactions. Annales Universitatis Mariae Curie-Skłodowska, Lublin-Polonia, 188-192.

Brol K., 1989. Znaczenie i współzależność techniki i zdolności czynnościowo-ruchowych. Praca magisterska. AWF Katowice.

Cashen E.R., 1977. Fencing with psychology. Fencing 2.

Celejowa I., 2001. Żywienie w treningu i walce sportowej. COS Warszawa.

Cheris E., 2002. Fencing: Steps to Succes, Human Kinetics Publ., II.

Crosnier R., 1956. Fencing with the Sabre, London.

Czajkowski Z., 1968. Teoria i metodyka współczesnej szermierki, SiT, Warszawa.

Czajkowski Z., 1970. Elementary conception of reaction in fencing, "Fencing Master", 6. 61-78.

Czajkowski Z., 1975. Trening sportowy w świetle teorii stresu. Sport Wyczynowy 11.

Czajkowski Z., 1984. Taktyka i psychologia w szermierce. AWF, Katowice.

Czajkowski Z., 1991. Z badań nad czynnikami wpływającymi na wynik sportowy w szermierce. Podstawowe problemy badawcze w naukach kultury fizycznej. AWF, Katowice.

Czajkowski Z., 1995. Nawyki czuciowo-ruchowe w działalności sportowej. ZSKFMŚ, Katowice.

Czajkowski Z., 1996. Psychologia sprzymierzeńcemm trenera. RCM-SKFiS, Warszawa.

Czajkowski Z., 2001. About the Specificity of Energy and Co-oordination Abilities, "Sport Wyczynowy," 11-12. 37-43.

Czajkowski Z., 2001. Theory, Practice and Methodology in Fencing. Advanced Course for Fencing Coaches. AWF, Katowice.

Czajkowski Z., 2005. Understanding Fencing: the Unity of Theory and Practice. Staten Island, NY. SKA Swordplay Books.

Dryukov V., Pavlenko Y., Shadrina V., 2003. Training Process Intensification for Skilled Athletes in Fencing at Pre-competitive Stage of Preparation, 8th Annual Congress ECSS. Salzburg. 58

Eberle S., 2000. Endurance Sport Nutrition. Eating plans for optimal training, racing and recovery. Champaign. Human Kinetics.

Enoka R., 2002. Neuromechanics of Human Movement, "Human Kinetics."

Ericsson M., Kilbom A., Wiktorin C., Winkiel J., 1991, Validity and reliability in the estimation of trunk, arm and neck inclination by observation. Proceedings of the International Ergonomics Association conference. Paris: International Ergonomics Association, 245-247.

Evangelista N., 2000. The Inner Game of Fencing: Excellence in Form, Technique, Strategy and Spirit. Master's Press, Lincolnwood, Illinois.

Exner S., 1873. Experimentelle untersuchung der einfachten psychischen Processe. "Pflug. Arch. Physiol." 7. 601-660.

Eysenck H.J., 1975. Fact and Fiction in Psychology. Penguin Books, London.

Eysenck H.J., 1985. The Scientific Study of Personality. Routlege and K. Paul, London.

Gulbin J.P., 2004. Paradigm Shift in Talent Identification, Proceedings, Pre-Olympic Congress, Thessaloniki, 77.

Heroux P., 1974. Some Aspects of Fencing Psychology. "The Sword" 4. 16-27.

Héroux P., 1979. Some aspects of fencing psychology. "The Sword" 4.

Johansson & Westling, 1984. Roles of glabrous skin receptors and sensorimotor memory in automatic control of precision grip when lifting rougher or more slippery objects. Experimental Brain Research, 56. 560-564.

Keele S., 1986. Motor Control, [in:] Handbook of perception and performance, L. Kaufman, J. Thomas, K. Boff (Eds.), New York.

Keele S.W., Hawkins H.L., 1982. Explorations of Individual Differences Relevant to High Level Skill, "Journal of Motor Behavior" 1. 112-128.

Keller S.W., Tyshler D.A., 1970. Fiechtowanije po sablach, "Zdorowje". Kiev.

Kevey J., 1952. Szermierka na szable, GKKT, Warszawa.

Klapp S.T., Erwin C.I., 1976. Relation between programming time and duration of the response being programmed, "Journal of Experimental Psychology; Human Perception and Performance" 2. 591-598.

Kłodecka-Różalska J., 1993. Radzimy sobie ze stresem. RCMSzKFiS, Warszawa.

Kluka D., 1987. Visual skill enhancement, "Strategies" 1 (1). 20-24.

Knudson D., Morrison C., 2002. Qualitative analysis of human movement, second edition: Human Kinetics, Champaign.

Korfanty E., 1983. Analiza czasów reakcji psychomotorycznej szermierzy zaawansowanych i początkujących. Praca magisterska. AWF, Katowice.

Kurian M., Catering L., Kulhavy R., 1993. Personality characteristic and duration of ATA Taekwondo training, "Perceptual and Motor Skills" 76. 363-386.

Latash M., 1993. Control of human movement. Champaign: Human Kinetics.

Litkowska-Grzegorczyk S., 1983. Wpływ struktury osobowości czołowych szermierzy na efektywność treningu i walki sportowej. Praca magisterska. AWF, Katowice.

Luce R., 1986. Response Times:Their Role In Inferring Elementary Mental Organization.Oxford University Press, New York.

Lukovich I., 1986. Fencing. Alfoldi Printing House, Debrecen.

Lukovich J., 1975. Fencing, Sport. Budapest.

Lukovich, I., 1997. Fencing: the Modern International Style. Staten Island, NY. SKA Swordplay Books (reprint of the above).

Malina R., Bouchard C., 1991. Growth, maturation, and physical activity. Champaign, Ill. Human Kinetics Books.

Mańkowski W., 1929. Szermierka na szable. Lwów.

Marino G., 1982. Qualitative biomechanical analysis of sports skills, "Coaching Science Update" 9. 20-22.

McCormick E., Sanders M., 1982. Human factors in engineering and design, New York.

Paisey T.J.H., Mangan G.L., 1980. The relationship of extraversion, neuroticism and sensation-seeking to questionnaire-derived measures of nervous system properties. The Pavlovian Journal of Biological Sciences 15.

Pashler H., 1994. Dual-task interference in simple tasks: Data and theory, "Psychological Bulletin" 116. 220-244.

Pitman B., 1990. Fencing: Techniques of Foil, Epee, and Sabre. The Crowood Press, Gipsy Lane, Swindon, Wiltshire, SN2 6DQ.

Platonow W., 1990. Optymalizacja struktury treningu sportowego. RCMSzKFiS, Warszawa.

Posner M., 1978. Chronometric explorations of mind. Hillsdale, NJ: Erlbaum.

Proctor R.W., Dutta A., 1995. Skill acquisition and human performance. Thousand Oaks, Calif.: Sage Publications.
Quesada D.C., Schmidt R.A., 1970. A test of the Adams-Creamer decay hypotesis for the timing of motor responses, "Journal of Motor Behavior" 2. 273-283.
Rhodes R.E., Courneya K.S., Hayduk L.A., 2002. Does Personality Moderate the Theory of Planned Behavior in the Exercise Domain?, "Journal of Sport and Exercise Psychology" 1. 35-62.
Richman C.l., Rehberg J., 1986. The development of self-esteem trought the martial arts, "International Journal of Psychology" 17. 234-239.
Rosenbaum D., 1989. On the selection of physical actions, "Five College Cognitive Science Papers," 389-422.
Rosenbaum D.A., Patashnik O., 1980. Time to time in the human motor system, [in:] Attention and performance VIII, R.S. Nickerson (ed.), Hillsdale, NJ: Erlbaum.
Ryguła I., 1998. Taking Advantage of the Optimalization Model in Athletic Training. Sport Wyczynowy 11-12. 37-43.
Ryguła I., 2000. Elementy teorii, metodyki, diagnostyki i optymalizacji treningu sportowego. Katowice.
Ryguła I., Borysiuk Z., 2000. Conditions of Sporting Level of Fencers at Master Stage of Training. Journal of Human Kinetics 4. 67-85.
Ryguła I., 1993. Elementy sterowania i optymalizacji w treningu sportowym. AWF. Katowice.
Sage G.H., 1984. Motor learning and control: A neurophysiological approach. Dubuque, Iowa; w.W.C. Brown.
Salczenko I.N., 1980. Dwigazjelnyje wzaimodiejstwija sportsmienow. Zdorowje, Kijew.
Schenker O., 1967. Szermierka na szable. SiT. Warszawa.
Schmidt R., 1991. Motor Learning and Performance. Human Kinetics Publishers, Champaign. Illinois.
Schmidt R., Wrisberg C., 2004. Motor learning and performance (3rd ed.) Champaign., IL; Human Kinetics.
Seat J., Wrisberg J., 1996. The visual instruction system, "Research Quarterly for Exercise and Sport" 67. 106-108.
Shestakov M., Averkin N., Molchanov N., 2002. Soccer as a Multi-agent System: Control, Simulation Modeling, Perspectives of Development, "Medicina Sportiva: Trener piłki nożnej", 214-215.

Shiffrar M., Freyd J., 1990. Apparent motion of the human body, "Psychological Science" 1. 257- 264.
Starkes J.L., Ericsson K.A., 2003. Expert Performance In Sports. Human Kinetics. Champaign.
Starosta W., 2006. Globalna i lokalna koordynacja ruchowa. MSMS, Warszawa
Starzewski J., 1932. Ze wspomień o Michale Starzewskim. Kraków.
Stawowska L., 1989. Psychologiczna diagnoza w sporcie wyczynowym. AWF, Katowice.
Sternberg S., 1969. The discovery of processing stages: Extensions of Donders' method, [in:] Attention and performance II, W.G. Koster (Ed.), 117-152.
Strelau J., 1985. Temperament, osobowość, działanie. PWN, Warszawa.
Szabo L., 1977. Fencing and the Master. Corvina Kiado, Budapest.
Szabo L., 1998. Fencing and the Master. Staten Island, NY. SKA Swordplay Books (a reprint of the above).
Szopa J., 1989. Nowa koncepcja klasyfikacji struktury motoryczności człowieka. Antropomotoryka 2.
Szopa J., Mleczko E., Żak S., 1996. Podstawy antropomotoryki. PWN, Warszawa-Kraków.
Szyguła Z., 1997. Choroba cieplna u sportowców i sposoby jej zapobiegania. Sport Wyczynowy 7- 8 and 9-10.
Szyguła Z., 1997. Choroba cieplna u sportowców i sposoby jej zapobiegania. Sport Wyczynowy 7- 8 and 9-10.
Tyshler D., Tyshler G., 1995. Fencing, Physical Education and Science Press. Moscow.
Tyshler D., 1995. Fencing. Physical Education and Science Press, Moscow.
Ulatowski T., 1995. Praktyka sportu, PTNKF, Warszawa.
Ward W.B., 2002. Visual search and biological motion perception in tennis, "Research Quarterly for Exercise and Sport" 73. 107-112.
Ważny Z., 1995. Leksykon treningu sportowego, AWF Warszawa, Wyd. I.
Ważny Z., 1997. Rozważania na temat metod analizy obciążeń treningowych. Sport Wyczynowy 3-4. 7-10.
Welford A., 1980. Motor skill and aging, [in:] Psychology of motor behavior in sport, Nadeau C., Halliwel W., Newell K., Roberts G. (Eds.), 253-268.

Wężowski J., 1976. Szermierka. Sport i Turystyka, Warszawa.
Williams A., Davids K., Burwitz L., Williams J., 1992. Perception and actions sport, "Journal of Human Movement Studies" 22. 147-205.
Williams A.M., Grant A., 1999. Training perceptual skill in sport, "International Journal of Sport Psychology" 30. 194-220.
Williams A.M., Reilly T., 2000. Talent identification and development in soccer. Journal of Sports Science 18. 657-667.
Wood J., Abernethy B., 1997. An assessment of the efficacy of sports vision training programs, "Optometry and Vision Science" 74. 646-659.
Zelaznik H., Schmidt R., Gielen C., 1986. Kinematic properties of rapid aimed hand movements, "Journal of Motor Behavior" 18. 353-372.
Zuchora K., 1965. Próba poszukiwania metody obiektywnej oceny gry w koszykówkę. Kultura Fizyczna 6.
Zukowski N., 1995. Influence of surprise on reaction time (in Polish: abstract in English), „Sport Wyczynowy" 11-12. 21-26.

Made in the USA
Middletown, DE
30 March 2015